Maurice Ronayne

God Knowable and Known

Maurice Ronayne

God Knowable and Known

ISBN/EAN: 9783337217396

Printed in Europe, USA, Canada, Australia, Japan

Cover: Foto ©Lupo / pixelio.de

More available books at **www.hansebooks.com**

GOD KNOWABLE AND KNOWN.

BY

MAURICE RONAYNE, S.J.,

Author of "Religion and Science: Their Union Historically Considered."

NEW YORK, CINCINNATI, CHICAGO:

BENZIGER BROTHERS,

Printers to the Holy Apostolic See.

1883.

Copyright, 1888, by BENZIGER BROTHERS.

PREFACE.

In this book I have attempted to draw out, in English, arguments that bear on the existence and knowableness of God. By so doing, I do not pretend to offer to the reader anything new; I have neither invented nor discovered the arguments. In their general outlines they have been before the human mind during all the ages. My only aim has been to show that, in the warfare with infidelity, those arguments are as available at present as in any period of the past, and that as weapons of defence they need only, as it were, to be refurbished anew, that they may be perfectly well fitted for modern use.

To give to the reasoning greater point, and to answer objections on different subjects, I have cast much of the book into discussions. In these the scenic part is altogether imaginary. Places, time, and persons, I have feigned, in order vividly to formulate doctrines which were my principal, I may say, my only concern.

Besides the authors quoted in the work, there are

others whose suggestions on various topics have helped me. There being question of the fundamental truth of all truths, I sought light wheresoever I thought I might find it, and deemed it not unseemly to help my weakness with the strength of those who in the same great cause fought valiantly against the infidel.

If this book will give security to some souls, and in any measure contribute to stem the tide of infidelity, the author shall consider himself amply rewarded for his labor.

CONTENTS.

		PAGE
PREFACE.		iii

CHAPTER
- I. Nature Witnessing to God. — 7
- II. The Data of Natural Knowledge. — 67
- III. God the Creator. — 94
- IV. "The Vestiges of God in Creation." — 137
- V. The Human Race Bearing Testimony to God. — 186
- VI. Buddhism. — 210
- VII. God in the Moral World. — 261
- VIII. The Nature of the Human Soul—Its Immortality. — 311
- IX. Conscience as a Witness to God. — 334
- X. The Proofs of Conscience Confirmed. — 364
- XI. The Knowledge of God Attainable by all Men. — 369
- XII. St. Augustine's Soliloquy with God. — 376

APPENDIX. — 381
- A Refutation of Darwinism. — 381
- "Encyclopædia Britannica." Art. Theism. — 384
- "The Sacred Books of the East." — 388
- Different Names of God. — 394

GOD
KNOWABLE AND KNOWN.

CHAPTER I.

Nature Witnessing to God.

ON the forenoon of the day on which the death of Mr. Darwin was announced, some half dozen gentlemen were reading the morning papers in one of the parlors of the Fifth Avenue Hotel, New York. Each of them seemed to be deeply interested in some item of news; when on a sudden the door was opened and Mr. Maxwell entered, exclaiming, as if in soliloquy, "bad news; one of the great lights of the age gone out." No one seemed to heed him, though his obtrusiveness of manner and tone drew all eyes towards him for a moment. He wished, no doubt, to elicit sympathy for the loss which, in his opinion, the world had met with, but none was shown. On other occasions, some of those present, admirers of Mr. Darwin, would have joined in his eulogy, but just then they were too much taken up with news touching their own mercantile or political interests. To Mr. Maxwell, who amid this silence felt somewhat embarassed, it was a relief to be addressed by Mr. Jennings.

"I perceive, sir," said he, "that you are an admirer, perhaps, I may say, a disciple of Mr. Darwin."

"An admirer I am," rejoined Mr. Maxwell, "but a disciple of the great deceased scientist I never have been. He was never explicit enough for me. In the domain of science he has opened up vast fields;—with the acutest observation he has followed nature in her different by-ways; he has shown how she varies her work by giving new forms to things, and how, step by step, through the course of ages, she has changed species into species. This work of taking down false landmarks through nature's realm and of putting up new ones will remain his great title to immortality. But I like to see men 'thorough' in their views; with the domain of nature, enriched as it is with every beauty and power, he ought to have been content, and not to have gone beyond it in search of its cause. Nature is self-sufficient; this universe, to my thinking, is the one, self-existing, eternal being."

This last phrase, spoken with a tone of defiance, startled all present; immediately they let their papers drop, and turning round on their chairs, looked steadfastly at the speaker, while the features of Mr. Jennings assumed a stern cast.

"I am unwilling," said he "to withhold from Mr. Darwin my word of praise for his minute zoölogical researches, though I do not admit that he has made his name immortal by any real original discovery. But, waiving that point at present, it is the view expressed in your last sentence which I dispute, nay, which I emphatically deny; your assertion puts on you the burden of proof."

"The proof," replied Mr. Maxwell, "is not far to seek; it is supplied by the universe itself, since the matter of which it is made, all scientists acknowledge, is indestructible: no known agency can destroy a particle of matter; it will be to the end what it has been from the beginning."

"Excuse me, sir," said Mr. Jennings, "the major premise of your argument is out of place; there is question of the cause of the universe, but your reasoning turns on its continuity. Because matter is indestructible, you conclude it had no beginning;—which is equivalent to saying, that you yourself were not born because in another state you will live forever. The pyramids of Egypt, we may well affirm, will last till the end of time, would you thence infer that they had no beginning?"

"The case is not a parallel one," spoke out roughly Mr. Maxwell; "the one is artificial, the other natural; all know that the pyramids were built by men, matter built itself."

"I used the comparison," said Mr. Jennings, "to point out the logical force of the argument, and as such I hold it to be valid; the inference in the one instance is exactly similar to that in the other."

"But my inference," was the reply, "is based on induction, yours on assumption."

"Let us see," said Mr. Jennings; "the argument from induction we base on single facts or judgments, and from the peculiar nature of these we ascend to the universal and formulate an analytic principle applicable to all facts and judgments of the same species. In the particular, for instance, we know that things which are equal to the same are equal to each other; then, by our abstractive power, we formulate the same as a principle of universal application. By induction, then, we proceed from the particular to the universal,—and this is the analytic method; by deduction, we descend from the universal to the particular,—and this we call the synthetic method. Your reasoning follows neither. Experiments have indeed shown that matter, though transformed, remains in quantity the same. This is a legitimate conclusion, drawn from actual facts, and relates to the actual constitution of matter, but it in nowise touches the point at issue. Induction only teaches that no human agency can destroy matter, but the problem of the origin of matter itself lies altogether outside the scope of the argument."

"I confess, sir," said Mr. Maxwell, "that I am no adept in the subtleties of logic, but when I find truth I hold to it to the last. The universe furnishes me with a firm basis for my reason and denotes, by its very features, its absolute, independent existence."

"You surely, sir," answered Mr. Jennings, "would not consider it a subtlety of logic, to point out the rules of logic, or to explain what a process of reasoning must be, in order to be valid. This is all that I have endeavored to do. But as to your statement that the universe bears on its face the proof of its self-existence, I maintain, that, so far from that, the universe, through all its domains,—in every particle of matter, in every manifestation of force, and in every germ of life, proclaims unmistakably that its cause is external to itself,—that God is its author."

Nature Witnessing to God.

"I should like to hear you prove it," said Mr. Maxwell abruptly.

"While I endeavor to do so, gentlemen," replied Mr. Jennings, turning to his hearers who were eagerly attentive, "I shall claim your patience."

"In the kingdoms of nature, all observation shows, that there are continual changes; one thing produces another, and this in its turn is the cause of a third, and all through the ages, in every land, recorded experience teaches that the same order of cause and effect has always reigned. The produced has come from a producing power,—new existences or new modes of existence springing from some causal energy,—the purely material phenomenon from a preceding one,—the plant from the seed, and the seed from the plant, back to the last border of nature. The first seed did not produce itself; the first particle of oxygen did not generate itself; dead matter was not its own cause. How then did it come to exist? Following back the causal history of existing things through the cycles of past time, we come to the same goal and have to ask, whence this first finite cause of element, of plant, or of animal? No matter how you may fancy the arrangement of these causes and effects, whether it be in a line of regular succession, stretching backward indefinitely, or in a circle whose circumference encloses the remotest causes or the first changes of matter, the same question recurs:—Whence came the first link in the chain of the series, or the first point in the formation of the circle? The length of the series or the breadth of the circumference does not change the nature of the finite. Tracing back, then, dependent effects and causes through all time, in any series, reason on the farthest limit of their physical existence necessarily perceives that there exists a first independent cause, from which all subsequent, subordinate causes necessarily depend. This first cause, since it cannot be prior to itself, cannot have produced itself. Of its own nature, it is independent, and is absolutely self sufficing. In other words, it is God.

The argument briefly stated is this. Since no creature can be its own efficient cause, everything that is produced must be produced by another. Again this latter in turn is either caused by another or if not, it exists of itself. If it is produced, the same question of dependence recurs, and since it is impossible to go back indefinitely from cause to cause, there must be an uncreated being from whom, as first cause, all subsequent causes depend."

"To the argument just given," said Judge Jefferson, "this objection occurs to me. In any line of beings we may suppose an indefinite or perhaps an infinite series, and hence that the first being of that series is the first cause of the same."

"It is numerically the first cause in the series," replied Mr. Jennings, "but since it cannot be its own cause, beyond it we must look for a cause of an altogether different nature, a cause which is absolutely the first. The same answer will hold even though without reason you claim that the series can be infinite, since, however placed, whether in a series or separately, the finite never ceases to be contingent; from itself it has not the sufficiency of its own existence. I say, *without reason*, since to make the infinite consist of a number of units, as Locke does, is to add the finite to the infinite. But besides this succession of cause and effect along certain series, there are other causes in the physical world, which are interlaced with their effects only by certain cosmic influences. The plant, for instance, will not grow nor produce fruit without the sun's light and heat. In such causes and effects the same reasoning holds as in the former case. Dependent causes lead up necessarily to the first Supreme Cause, who gives their efficiency to them."

"Notwithstanding the explanations just given," said Judge Jefferson, "I think the proof of the thesis is not comprehensive enough. It is based exclusively on the animate organic world, but touches not that vast expanse of inanimate matter which lies outside the domains of life. I should, therefore, like to hear it proved how matter, or this solid earth on which I stand, bears witness to the existence of a first Supreme Cause."

"Pardon me, when I say," replied Mr. Jennings, "I think, you have not seized on the precise bearing of the proof presented. In its application it is not restricted, as you suppose, to animate nature, but extends to all matter, inorganic as well as organic, or to wheresoever natural causes operate. From all material effects, we can reason to their material causes, and from these again, considered as effects, we can ascend to the elements which compose them, and thus backward along the line of material efficiency, until we come by analysis to the first simple elements. Arrived at which barrier we ask, whence came these elements?

"But to answer directly your request, an argument for our thesis can be formulated from the very matter to which you appeal. I say, then, that matter, or this solid earth, must have come into existence only in one of two ways. Either it was produced by a pre-existing being, altogether independent of it; or it exists of itself as an absolutely necessary being,—one whose nature it is to exist. In this latter case, not only is the existence of such a being absolutely necessary, but its mode of existence must also be so. A self-existing being cannot exist otherwise than it exists, since its mode of existence is necessarily implied in its existence, it is absolutely unchangeable. Now, how is it with matter? is it unchangeable in its substantial mode of existence? Your own observation, I am sure, sir, teaches you, that matter can exist in three states altogether different, in the solid, gaseous, and liquid states. Moreover, you must have observed that the elements which go to make matter are different in the simple from what they are in the compound; oxygen and hydrogen have separately quite different qualities from those which they have in water, their compound. Marble to the eye seems to be but one ingredient, but let it only be submitted to the glowing heat of the lime-kiln and it is immediately decomposed into two totally unlike substances, quicklime and carbonic acid gas. Now send a current of electricity through the former, and you have calcium, a light yellow metal, and oxygen; while the latter, if suitably treated, gives charcoal and oxygen. But farther back than calcium, charcoal, and oxygen we cannot go:—in them matter has found new modes of existence. Even a diversity in the relative proportions of material constituents connotes a specific diversity in their compound. Thus oxygen and nitrogen in different proportions, in five different combinations, will produce five different substances, each with its distinctive properties. Matter, then, continually changes its modes of existence, and thereby with the clearest evidence shows that it is not self-existent;—its changeableness of substance is proof convincing of the dependence of its origin. It proclaims unmistakably that whatever is in it, it has received from one outside itself, who is the independent, unchangeable first cause of all things."

"The proofs just proposed," said Mr. Maxwell, "sufficed for the Middle Ages, but have been in our age set aside by the progress of science. The physical basis on which they rest being found to be spurious, they forthwith, of course, lost all their force."

"I fear, sir," answered Mr. Jennings, "that you have not examined the subject closely. The basis of the proofs given is not any scientific analysis but reason and that knowledge of the physical world which all men have. Now an argument based on such a foundation is good, I submit, not for one or other age, but for all ages. Furthermore, I will add, that it has been conclusively shown that real modern science, so far from being in conflict with mediæval teaching on the constitution of matter, has but confirmed it in its principal points. Chemistry, as an experimental science, remaining strictly within its proper sphere, has not disapproved any of the doctrines taught in the schools of the Middle Ages,—in regard to the elementary forms and combinations of matter. The proper object of chemical analysis is the sensible, or the facts and phenomena that fall under the senses, but when, passing beyond these, it undertakes to investigate the efficient causes of things, it uses instruments which are not within its competency and is invading the domain of metaphysics.[1]

"But," retorted Mr. Maxwell, "does not metaphysics do the like? it uses physics for its own purposes."

"It uses physics," answered Mr. Jennings, "as science uses them, for the acquisition of knowledge, but not as going outside its own sphere to reject or contradict the laws that regulate physical combinations. As the superior science, metaphysics has a right to use for its purposes the certain results of physical investigation."

"Would you not consider, sir," inquired Mr. Ferguson, "that the theory of evolution has greatly weakened the cogency of the argument stated? Within the realm of nature, it accounts for all new existences and explains every change in the world as being merely consequent on a former change."

"I think, sir," answered Mr. Jennings, "that the argument has in nowise been weakened by the theory of evolution. And first I would remark that the theory itself, as maintained by some physicists, looks to me like a forgery put upon nature. It has not been demonstrated; even some of its most zealous advocates admit that it is only a hypothesis, grounded they say, but still a hypothesis. A form of evolution, indeed, is traceable in this material earth on which

---

[1] See the Metaphysics of the School. Vol 3, p. 80 and the following. By Thomas Harper, S. J.

we live, in the development of nature from lower to higher conditions, through the various geological strata; but that is all that seems to be certain in this theory. Granting, however, all that it supposes: that the world, for instance, has been evolved from the fiery cloud, and force, and that all living things have been developed from the lowest germs of life, the question again returns, whence came the cloud, and the force, and the germs? And if for these again another finite cause be feigned, that cause, in its turn, will have to be accounted for. To the same barrier we come by analyzing all natural substances, and when in our search we have got, if that could be, to the first atom or to the first element, reason, peering through the void, will recognize the first great, absolute cause of all things."

"In a certain sense," rejoined Mr. Ferguson, "the answer is conclusive, but under some respects it does not seem to me to be altogether clear. The changes which take place in nature, you call effects, and thereby suppose their causes, while these causes in their action you appear not to distinguish from the first cause. The latter and every cause that is the result of will I would qualify as truly efficient causes; the former, namely those in nature, I would call a sequence of changes or conditions produced by natural growth."

"With the explanations given, sir, I presumed that I might use the term 'effects' without implying a begging of the question. The argument turned on these new products which meet us everywhere in the world, and which postulate three conditions for their existence, 1. That the things produced be preceded by the power producing, 2. That the latter is necessary for the production of the former, 3. That it suffices for the same end. These conditions, to be sure, are not verified to the same extent in all causes; in intelligent causes, they have their full efficiency; in material causes, though working differently, they are no less real. I perceive as quickly that heat has caused water to boil, as that intelligent man has constructed the Brooklyn Bridge. There is, I acknowledge, an essential difference between the first cause and all secondary causes: the former is absolute, and self-existent; the latter, though real, are dependent or relative; the former is absolutely required for the production, not only of the existence, but also of the essence of the finite; the latter are not in themselves absolutely necessary for the existence of their effects, since these could be produced by other means by the Creator. He alone holds the first link in the chain of finite causes, gives them productive strength, and supplies the mind with that light whereby it perceives that whatever exists must have a sufficient cause.

"Another view of the physical world," added Mr. Jennings, "will present this same truth to us under another and perhaps a more striking aspect. There is no lesson of nature which perhaps it emphasizes so strongly as that derived from the dissolution of things. Over its domains are continually passing in succession the glow of life and the shadow of death. To day we have life germs, growth, and florescence, to morrow decay, corruption and dissolution, so that no other truth is brought home to us so forcibly as that of which the poet wrote,—

>   . . . . . 'all that is, must die;
> Passing through nature to eternity.'

"All that is, once was not, and sometime hence will be no more. Nothing in this world can hold back death's strong arm; in time, its reign has been universal; on every living thing it has put its mark. With the inherent perishableness of all things before us, then, we can conceive in the far off past a point of time when nothing lived. Farther back, therefore, than the epoch of the Laurentian bed, let us gaze, if you will, through the mirror of fancy, on the bald, black, dreary world. There is not the least token of vital power in either earth or air or water; not the rustling of a leaf, not the fragrance of a flower, not the chirp of a bird, not the buzz of an insect through that vast waste of a dead world. Where shall we find life? Not in the cold, dead clay, not in the hard grained rock, nor in the subtile atmosphere, nor in the boundless ocean. We look beyond the verge of nature, and reason directly grasps the conclusion—life must be from One who Himself is self-living, an absolute, independent, necessary Being—God."

"Multiply the contingent as much as you like, it will never lose its nature. What cannot be as well as be, needs a cause to determine its existence, since nothing can give existence to itself, and undetermined being as the contingent by nature is, must have a determining cause. Fancy the perishable in a series of changes through life and death, reaching back eternally, if that were possible, and even then it would require a living cause to make it pass from the non-existent to the existent,—a Being who would determine the indeterminate, would limit the indefinite, and would cause by an act of his will the possible to pass into the actual.

"In another form, the same argument may be thus proposed. In the physical world, all observation shows that things may be or not be; contingency is of their nature. Let us suppose, then, that nothing but the contingent existed in time or eternity; and according to that hypothesis, what was possible not to be, since it could not be its own cause, was not at one time. Taking into account, then, the universality of contingent beings, we can logically say, since it is possible for them not to be, that there was an instant when they were not, and all was emptiness through the immeasurable void, since nothing was. But if nothing was in the abyss of the past, then, I say, nothing should be in the present. The non-existent or the possible cannot become the actual, but through the activity of a living agent. If, then, all existence were eternally a blank, a blank it should always remain. Now, however, since things innumerable do exist, they proclaim that, before the existence of all perishable things, there was always a Being not liable to decay or death, who, having in Himself the principle of His own existence, is a self-existent necessary Being, from whom are all existences—who is God."

"I am at a loss to see," remarked Mr. Maxwell, "how you conclude from the finite to the infinite, from the contingent to the necessary, and from the relative to the absolute."

"You will allow, sir," was the reply, "that in civil life the notion of an inferior or dependent naturally suggests the notion of a superior or master; and so too in the argument just stated, the idea of the finite and dependent, by a sort of natural necessity, suggests the idea of the infinite and absolute. And with this idea before it, the mind again judges, that what depends on another for its existence cannot be the first cause of all existences, or that beyond the range of the finite, there exists a Being from whom the finite came to be."

"I see no necessity," said Mr. Maxwell, "for looking for a first cause of things outside the world as we know it, since it accounts for its own existence."

"To answer by an illustration," answered Mr. Jennings, "Brooklyn Bridge, sir, as we know it, holds itself together and nobly spans the river; would you say that its present existence postulates its self-formation?"

"I would not, sir," was the reply, "because the case is not parallel. In the world we have matter, force, and gravitation, and these suffice for the building of the universe."

"But have we not the same in the bridge?" was the answer; "we have iron, which is matter; force also we have under various forms, and gravitation, as a general law, acting on the bridge. I am willing to grant, of course, that these have been balanced against one another by the power of genius, but still they show that for the argument the case is parallel. Besides, sir, you begin by assuming the whole subject. The question is about the origin of the world, but not caring for that, to start with, you take the world for your fulcrum and then proceed to use the lever."

"I do not assume," said Mr. Maxwell, "I take the data furnished by science. It has been satisfactorily proved that the world is the result of the combination of atoms."

"But," answered Mr. Jennings, "supposing that to be the case, the further question is, whence came the atoms? Moreover, sir, the atomic theory is in direct conflict with some chemical laws. It proceeds on the supposition that the combinations of atoms took place by blind attractive force. How then does it happen that the atoms of oxygen and hydrogen essentially distinct combine in due proportion to form water? And how is it, if the measure of that proportion be not observed, they will not combine? And again, that other combinations of atoms for such a purpose are not formed? If the combination of atoms explain every physical process, what are we to say of the necessity of generation and corruption for the production of living things? The collocation of atoms in a dead and a living body is the same; change it as you may, you cannot make the dead live."

"It seems to me," said Mr. Ferguson, "that the only conclusion we have reached by the argument from causation is, that beyond the range of cosmical causes there is an independent cause, impersonal it may be, as far as the proof goes."

"Not at all," replied Mr. Jennings promptly; "we conclude not merely from effects in the inanimate creation, but also from those in the realms of animated nature; from all that has life and sensations; from men endowed with mind, morality, and will, and personality, we rise by reasoning to the conception of the living, intelligent, moral, personal, first cause of all, who is God."

"It is Mr. Mill, I think, sir," said Mr. Webber, "who maintained that the development of inferior orders of existence into superior ones is the general rule of nature. Out of the lifeless earth grow vegetables and plants of various beauties. Is not that a reversing of the order of causes?"

"Undoubtedly, if true," was the reply. "It is not the bare earth that produces the vegetable or plant, but the seed. In it is the life-principle of vegetable and plant, a principle immaterial as it is, that assimilates nutriment from the soil and builds up the living stem or sprout. The beauty, then, of the rose or of the lily is, by way of germ, in their seed."

"But, sir," asked Judge Jefferson, "does not the doctrine of forces cover the ground of the origin of life, vital force being only, according to eminent physicists, the result of the combination of various other forces? Your argument, however, seems to depend mainly on the contrary hypothesis."

"I would say, sir," replied Mr. Jennings, "that, even were the origin of life such as you represent it, my argument would not lose its conclusiveness. Life then would be the effect of force, but force itself, potential or active, traced back to the origin of things, whence did it come? and whence did that atomic force or activity of nebulous matter get the special law of grouping elements around different centres? Here, indeed, Mr. Darwin, to meet the emergency, calls in "pangenesis" or a creative energy as pervading organic bodies, while Mr. Herbert Spencer has recourse to 'physiological units;' but still the same query comes up: whence come the 'pangenesis' and 'the physiological units'?

"But the supposition itself, that vital force is the outcome of physical forces, is entirely gratuitous; no conclusive proof of it has ever been given; physicists, no matter what they may say, have never succeeded in producing from any combination of force or matter even the lowest form of any living thing. It has been shown, indeed, experimentally, that all physical inorganic forces are correlated and that one is convertible into the other, but nowhere and by no one has it been shown that any physical force is convertible into vital force. Between them there is 'an incommunicable gulf,' to use the words of Sterling, —'the mighty gulf between death and life.' But physicists have a logic of their own when they wish to reach a conclusion. One writer, for instance, tells us that 'life is a complex term,' and includes all the phenomena which a living body exhibits, which is as much as to say that life is life; then he goes on to state that he uses 'the term vital force to express only the actual energy of the body, however manifested.' This being supposed, vital force is convertible into actual energy, and energy in the body is the same as energy without the body, and on these assumptions, 'the conclusion is reached that vitality is the sum of the energies, both potential and actual, of a living body.' Of the confusion of thought in some quarters on this same subject an apt illustration is given by the Bishop of Carlisle in the Contemporary Review for September, 1885. He is examining the definition of life, and, in order to show how difficult it sometimes is to put a practical conception of it into definite words, quotes a passage from Professor Drummond's work,—'Natural Law in the Spiritual World.' The Professor stated that, according to biologists, the characteristic of the living organism is 'its vital connection with its surroundings,' or, put scientifically, ' to be in correspondence with its environment,' and that it is in virtue of this correspondence that one is said to be called alive, upon which views the bishop writes, (as I find by my note book) 'Now, if this biological language be of any value, it ought (one would think) to explain itself and not require to be explained, but Professor Drummond cannot trust it to itself and he follows it up with a 'that is to say.' And what is there to be said? Why this, that the meaning of being ' in correspondence with his environment' is, that ' he is in active and vital connection with them;' in other words, that he is alive. Thus life means vital connection; vital connection, 'in biological language,' means 'correspondence with environment;' correspondence with environment means vital connection; and vital connection put into English means life.'"

"That certainly is laughable enough," said Judge Jefferson ; " but are there not grounds for supposing, from discoveries already made, that life may be only the result of physical and chemical changes? Respiration, for instance, has been discovered by Lavoisier and others to be reducible to the general laws of combustion; by experiments also, begun by Spallanzani, it has been shown that digestion is a chemical process, and that the strength of the muscle is only 'the potential energy of the carbon of the food,' assimilated."

"Certainly," said Mr. Jennings ; " but it is the life

principle that vitalizes these physical or chemical processes, which co-ordinates them and makes them work for the same end, the building up and support of the organism. Apart from the vital principle all the science of the age could not form the almost structureless amoeba. The experiments of Pasteur in France and of Dallinger and Drysdale have put this subject out of controversy,—'omne vivum ex ovo' is the formula that touches nearest of all definitions to the principle of life."

"You would admit, however," rejoined Judge Jefferson, "that since the time of Lucretius, the greatest scholars, and some of them renowned for piety, held that matter under certain conditions can produce the lowest forms of animal life."

"They did, I acknowledge, hold such views, said Mr. Jennings; "but that they were mistaken, microscopic investigations and other experiments have clearly shown. Their opinion, however, does not in the least militate against my argument, since they referred the generation of life ultimately to God as to its primary source."

"Still," it was again urged, "the difference between the elementary composition of organic and inorganic bodies may very well account for their character as vital and non-vital."

"No such difference exists," replied Mr. Jennings. "That there is such a difference was a theory of Lord Bacon which modern science completely negatives; it is now admitted as a postulate by scientists that matter in the organic and inorganic state is composed of the same identical elements; namely oxygen, hydrogen, azote, carbon, together with something of phosphorus, sulphur, iron, etc., with, of course, in living things the additional vital principle. By a combination of some of these or of other elements chemistry has succeeded in forming chemical compounds, but not the smallest vital organism; it has never produced and will never succeed in producing a living leaf or a nerve, or a life-cell. In inanimate matter, for instance in crystals, the formation is from without; the forces in them, by their interaction under the directing influence of the substantial form, give to them a geometrical harmony by fitting angle to angle, and side to side, so that there is a mechanical response of one part to another—but in the living body, the formation goes on from within, not by putting layer after layer in juxtaposition, but by a constant assimilation of new matter, by an exchange of the molecules from within for those from without, by harmonious growth from one vital principle that subjects to itself the chemical action and the physical forces of the organism."

"But may not the elements of the primitive world," asked Mr. Jefferson, "have been different from those of the finished universe? And in that hypothesis, we could well suppose that life sprang from the interaction of material forces."

"To make such a hypothesis," said Mr. Jennings, "would indeed, be in keeping with the theories of many scientists, but would surely be in no wise science. Besides, it would put scientists in contradiction with themselves in regard to the invariableness of matter and force, and would upset the very equilibrium of things. Let the proportion of gases in the composition of bodies be changed, and their constitution is reversed; or let these gases be different from what they are, and you shift the grounds of the argument. You may be speaking of the temperature of Mars or Uranus, although you pretend to speak of that of the earth."

No other objection having been raised, a conversation ensued on the opinions of some modern writers in relation to the subject of the present discussion. Locke, it was admitted, broached views on the source of our knowledge which led to materialism. The intellect he looks upon in some passages of his essay as a mere faculty for perfecting sensations, while these again he identifies with ideas. There runs through his work, it has been remarked, a twofold philosophic system. "At one time, he seems to be a thorough-going phenonomist, at another, an out and out realist: now he appears to do away with all substance in things, and again zealously maintains it." But, unsafe as he is as a guide in philosophy, he has drawn out with great force a proof for the existence of God.

(Here Mr. Walters read from his note-book) "'To show, therefore,' writes Locke, 'that we are capable of knowing, that is, of being certain that there is a God, and how we may come by this certainty, I think, we need go no further than ourselves, and that undoubted knowledge we have of our own existence.'

"I think it beyond question that man has a clear idea of his own being; he knows certainly that he exists, and that he is something. He that can doubt whether he be anything or no, I speak not to, no more than I would argue with pure nothing or endeavor to convince nonentity that it was something. If any one pretends to be so sceptical as to deny his own existence (for really to doubt of it is manifestly impossible) let him for me enjoy his beloved happiness of being nothing, until hunger or some other pain convince him of the contrary. This, then, I think, I may take for a truth which every one's certain knowledge assures him of, beyond the liberty of doubting, viz., that he is something that actually exists.

"In the next place, man knows by an intuitive certainty, that bare nothing can no more produce any real being, than that it can be equal to two right angles. If a man knows not, that nonentity or the absence of all being cannot be equal to two right angles, it is impossible he should know any demonstration in Euclid. If, therefore, we know there is some real being, and that nonentity cannot produce anything real, it is an evident demonstration that from eternity there had been something, since what was not from eternity had a beginning, and what had a beginning must have been produced by something else.

"Next it is evident, that what had its being and beginning from another, must also have all that which is in and belongs to its being, from another. All the powers it has must be owing to, and received from the same source. The eternal source, then, of all being must also be the source and original of all power. And so this eternal being must be also the most powerful.

"Again, a man finds in himself perception and knowledge. We have, then, got one step farther;

and we are certain now that there is not only some being, but some knowing, intelligent being in the world. There was a time when there was no knowing being and when knowledge began to be; or else there has been a knowing being from eternity. If it be said, there was a time when no being had any knowledge, when that eternal being was void of all understanding, I reply, that then it was impossible that there ever should have been any knowledge; it being as impossible that things wholly void of knowledge, and operating blindly and without any perception, should produce a knowing being, as it is impossible that a triangle should make itself three angles bigger than two right ones."

"The form of the argument is good," said Mr. Jennings, "but it is not original; it was given in the 12th century by Richard of St. Victor.[1] He lays down the very principles from which Locke argues. Given, he says, the contingent, or that which so exists that its non-existence is possible, and, since it could not give itself existence, there must be a self-existing eternal being from which it received its existence. If nothing were from itself, then there had been nothing from eternity; and then there was no origin or succession of things. Summing up the whole argument, Cardinal Newman thus writes: 'For if (to suppose what is absurd) the maker of the visible world was himself made by some other maker, and that maker again by another, you must anyhow come at last to a first Maker who had no maker, that is, who had no beginning. Else you will be forced to say that the world was not made at all, or made

[1] Lib. 1 De Trinitate, Cap. 8, 10, 12.

itself, and itself had no beginning, which is more wonderful still; for it is much easier to conceive that a spirit, such as God is, existed from eternity, than that this material world was eternal. Unless, then, we are resolved to doubt that we live in a world of beings at all, unless we doubt our own existence, if we do but grant that there is something or other now existing, it follows at once that there must be something which has always existed and never had a beginning.'"[1]

In the course of the conversation, the name of Hume was next brought up, and his teaching in relation to Theism examined. It was admitted that in psychology he was a sensist,—denying also that we have any intellectual perception of the law of causality. We do not know things but impressions, was one of the maxims of his teaching. The natural consequence of such a doctrine, if carried out, would be a denial of the existence of God. Still, in his treatise on Natural Religion, Hume writes: "The whole frame of nature bespeaks an intelligent author; and no rational inquirer can, after serious reflection, suspend his belief a moment with regard to the primary principles of genuine Theism and Religion."

The inheritors of the teaching of Locke and Hume have taken it to its farthest lengths. Out of it and its interpretation by scepticism they have developed what has been called "the philosophy of nescience,"—a philosophy whose special advocates profess to be downright know-nothings or agnostics, as they wish to be called. Their one and sole dogma is, that we know nothing but pheno-

[1] "Discourses addressed to Mixed Congregations." p. 197.

mena; or that it is only the appearances of things that we know, but of things themselves we have no knowledge.

On this teaching the comments of the gentlemen were various. Mr. Webber pointed out that the theory itself was self-contradictory, since, while denying the certainty of knowledge, it professed to be certain of the falsity of other theories, as well as of its own truthfulness. Besides, its supporters steadfastly contradict themselves in practice. They do not take gold for silver, nor silver for copper, because these metals differ in the phenomenon of color, but because of something beneath that color and partially manifested by it. As sane men, too, they are certain of their own existence, and they know that, though professing extravagant views, they are not simply phenomena but human substantial beings, and this, not for to-day or yesterday, but perhaps for dozens of years. Prominent in the school of nescience is Mr. Herbert Spencer, who, notwithstanding his connections, knows a great deal and often thinks for himself. In his "First Principles," having refuted with great force of reasoning the illogical statements of Sir William Hamilton and Mr. Mansel on "the absolute" or "unconditioned," he undertakes to define what he himself means by the absolute. And, in the first place, he insists that it is not personal nor self-existent, nor infinite; still it is the "ultimate cause," is omnipresent, indefinite, and "in every respect greater than can be conceived." It does not of its nature exclude limits, but can be conceived in some imperfect way as being without them. From these views it is clear that the absolute in Mr. Herbert Spencer's sense is nothing but abstract, universal, indeterminate being; that as such it has neither existence nor intelligence, nor will, but that it underlies the world and is identified with it. Further on in his work, feeling that he must be more definite, he confesses that the "absolute" of which he spoke is, in plain words, "the Persistence of Force," in capital letters. It is a cause which, he says, transcends our knowledge and conception. In asserting it, we assert an "Unconditioned Reality, without beginning or end." "Thus, quite unexpectedly, we come down once more to that ultimate truth, in which, as we saw, religion and science coalesce."[1] As an expression of his belief, this is satisfactory. It is clear that Mr. Spencer's god is "the Persistence of Force." This is "passing strange;" but stranger still to understand how he can know this god. The great source and test of knowledge, he says, is experience; we know only what we see, or hear, or touch; but here is a being that is above our knowledge and conception, or "which transcends experience by underlying it." Mr. Herbert Spencer then knows the force-god, though he cannot conceive him; he knows him to be "without beginning or end," though he flouts the idea of his being self-existent or produced. He takes him also to be formless and indeterminate and yet to be determinate in his manifold manifestations. He is no definite reality and is all reality at the same time. As blind as the stone and as impersonal as the air, this "Persistence of Force" is, however, the cause of beings that live, or feel, or think, and

[1] First Principles, p. 192 d.

reason, and will. Such, then, is the self-contradictory, first principle of the "First Principles" and the basis of the synthetic philosophy of Mr. Herbert Spencer. A philosophy, be it remarked, that has been pronounced to be specially fitted for the needs of the rising generation.[1]

When Mr. Webber had finished speaking, Judge Jefferson remarked: —

"In connection with this subject I may be permitted to narrate a dialogue which I once heard in a railroad car. A Darwinian maintained that the environment in which anything grows is the great factor in creating and diversifying its organs. This assertion he tried to prove by instances taken from the habits of various animals. Whereupon the Cincinnati merchant whom he addressed retorted much after this manner:—

"'There are certain animals, sir, which breathe through their lungs, others which breathe through their gills,—would you have me believe that air created the former and water the latter? Or could you tell me what medium or environment formed the heart, which, pump-like, receives blood from the organs through one channel and gives it back to them through another? Or again, would you venture to say that it is light which has formed the wonderful apparatus of the eye, whereas it was actually

---

[1] "The invigorating influence of philosophical studies upon the mind, and their consequent educational value, have been long recognized. In this point of view the system here presented has high claims upon the young men of our country—.... We say, the young men of *our country*; for if we are not mistaken, it is here that Mr. Spencer is to find his largest and fittest audience. There is something in the bold handling of his questions, in his earnest and fearless appeal to first principles, and in the practical availability of his conclusions, which is eminently suited to the genius of our people."—Preface to the American Edition of "First Principles," p. 8.

formed in the darkness of the womb? Newton asked: "could He who made the eye be ignorant of the laws of optics?" Scientists of your school, sir, would answer, 'yes,' and that he was not only ignorant, but was not even conscious of his action, since this is but the result of the unknowable, whatever that may be, evolving itself by blind, indiscriminating tendencies."

As the conversation went on, Mr. Walters, turning to Mr. Jennings asked,—"Would you not think, sir, that your primary argument has been much weakened by the Association Philosophy, as taught by Hume?"—"I do not understand," answered Mr. Jennings.—"Hume," continued Mr. Walters, "maintained that, as we see only the sequence of things, our idea of one thing being the cause of another has come from the custom of our taking the sense of that sequence to be the perception of the necessary connection between them."

"I think, sir," said Mr. Jennings, "you will admit that we know more than our senses tell us. Our knowledge is surely greater than that of the brute creation. We surely know ourselves. Sensible impressions tell us of the sequence of things, but that one thing produces another, is apprehended spontaneously by the intellect. Cause, no more than substance or vitality, is reached not by sense but by reason. Outwardly, the sequence of things is perceived, but inwardly the mind, by a law of its nature, perceives the causal connection between them. A man, I suppose, removes a chair from one part of a room to another; my senses tell me of the sequence of change, but my mind clearly apprehends that the man is the cause of it. And thus I am made conscious of a faculty within me which can know causal action, in itself unattainable by sense."

"But," resumed Mr. Walters, "the recurrence of natural phenomena generates the idea of law; may we not say the same of the law of causality?"

"I have no difficulty in admitting," said Mr. Jennings, "that the recurrence of similar successive events facilitates the perception of the causal relation between them, but it does not generate it. A single case often suffices to enable the mind to perceive the relation of cause to effect. While skating, let us suppose, a man falls and fractures his arm; it was his first experience of that kind, nevertheless, he clearly sees that his fall was the cause of the fracture. I admit, however, that the idea of causality is brought home to man by his own consciousness; we all feel and know that the motives which we form inflow into the will, and that by these it freely determines itself for action. When I wish to move my arm, I move it, and therein I perceive that the determination of my will is necessarily connected with the motion of my arm, is its cause. When, then, in nature, I see a series of changes taking place by way of sequence, I naturally infer that a cause is required in order to account for that sequence."

"I can very well understand," suggested Mr. Ferguson, "how, with materials to work from, a being can produce effects, and, therefore, be a cause in various circumstances, but how a being without matter could have produced the world is more than I can fathom."

"I think, sir," replied Mr. Jennings, "the point of

the argument has escaped you. We are discussing the *fact* of the existence of the First Supreme Cause of things, and now you turn aside to discuss the '*how*' of the world's origin. I need hardly tell you, sir, that the one is entirely distinct from the other. Every moment we are dealing with facts the intrinsic plexus of which we know nothing of. For instance, you know that you think and will, but *how* you do so, you cannot distinctly say; still you would not, for all that, deny the fact. Science also has taught you that bodies in the system of the world are kept in their orbits by the force of gravitation, but what precisely in itself gravitation is, you do not know. Facts we know, but the ultimate reason of these facts we know not. The first principle, the dynamic force, the vivifying power, the efficient causes of those successions, which we term natural laws, elude the utmost efforts of our research.

"I cannot, then, conceive *how* God made the world, but I can conceive *the fact* of His having made it. All nature cries out to me that He made it, and reason distinctly teaches me that there is no objective repugnance in things to His having done so."

"I admit," said Mr. Harrison, "that along certain lines reasoning will lead up to a first, independent cause, but from these particular facts as premises to reason to an universal cause is not logical."

"Certainly," said Mr. Jennings, "if *these* only furnished the ground for the conclusion; but everything that exists, plant, element, animal, man, furnishes the same. All the phenomena of animate and inanimate nature are like so many streams, which, when traced to their fountain-heads, direct us onward and upward to their eternal source. Besides, sir, the world is not like a bundle of distinct and separate sticks, but so forms one compact whole, that between its parts there exists an interdependence or a mutual interlacing that makes them to be one system governed by uniform law. An argument, therefore, derived from the constituent parts of the world, is also logically equivalent to an argument from the whole. 'The System of Nature,' writes the Duke of Argyle, 'in which we live, impresses itself on the mind as one system.'[1] It is under this impression that we speak of it as the universe..... I have already indicated the sense in which the unity of nature impresses itself on the intelligence of man. It is in that intricate dependence of all things upon each other, which makes them appear to be parts of one system. And even where the connection falls short of dependence, or of any visible relation, the same impression of unity is conveyed in the prevalence of close and curious analogies which are not the less striking when the cause or reason of them is unknown.'"

"Has not God," asked Mr. Maxwell, "received an addition to His being by creation? How, then, can the theory of Mr. Spencer be so faulty?"

"Since creation there are more *beings*," answered Mr. Jennings, "than before it, but not more *being*. You would not say, sir, that a man who has painted a hundred pictures is more of a man after his work than before. His pictures do not add to his being, neither do the works of God add to the being of God."

"I think, sir," resumed Mr. Maxwell, "if you

[1] The Unity of Nature, pp. 1-5.

escape Scylla, it is only to fall into Charybdis. God being infinite in nature is, you say, the cause of all other beings; then, I conclude, all things, good, bad, and indifferent, exist in God."

"By way of retort, I ask," was the reply, "would you say that the house which the architect has built exists as such in him? But answering the objection directly, I hold that all things are in God, but after different modes. Perfections simply and purely such are in God formally or according to their definite nature; life, intelligence, goodness, justice, etc., exist as such in God; but material things, and those that are made up of the perfect and imperfect, exist in Him *eminently*, or in His supreme, creative, and conservative power.

"In creatures their perfections exist in finite proportion, narrowed as they are by matter or nature; in God, all spiritual and actual as He is, perfections exist in all their fulness; in creatures perfections exist as qualities, in God they are one with His substance; hence, man is said to be good or just, but God is justice itself and goodness itself. We cannot, therefore, affirm perfections in the same sense of God and of man; but by a certain analogy, the perfections of the creature we predicate of God, in whom in their infinite grandeur they formally exist, and from whose plenitude all have received.

"The bad, it is evident, cannot exist in God, it is of man's making.

"In conclusion, I say that the eternal Being of God cannot be added to, even in thought; it cannot be developed."

"But," rejoined Mr. Walters, "if the perception

of causality be so evident, how is it that some persons doubt of it?"

"I would say," answered Mr. Jennings, that "some persons may doubt for want of reflection; the concrete, and not the abstract, is all they think of. Others doubt theoretically, but not practically; in actions they contradict what they express in words; and others again doubt, because they will it. They can close their minds to the truth, as easily as they close their eyes to the light."

"I suppose, then," said Mr. Walters, "that I must accept a proposition as true, when I cannot conceive its contrary."

"Not at all," answered Mr. Jennings; "that would not furnish you with grounds for accepting it. The proposition must contain in itself the evidence of its own truth. I accept as true the proposition that the whole is greater than its part, on its own internal evidence, and not because I cannot think the contrary. The inability to think is one thing, the perception of the impossibility of a thing is quite another. I also accept the law of causality as true, because it clearly recommends itself to my intellect."

"If you allow me, sir," said Judge Jefferson, "I think we prove too much at a time. Our argument led us to the first cause, and from that we proceed to formulate a religious view and call that cause God. Now, would it not be well to wait, before thus defining, until we have examined the moral, emotional, and æsthetic nature of man, on which principally theistic belief rests?"

"All the proofs for God's existence, I admit," answered Mr. Jennings, "by different processes, reach their conclusion, considered under this or that aspect. One proof directly leads to God as to the supreme first cause, another, to Him as a necessary Being, another again to Him as unchangeable, and still another takes us to Him as to an infinitely perfect Being. But all the while, by different ways, it is God Himself that is reached. When I ascend to Him as the first independent cause, I realize not an impersonal force, or indeterminate power, or merely universal energy, but the one, living, eternal God, the cause of all things. Under this latter aspect I directly view Him, and then by reflection recognize in Him the attributes of the Godhead. Now, from such premises, we can certainly form a religious conception of God. By acknowledging our dependence on Him as the first cause we frame the first article of our religious belief. This to Him is our '*reasonable* service,' based on our intellectual nature or on the two great characteristics of intellect and will, that are peculiar to man alone. True religion in man, then, is not, sir, as you seem to suppose, a thing of emotion, or of taste, or of æsthetics, but the dutiful homage of his whole being to 'the Creator of heaven and earth,'"

Scarcely had Mr Jennings finished speaking, than Mr. Taunton, who all along had been quite thoughtful, said: "I need hardly remark, gentlemen, that the testimony of nature to God is not exhausted by the evidence which cause and effect or life and death afford. Through her domains she furnishes, under thousands of forms, grounds for the same evidence. The change which underlies the causal process or that of dissolution is only one phase of that universal movement that reigns through creation. For myself, I confess that the physical phenomenon which takes my mind back to God, as it were on the wings of lightning, is the motion that has everywhere sway around me and is even in me. By the study of its pulsations in things animate and inanimate I can reach its source, judge of its nature, and discern how it must be immovable because all other things are movable. The argument was suggested by Plato in his Phædrus, and again in his treatise on laws, but it was Aristotle who, we may say, gave to it a scientific form in his two last books on Physics. 'Everything that is moved is moved by another' is the principle on which he bases the argument. And by motion he means not only the transition by external force from the passive state to the active, as we see it in the local changes of material bodies, but also the transition from the potential to the actual, as we witness it in the external and internal acts of living beings. The analysis of motion, therefore, gives us these data, namely, the capacity of a being for receiving motion as a perfection of its nature, and also the power of a being of conferring that perfection, either instantaneously by one act, or successively by different acts. A being, consequently, that by his very nature can receive no perfection by change, is necessarily immovable, and perfect. In animals, their bodily motion springs from the vital principle in them, and this again is moved to act by the influence of external objects; vegetative growth, also, comes from the vegetative principle of life, and this is stimulated to action by material elements, by temperature, and by sun-light. In man his will is moved to act by what the intellect proposes to it as desirable, and his intellect is roused to activity only by the intelligible properly presented to it. The Being, therefore, who Himself is truth for His intellect, and goodness for His will, is alone not acted on by another, but is 'truth understanding itself, and goodness wishing itself in one eternal, inimitable act.'

"Looking only to experience, we say rightly that every living creature is self-moving; but analyzing its act, we learn that, as a whole, it does not move itself, since part only moves part, the vital principle, for instance, the body; or again the intellect, the will; the will, the nerves; the nerves, the members. Not infrequently, however, the word motion is, in a general sense, taken for any immanent vital operation, and also, as in man's case, for his free acts; and then every living being is self-moving, not only because it is endowed with immanent vital activity, but also because it is influenced from without.

"So much being premised, I say, all things in the world in which we live are changeable and movable; everything that is moved, we have seen, is moved by another; all nature is continually drawing on its powers and urging them to activity,—that which was moved, imparts in its turn motion to another. Following back in any series of motions the moved and the moving, to the remotest rim of nature,—and since there cannot be an infinite series, we come to the first thing moved or that which first passed from the passive or the potential to the active and the actual. We examine;—it could not have brought itself over the abyss that stretches between the passive and the active, or between the potential and the actual, since it did not exist; it could not have been brought by other finite things, since they were not. In default, then, of any sufficient ground for the existence of that which was first moved or actuated, we necessarily conclude to a Being, who, immovable Himself, is the first cause, immediate or mediate, of all that moves or is moved. Thus all the changes or movements which we perceive in nature, followed back, bring us ultimately to the first cause from which all mutable and actual beings receive the perfections they possess. 'They shall all grow old as a garment, but Thou art the self-same, and Thy years shall not fail.'"

"Perhaps," said Mr. Harrison, "I did not take in the full meaning of the argument, and hence, no doubt, it sounds to me sophistical. Science, I think, has proved that motion is of the essence of matter; if that be so, then, I say, since matter moves itself, that the argument is a begging of the question."

"Allow me to say, sir," answered Mr. Taunton, "that all physicists admit that matter has two great properties, one passivity, or the capacity of being acted upon; the other, 'inertia' or the incapacity of self-motion: it has been acknowledged as a law of universal experience that want of spontaneous motion is a property of all inanimate nature."

"You do not mean to deny," said Mr. Harrison, "the existence of the laws of attraction, as discovered by Newton."

"No, sir," was the answer; "all that those laws teach me is that material bodies naturally attract each other, but not that they move themselves. I will add even, that, if you do not admit inertia, you cannot estimate attraction. If the planets were self-moving, their relations and orbital disturbances, their influence and existence could never have been determined. If Uranus were the cause of its own motion, *a priori*, it could never have been conjectured by Leverrier that, as an explanation of its variations, the planet Neptune, which caused them, must exist; if the heavenly bodies were their own motors, Laplace, as he himself insinuates, could never have composed his *Méchanique Céleste*.

"Newton himself does not call attraction a physical force, or one inherent in bodies, but strives to explain its influence by supposing the existence of a subtile fluid, in which the heavenly bodies are immersed. Writing to Bentley on the doctrine of Epicurus, who taught that motion is innate to matter, he uses the following words: 'That gravity should be innate, inherent, and essential to matter, so that one body may act on another, at a distance, through a vacuum, without the mediation of anything else, by and through which their action and force may be conveyed from one to another, is to me so great an absurdity, that I believe no man who in philosophical matters has a competent faculty of thinking can ever fall into it.'"

"Well, then," said Mr. Harrison, "you hold that all bodies are only dead matter, that they have neither energy, nor force, nor activity."—"That is not my opinion," replied Mr. Taunton; "I hold that all bodies have an activity peculiar to them, and that their very essence is the principle of their activity. They possess resistance, impenetrability, quantity, and other properties, and by means of these they influence other bodies. But that is quite a different thing from spontaneous motion; the rock of itself will always remain immovable, and the earthen mound will never give a sign of motion. But let us take two bodies which, though they cannot move themselves, can move each other, then that which moves, is itself moved by another, and this again by another, and so on indefinitely. Thus all the movements in nature are linked together and form, as it were, a chain, the first link of which, since it cannot cause itself, must have its cause beyond it."

"All this," said Mr. Harrison, "seems to me to conflict with what had been affirmed of the passivity and inertia of matter."

"The words that were used," replied Mr. Taunton, "if understood with the meaning in which they were taken, exclude all contradiction. That bodies have 'passivity' or a capacity of being acted upon is a fact of universal experience. 'A body is composed of potency and actuality, and hence is active and passive.'[1] It is passive, inasmuch as it can be acted on by other bodies; it is active, inasmuch as it acts on them. The oak, for instance, will bend before the storm, but will not suffer itself to be easily uprooted; iron in the furnace will become malleable, and water under a burning sun will become vapor, but iron will not yield to every heat nor water to every sun-ray.—Inertia implies that matter in itself is not self-moving,—a truth, I presume, which requires no proof."

[1] "Corpus componitur ex potentia et actu et ideo est agens et patiens." St. Thomas.

"It is now admitted," said Mr. Harrison, "by almost all physicists, that bodies are formed from molecules, and that these attract one another; would not this fact go to prove, sir, that matter is self-moving?"

"I fail to see that it would, even if I admit the hypothesis which you make," replied Mr. Taunton, "and you yourself have suggested the refutation. You tell us truly that two molecules attract each other; note, you require two,—one, you grant then, has no self-motion, has not in itself the power of ruling itself, but for movement needs the attraction of another. The same holds good of all the other molecules that make up the universe; they are held together by reciprocal attraction, and as they do not possess in themselves the reason of their motion, we must go outside and beyond them for the cause of it."

"But," asked Mr. Ferguson, "does not the earth move, and do not all things move with it?"—"Certainly," was the answer, "the earth with all things moves with planetary rotation, that is, it receives its movement from some influence, or impulse, or power outside it, but this no more proves that motion is essential to matter, than that a railroad car is self-moving because it is drawn by a steam-engine. Matter in itself, inert, as all experience shows, is not motion and neither is it force."

"I have always admired," interposed Mr. Webber, "the idea of Lord Bacon of England in regard to the construction of the universe. According to him, love is the great cement of the world; it was love, which, when only chaos existed, united atoms to atoms, and thus built up earth, and water, and firmament. This affection of atom for atom is inherent in them, and has no cause within nature; and albeit that it is stone-blind, as being love, it sorts things nicely, and balances all things with just measure. Now I submit that this system leads up to an intelligible way of explaining the origin of things, and bridges over for me the abyss between my finite thought and God's infinite nature."

"The remarks just made," said Mr. Jennings, "remind me of what Sextus Empiricus relates of Epicurus. In his youth, so the story goes, Epicurus, as he was reading with his teacher the cosmogony of Hesiod, came to the lines:

'Eldest of beings, chaos first arose;
Next earth, wide-stretched, the seat of all.'

and having listened to the explanation given of the origin of things and of chaos, then pointedly asked: —'and whence came chaos?' The teacher was fairly tripped up by the question, and candidly told his pupil that for its solution he must go to the philosophers. He went, and as an explanation of the origin of the world, adopted the atomic theory of Leucippus and Democritus. It never occurred to Epicurus, that one of his own pupils might very well have asked him,—'and whence came the atoms?' But to be just, though Bacon attributed a native affinity to atoms, he never maintained that the atoms themselves were uncaused, but continually in his essays recurs to God as the Creator of all things. Here are words of his," continued Mr. Jennings, as he read from his note-book: "'I had rather believe all the fables in the legend and the

Talmud and the Alcoran, than that this universal frame is without a mind; and, therefore, God never wrought miracles to convince atheism, because his ordinary works convince it. It is true that a little philosophy inclineth man's mind to atheism, but depth in philosophy bringeth men's minds about to religion; for while the mind of man looketh upon second causes scattered, it may sometimes rest in them and go no further; but when it beholdeth the chain of them confederate and linked together, it must need fly to Providence and Deity..... The Scripture saith: "The fool hath said in his heart, there is no God:" it is not said, the fool hath thought in his heart; so as he rather said it by rote to himself, as that he would have, than that he can thoroughly believe it, or be persuaded of it; for none deny there is a God but those for whom it maketh that there were no God.'

"Your chief difficulty, however, sir, as I understand it, comes from our mode of conceiving God. The difficulty is not a new one, but in modern times it has been popularized by Sir William Hamilton and has been adopted and repeated by Mr. Herbert Spencer and his school. To them God is 'inconceivable' and therefore 'unknowable,' and thus, from the meaning which they attach to words, they rush into the denial of the basis of all truth. In their opinion, we cannot conceive God, unless we put, as it were, our minds around Him, see Him through and through, or comprehend Him. And surely, in this sense God is inconceivable. But is this sense really required in order that we should conceive God? If it be, then I say, most things are to us inconceivable, because we neither fathom all their properties, nor can we, from mere actual sensible phenomena, measure the fulness of their nature. I conceive the ocean and space, although I have not seen their limits, and the magnet, though I do not know the cause of its magnetic power, and light, though I do not know its nature. Of these I have a distinct idea, though not an adequate one; I know that they exist, but I cannot furnish the summary of all the qualities of their existence. To know the fact of existence is one thing, to know the reason of that existence is another. Through my senses I am brought in relation with them, but it is by their essence I conceive them. It is the essence or the substantial form of things, or that in them which makes them to be such or such,—it is this, I say, which the mind primarily apprehends. The incompleteness of our knowledge of a thing, therefore, does not hinder us from having a conception of the same. Now the physical world has led us to God as the first cause; the contingency and limitation of all finite things have directed us to Him as a self-existing, absolute Being, and the motion that exists through the universe has postulated Him as its unchangeable, immovable Author. Under this threefold aspect, then, to remain within the compass of the arguments hitherto drawn out, we have a distinct idea of God—we conceive Him; we know of His existence from the visible things of nature, much in the way that we know of the existence of the soul of a man from his sensible actions."

"Still," said Mr. Walters, "it is not so clear to me how the finite mind can conceive the infinite. To do so it should in some way include it, it should take it in by its mental power from the representation of it given by the imagination. This I consider to be the rational order of knowledge."

"Your difficulty, sir," said Mr. Jennings, "arises from not observing the different relations which the mind bears to objects, or how one object may be included in another after a twofold manner. When I predicate animality of man or horse, I mean that they possess it in their substantial nature (entitative); when, again, I say of such or such a picture that it suggests this or that painter, I mean that it has certain features which clearly point to him. The finite understood in the former sense does not, of course, stand for the infinite, but taken in the latter sense, it does; that is, visible things, lit up by the light of the intellect, are for men signs wherefrom they may infer the existence of their Author. The vestiges of His attributes they perceive in creation, and then, by the force of reason, they conclude to His existence as the First Great Cause of all things, the self-existing Supreme Being."

"It is only then," said Mr. Maxwell, "those who are versed in reasoning processes who can have a knowledge of a Supreme Being; which is tantamount to saying that the belief in His existence comes from art and not from nature; that, I think, ought to suffice to discredit your argument."—"By no means," answered Mr. Jennings; "one of the occasions that call for the use of the art of logic is the abuse of logic; when men strive to misinterpret nature, their efforts have to be laid bare by art derived from nature. Men who follow the leading of reason conclude to God's existence,—common sense pointing out the way. For this natural process, there is no need of any chain of reasoning: reason directly infers that back of force and matter, or this external world, there is a power that originated it and upholds it."—"That," said Mr. Maxwell, "would not be common, but uncommon sense, since it would find a cause where a cause was not necessary. Whereas force would suffice, it would call in God."—"You will admit, sir, I presume," was the reply, "that force does not exist independently of matter, or that it must have a subject to which it adheres." Mr. Maxwell assented. "Well then," continued Mr. Jennings, "it is not only of force but of matter that you have to explain the origin; and as matter is not self-existing, has not produced itself, it postulates a cause outside itself. If you say that force produces matter, then you abandon the argument from induction and maintain what reason and observation pronounce to be absurd."—"I did not say," retorted Mr. Maxwell, "that force makes matter, but it has made the world."—"The same difficulty recurs," answered Mr. Jennings, "since the world is made of matter. But, besides, you will have to explain how forces repulsive and attractive put themselves in equilibrium; if they exist equally they neutralize each other; if unequally, then nature becomes unbalanced. When men conclude that behind force, followed backward to its ultimate analysis, there must be substance, and that this primordial substance has not created itself, they are going by reason towards God. But still scientists will beat the air and let it be understood that they themselves alone know everything about the subject."

"The same charge of self-assertion," screamed out Mr. Maxwell, "might be more fairly brought against those who claim that they know God with means not proportioned to that purpose. I like consistency in argument and logic carried to its ultimate conclusions, be these what they may. It has been assumed that the sensible is a necessary condition for thought, or that ideas must rest on some objects presented by sense or by imagination or by sensible memory. In a word, that every concept must be labelled with some sensible mark. Now, from this position the gentleman recedes, since he tells us that the idea of God, infinite as it is, can have no adequate, sensible token of itself, in *rerum natura*. I agree with him; what is beyond my senses, or what I cannot imagine, is to me inconceivable."

"Not so quickly," replied Mr. Jennings; "in the case, I appeal to your own convictions. You will not, I suppose, refuse to admit that I can have an idea of your soul or, for that matter, of an angel, though I can clothe neither with imagination; I can conceive abstract truth, or goodness, or power, though I cannot imagine it; I can also conceive the annihilation of the soul, though I can have no sensible image of it, and so also I can conceive God as a most pure, infinite spirit, though I cannot picture Him to my imagination.[1] By intellectual representations I can ascend to Him; the various truths that I know of Him I can combine and examine by mental acts; but I cannot imagine them as they are in His one,

---

[1] "That which is unpicturable may be conceivable, and the abstraction which is impossible to imagination is easy to conception." Problems of Life and Mind, vol. I., p. 430. By George H. Lewes.

indivisible nature. His adorable name, however, as expressed in words, I can use as a sensible support for thought. His nature and attributes, as stated in propositions, are something for the imagination to gaze upon;—the propositions, 'the Son is God,' or 'the Holy Ghost is God,' appeal to my imagination as well as to my intellect. By the imagery conveyed by the words I find an object for the former; by the revealed truth that is in them, I find food for the latter.

"As a preliminary for thought, the sensible is necessary; it is, as it were, a stimulus to the activity of the mind, and the source from which the imagination draws its imagery; but it is neither an ingredient of rational thought, nor does it make sensations to be equivalent to ideas. On the other hand, conscience tells us that the mind can rise above fancy, and by its own native power can perform a thousand operations beyond the range and realm of sense. Imagination being a sensitive faculty, represents only the sensible; it can photograph, so to say, objects presented by the senses, and out of the slightest sensible sign can construct a fancy image; it can unite, compare, and divide the features of things, and by the force of some analogy can furnish the mind with a certain sensible prop for the grasping of the immaterial. What is subtile and active and ethereal it can so use that the mind may be aided to apprehend the spiritual;—the power, the goodness, the wisdom, and the other qualities which the mind gathers from creatures, it can magnify indefinitely, and thus by analogical reasoning rise to some knowledge of them, as they exist in infinite intensity in

God. But the contradictory or impossible, as being nothing, for the life of me, I cannot know; I cannot form an idea of a square circle or a thinking stone; and for the like reason, I cannot conceive a thing to be and not to be at one and the same time; or to be essentially inert, and self-moving; to be perishable, and self-subsisting; to be contingent, and necessary; to be possible, and actual. These are chasms which I cannot span by any stretch of thought, which, however, I would have to do in order to conceive a self-existing universe.

"It is otherwise when I think of a self-subsisting infinite Being. His power and divinity and wisdom and glory appear through creation; they are, so to speak, food for the senses and materials for the sketching of the imagination. Through them I ascend to their source, and form a distinct idea of that self-subsisting Being, who, by the very reason of His self-subsistence, is limitless by nature, and is, to use a word of St. Gregory of Nazianzen, 'the sun of the intelligible.'"

"Might it not be inferred, sir," asked Judge Jefferson, "that the imagination, since it has such a sway over the human mind, has led it also to imagine God? We know how savages, in whom the imaginative faculty is uppermost, ascribe, through ignorance or fear, the phenomena of nature to some presiding deities."

"This objection, urged by some writers," answered Mr. Jennings, "runs altogether on false premises. First, it supposes an abnormal condition of the imagination, when reason is, as it were, in abeyance, whereas the argument given regards the normal state of the human faculties; secondly, that the idea caused by the terror of natural phenomena does not outlast them, or that, when the imagination becomes settled, the notion of God ceases; thirdly, that this notion has come only out of the unwonted excitement of the fancy, such as savages experience, no account being taken of civilized nations, or of those great scientists, who, the more they became acquainted with the laws of nature, the more they reverenced the stupendous wisdom and power of God. Fourthly, besides, the hypothesis that savagery was the first condition of our race is a view that has been clearly refuted; and fifthly, I would say that the poor savage is only following the instinct of nature in striving to trace effects to their cause, and errs by giving loose reins to fancy when he should hold to the stern dictates of reason. He could never have conceived the idea of God from fear, had he not engraven on his heart the habit of what is just and unjust, or of a law which suggests to him a Supreme Ruler."

The argument having been apparently exhausted, the conversation turned on the relative influence of reason and imagination on the conduct of life in the nineteenth century. Mr. Ferguson was of opinion that the distinctive feature of this age is reason. To maintain his view he instanced the sciences, old and new, in which cultivated minds have enlarged what was known, have opened up new views of knowledge, have explored the data and the very sources of history, or again examined and sifted by analysis the different religions of the world. In philosophy, he maintained, in legislation, in literature, and morals, reason's influence in this century is clearly traceable. From these appreciations of Mr. Ferguson, Mr. Walters dissented, and went on to show, by a sort of arithmetical process, that by subtracting the imaginative quantity from the sum total of the labors of this age of ours, all that remains for reason is not considerable. He dwelt at some length on the scientific *abuse* of the imagination, and how in all the fields of science students have been ploughing and harrowing, and after all have frequently produced nothing but stubble; and again, how it was that in the British Quarterly for April (1884) Mr. Mivart, a distinguished scientist, himself admitted that many of the scientific theories of our day have been completely upturned by the work of Stallo. They were bubbles,—inflated by imagination. "Reason, of course," Mr. Walters observed, "can be exercised for very unreasonable purposes and on very fanciful and base subjects, or can be wasted on futile scientific hypotheses. It is certainly a strange recoil of modern so-called science on itself, when, as Mr. Huxley tells us, "There is much reason to believe that science is going to make a still further journey" (than that from Dalton's hypothesis of ether to that of Descartes) " and, in form, if not altogether in substance, to return to the point of view of Aristotle."[1]

Other gentlemen having taken part in the conversation, Mr. Walters, after some reflection, said: "Gentlemen, a few thoughts occur to me on the main question of discussion, which I would make

[1] "The Advance of Science in the last Half-Century." By T. H. Huxley, F. R. S., p. 55,

bold to propose to you. It has been said that through nature there are many ways that lead to God; the one that I point out, is that which stretches from finite to infinite being. It is based on a contrast between the grades of perfection in existences, or on a scale of finite, graduated excellence that, like Jacob's ladder, reaches from earth to heaven. The scale, remember, is not made up of the nature or essence of things, but of these perfections, which either mark the essential difference between them,—such for instance as subsistence, life, feeling, intelligence, or are attributes of creatures, such as truth, wisdom, power, beauty. Now, all observation shows that in the domain of nature there are different degrees of perfection in beings. Life in man is superior to that in the brute, and that of the brute superior to that of the plant. In like manner, power has its different degrees in beings; so also have beauty and wisdom. Everywhere and through all species of beings, there is a scale of perfection, and according to this men estimate them. Matter is inferior to life, bare life is inferior to the sensitive faculty, and this again to intellectual power, which we can conceive greater and greater. Since, then, in the physical order there are a good and a better, limited in their extent, there must be the best, from which the better is derived. In any line of pure perfection, metaphysically, we can also conceive a Being possessing that perfection without limit, and a more perfect being than He we cannot conceive. Thus starting from the true, the good, the beautiful in creatures, we mount higher and higher on those lines, to their source, until we reach truth itself, goodness itself, and beauty itself, which is God. Or again, taking subsistence, life, intelligence as our starting point, by these grades of perfection we ascend to Him who is self-subsisting, who is life itself and intelligence itself."

"As I understand it," said Mr. Webber, "the force of the argument lies in this, that the perfections which we see in creatures we can conceive to be greater and greater and even unlimited. Let us suppose that we have done so, we have only conceived being in the ideal order, but not an actually existing being, in whom infinite perfections really exist."

"In the argument, sir," answered Mr. Walters, "we do not consider perfection in the abstract or simply ideal, but as it exists in creatures, and therefore real, actual perfection. This, in its distinctive species, we follow up to its ultimate grade, and as the creature postulates for its existence a first cause, so does the perfection of the creature demand for its existence an absolutely perfect Being. Now the perfection of such a Being, I say, is infinite. The limits of the perfection of finite beings come from the dependence of their nature. To the finite something can always be added, it can be rendered more and more perfect, and at least within the limits of species, is indefinitely perfectible. But a self-existing Being, as God is, whose very essence it is to exist, cannot be limited in His perfections, because He is dependent on no cause and He cannot be perfected, because, self-subsisting as He is, He possesses the fulness of perfection. He is not merely living, truthful, beautiful, but He is life itself, truth itself, and beauty itself."

"If the proof is to be considered valid," remarked Mr. Harrison, "it seems strange to me that it should have been ignored by nearly all the great teachers of the past."

"But it has not," rejoined Mr. Walters; "St. Augustine gives it in various passages in his works; St. Anselm draws it out with great subtlety of reasoning in his 'Monologium;'[1] Richard of St. Victor insists on it in his work on the Trinity; and it is one of the arguments given by St. Thomas Aquinas in his Summas, namely the 'theologica' and that 'contra Gentiles.'"

"To me, I must admit," said Mr. Harrison, "the argument does not as yet seem conclusive. The grade of virtue which each one has depends on himself; he is wiser or better because of his stricter observance of law."—"It is not the argument in itself that is at fault," replied Mr. Walters, "but, I presume, my presentation of it. That there is a gradation in the orders of beings will not be denied by you. The mineral, vegetative, and animal kingdoms clearly follow each other in a graduated scale and have from nature their inferior or superior qualities. But it is from man's position that your difficulty arises. He is wiser and better because of a law; then, I say, the law of the wiser and the better is before him and above him. He can become wiser and better still, and strive again to advance,—looking onward to the standard of the all-wise and

---

[1] Quum naturarum aliæ aliis negari non possunt meliores, nihilominus persuadet ratio aliquam in eis eminere, ut non habeat superiorem. Si enim hujusmodi graduum distinctio sic est infinita, ut nullus sit ibi gradus superior, quo superior alius non inveniatur, ab hoc ratio deducitur, ut ipsarum multitudo naturarum nulla fine claudatur. Hoc enim nemo non putat absurdum, nisi qui nimis est absurdus."
—Monologium, ch. 4.

the all-good which attracts him to itself. And the nearer he shall approach this standard, which is also the centre of wisdom and goodness, the more enlightened will he become, just as a body becomes more lightsome the nearer it approaches the centre of light. And as that centre of light is the cause of light in all other objects, 'so,' to speak with St. Thomas, 'there is something which is the most true, the best, and the noblest, and consequently pre-eminently being, which is the cause of being, of goodness, of truth, and of excellence, in all other things.'"

"The argument is valid," said Mr. Ferguson, "provided, all the while, the perfections are objectively in things, but this is exactly what the argument supposes."

"In stating an argument," said Mr. Walters, "a man is not supposed to prove what is self-evident; —and the existence of the physical world I assume to be such. Some idealists excepted, who in practice deny what they assert in theory, the human race has believed in, and acted on the conviction of the existence of an external world. You would not say, sir, that all men, at all times, and all places, have been under a huge delusion. They lived, as you would suppose, not on the mere husks of things, or on phenomena, but on strong, digestible, substantial food. The solidity, extension, and quantity of matter were to them proof unquestionable of its existence. With Dr. Johnson, they would have thought that kicking a stone was refutation sufficient of idealism."

"If idealism be as fallacious as you say," answered

Mr. Ferguson, "how is it that such scholars as Mr. John Stuart Mill, and Mr. Alexander Bain maintain it under some form or other?"

"To this I answer," said Mr. Walters, "that it is no business of mine to settle difficulties for these gentlemen. I shall only add that, while they deny the objective existence and reality of matter, they are manipulating the same in their scientific investigations, and supposing it therefore not to be a mere shadow. They even prove scientifically that, before man was, the physical world had been; or that, even according to their conclusions, materialism existed before idealism.

"I have no difficulty in admitting," said Mr. Jennings, "the objective reality of things more or less perfect in their nature. But hence I cannot see how the argument concludes to an infinitely perfect Being. Ideally I can conceive a being such, but therefrom I cannot conclude to his real, actual existence."

"Pardon me, sir," said Mr. Walters; "you not only can, but you should. But first, I would remark that, when I speak of perfection, I mean something real, that qualifies creatures and gives them grades of being. I also note that, when I speak of God as being infinite, I mean that He is infinite in perfection. Now in this world, as you must have remarked, everything that exists has a determinate being. A horse, for instance, is a horse, and a man is a man and nothing else. Thus they cannot be essentially other than what they are; or their nature is circumscribed by their essence. But they can have endowments greater or less and are in their respective species indefinitely perfectible; the addition which they can thus receive to the perfection of their nature tells that they are finite and dependent for their existence. On the contrary, in a self-existent Being, His essence, being perfection itself, is necessarily limitless, or infinite. It cannot be limited by another, since God is before all and independent of all, not by Himself, since He is not His own cause, but, as His essence is the self-same as His existence, infinite as He is in the one, He is also necessarily infinite in the other. Looking then to the grades of perfection that I see in creatures, and taking any one species of them, wisdom, for example, I ascend to its highest possible degree and seek to know whence it came. If not from an inferior grade, then from a superior one, the highest, which, not being dependent on another, is self-subsisting wisdom itself. Thus, what is the highest in perfection in the ideal order, or the infinite, is also the highest in the real order, as being its cause."

"It seems to me," said Mr. Webber, "that there is something wanting to this exposition, since, if God be limitless and not presenting to my mind any determined or definite existence,—how can I conceive Him?"—"Certainly," answered Mr. Walters, "nothing is so determinate or so definite as God. All actual, He is omnipotence itself, justice itself, perfection itself. But because He is infinitely determinate it does not follow that He is therefore limited. All that is limited is determinate, but all that is determinate is not limited."

"We have gone pretty far in this discussion,"

said Mr. Ferguson, "but what, after all, have we gained? We have chopped some logic but have demonstrated nothing. This, I admit, is not our fault, since demonstration turns on the relations of our ideas, and not on anything objective or real outside us. Without assumptions, the most we can hold in regard to our thesis is that it is one of those practical certainties which men fall back on in daily life, but which they care not to account for, or which perhaps they cannot account for by the force of logic."

"Excuse me, sir," answered Mr. Jennings, "the arguments hitherto given are strict demonstrations of our thesis. A demonstration, you will admit with philosophers, is the evident deduction of a truth from real and ascertained principles. Its mere logical process is the work of the mind, but the materials on which it is grounded are objective realities or principles; if our knowledge were purely subjective, or if we knew only thoughts and not things, your reasoning would be valid; but since the object and the mind are both necessary factors in knowledge, the demonstration of a proposition is also the evident proof of its objective truth and reality. The demonstration of a proposition in geometry is not a mere mental speculation, but the setting forth of a truth that objectively exists. To be sure, demonstration may run on two different lines, one, that which takes the cause for the root of its development, another, that which takes the effect as a premise for reasoning to the cause. The former is known as the *a priori* method, the latter as the *a posteriori*, and this is the more common. When Columbus, after many days' sail in his voyage of discovery, saw marine birds and noticed the debris of wood and sea-weeds floating on the waves, facts that were indicative of land, he inferred with a certainty that no opposition could shake, that land was not far distant. He had clear premises for his demonstration, and a day or so sufficed to enable him to realize fully the conclusion of his argument by the magnificent discovery of a new world. The birds, the wood, the sea-weed, his own cognitive faculties, were certainties and not assumptions; they were premises which nature gave to him and from which, in the light of reason, he grasped a truth before he was able to verify it. For ages and ages, that truth had existed in its grand, bare objective proportions,—not stimulating the activity of any human mind or energizing the power of any human will; for men it was as if it were not, but brought in contact with human souls by the discovery of the great Genoëse, it became a vast field for human thoughts, a fruitful germ of a new civilization, and a fresh revelation of some of nature's greatest grandeurs, through which men may clearly see 'the invisible things' of God, 'His eternal power and divinity.'

"The existence of God, is, sir, if you like, one of the practical certainties of life; it declares itself to the reflective mind in every work of the world; but it is one, too, which, when questioned, admits of the most convincing demonstration."

In the heat of the discussion time passed on unnoticed. The truths explained so engrossed the attention of all present, that on the occasion they lost sight of their professional or mercantile interests. But, by a word of Mr. Ferguson having realized the lateness of the hour, they quickly arose to depart. Just then, however, Judge Jefferson begged their attention for a moment.

"Gentlemen," said he, "the truths that have been brought home to my inmost convictions to-day I take to be of greater moment to me than all the wealth of the world. Our meeting here, the starting of our discussion, our interest in the topics debated, have for me a far-reaching meaning—but that I shall not discuss just now. I take the facts of the case as they are, and these, I claim, ought to be bonds of union and friendship among us. We have begun the discussion of momentous truths, surely we will not be satisfied with that beginning.

"Gentlemen, I am staying at the Brevoort House, on Fifth Avenue; I invite you all to luncheon on Monday next. Will you be so kind as to accept?" All cordially assented. "I thank you," added the Judge, "but allow me, I have this favor to ask of you, that each will invite a friend whose studies or tastes would be interested in our symposium."

After having become personally acquainted with each other, the gentlemen set off for their respective engagements in the city.

CHAPTER II.

THE DATA OF NATURAL KNOWLEDGE.[1]

MANY of the errors of our time have arisen from a misunderstanding of the data of knowledge. In the confusion of mind that has followed, persons have often confounded sense-impressions with sensations, sensations themselves with thoughts, and sensitive cognition with intellectual knowledge. Because the same word "knowledge" is often used in either case, they take it to denote that the things for which it stands are the same, and that the knowledge, therefore, of man does not differ from that of the brute.

Nature, however, plainly shows that the faculty of knowledge in irrational animals is sense-perception, while that of a man primarily is intellect. Animals know only the particular object; what they see, or hear, or touch is all that they know; by no power of abstraction can they universalize the nature of the object, nor can they, as all experience shows, improve their knowledge by new methods or by new instruments; they are now in regard to knowledge, what they were at the date of the most ancient historical records. They know only what their senses tell them—neither rising to

[1] A paper written, at the request of the gentlemen, by Mr. Webber.

any ideal knowledge, nor forming anything like a rational plan for bettering their condition. What their instincts prompt, that they necessarily do; the agreeable they seek after and shun the disagreeable or hurtful. Their senses, especially those of the highest kind, are strikingly developed. Besides their subtle organism of sense, animals have those strong innate instincts that lead them to fulfil their respective functions. These instincts are spontaneous and necessary, not deliberative and free,—invariable and determined, not modifiable and of universal scope. Under the sway of these instincts, animals reach their end, not knowing consciously how or why, and that with a directness and accuracy which man, by his selective power and with whatever instinct he has, can never attain.

To the level of the brute's knowledge, some writers have endeavored, in these latter times, to bring down the knowledge of man; they differ, they assert, in degree, but not in kind. In man, to be sure, they admit, there exists consciousness,—something to them inexplicable; but ignoring this, they content themselves with examining man's bodily organism. Sense-impressions in their sole relations to nerve and brain they specially study, but the phenomena of conscious sensation, as experienced by men, they do not care to investigate. There are, however, in every sensation two separate elements, one, the impression on the organ of sense, the other, the change or determination of the vital faculty by the sensible object. Physiology deals with the former, psychology with the latter. Thus the impression made on the organ of sense is not the sensation but is preliminary to it; this it is which arouses and determines the sentient faculty and links to it, so to say, the sensible object. How is this done? The object is material, while the faculty, as being vital, is above the range of gross matter; and, moreover, according to the received axiom, the object of knowledge is in the faculty of knowing, according to the nature of that faculty. It is clear, therefore, that the sense-impression must so represent the sensible object that the vital faculty can perceive it and be united to it. Now this it does by producing a likeness of the object through the mechanism of the sense-organ. This symbolic likeness need not, to be sure, be a complete copy of the object, though it sometimes is, but may be a sensible sign, or token, or word, or a reminiscence, that unites the object to the faculty by something common to both. Received into the organ of sense, the image presents the object in order that the faculty may be determined to action by it, and in its turn the faculty, now rendered active, produces the vital act of sensation itself. These operations seem long in the reading of them, but in reality they take place in the twinkling of an eye, known to us as they are by conscious observation. They are in direct variance with the theory of merely subjective sensations upheld by the sensists. These teach that it is not the external object that we see, but its likeness within us, and that we know the object only by a process of reasoning. It is the image of the sensible object, they say, that we see, and not the object itself. To men who follow the plain dictates of nature, such a theory clearly declares itself to be a delusion; everywhere and in every epoch, as history teaches, they have thought, and spoken, and acted with the convictions that they knew things themselves and not barely their representations within them. The theory, moreover, supposes that an organic sense, the eye, for instance, has a reflex power, or that it can look back into itself, and that, instead of looking outward, as nature intended, it looks inward; it also supposes that the wonderful structure of the human eye is in itself radically wrong. To escape, if possible, the distressing recoil of their own teaching, sensists tell us that it is not the eye which sees, but the brain. Now we do not deny that the internal sense, and brain, and nerves have much to do with sensation; they are conditions for the perfecting of it. It is through the brain that we become conscious of sensation, but it is in the organs of sense, that it is accomplished; it is with our eyes we see, and with our ears we hear. And since the intellect depends for knowledge on the senses, if these can give no true report of what is external, I can know nothing of the material world,—nothing of earth, nor of sky, nor of plants, of animals, of men,—nay, nothing of God Himself.

To sensitive nature also, whether in man or irrational animals, belong imagination, sensible memory, and the internal sense. The imagination, being a sensible faculty, depends on the senses for its materials; it can in no way picture what in no wise comes under them. But for its end the least sign or even the faint remembrance of a word suffices. Its function is not to show the nature of what we are to think of, but partly to stimulate the intellect to act, and partly to bring it to persevere in its actions. The sensible memory is, as it were, the store-house of sensations. It holds within itself impressions of the facts and persons of the past, and gives them up when required to do so by some sensible passing events, or by the recurrence of the objects or actions which produced them. By our dreams we can perceive how retentive that memory is, and how with its aid the imagination may revel in the world of sensible imagery. Back of the external senses is the internal sense from which, as from their source, the former receive their sentient power, and to which, as to a common centre, sensations are referred. It is this, which distinguishes sensation from sensation, and again associates them, making them, as it were, to cohere in the one, same, individual being. These different sensible powers the Phenomonist will readily admit and even exaggerate their capacity; in his opinion they alone suffice for the acquisition of knowledge, no matter of what kind. Sense-perception has been his constant study, and since on the observation of physical phenomena his mind has been centred, he cares not to examine anything above them. What he sees, or hears, or touches, is all he thinks of, though meanwhile, as if in spite of him, his mind is at work, joining facts together and drawing inferences from them. He will admit, however, that he knows more than the beasts of the field, and he cannot deny that science, practical and speculative, literature, art, morality, and religion, as possessed by the human race, suppose a faculty of knowledge which irrational animals do not possess. Their knowledge, being merely sensitive, springs from sense, which is an organic power, whereas man's knowledge is intellectual, formed by the intellect, which is an inorganic faculty. Enlivened by sense-perceptions their sentient faculty rises not above the sensible, but the human soul, through an intellectual light given to it, abstracts by its inherent power ideal representations from sensible things. In animals sense and imagination exhibit the sensible object, but in man the imaginative representation is followed by an act of the intellect. Sensible operations, as we have seen, fit the sensible object to the vital faculty, and now the same object, by intellectual activity, is fitted for the intellect. The sensible rendered intelligible by the working of the active intellect becomes, so to say, connatural to it, and thus brings it to pass that the intellectual act terminates, not in the sensible as sensible, but in the object directly as it is the intelligible. Thus the same object, presented to the animal and to man, gives rise to different kinds of knowledge, since the object known is in the faculty of knowledge, according to the nature of that faculty. The animal has a transient, superficial cognition of sensible things, man has a reflex, conscious knowledge of them and knows them in their very essence. What the special and formative data of that knowledge are, we shall learn from the study of ourselves and of our fellow-men. By it we shall know how exalted man is in the sovereignty of his reason and in the exercise of those powers by which he knows truth and the causes and relations of beings.

Looking therefore through the world of thought and desire within us, we find that the distinctive faculty of knowledge in man is, as before stated, his intellect. Taken in its widest sense, the object of the intellect is being, possible or actual. Now being can be predicated of all things,—of material objects, of plants and animals, of man and of angel, and, in a manner peculiar to His nature, of God. Being, as wound up with all of these, can be reached by the intellect, and becoming thus the intelligible, is to the human mind much what light is to the eye,—it is a medium for intellectual vision. In itself, indeed, created being is indeterminate; to be an object for definite thought, it needs to be centred in some definite, sensible subject, since the essence of sensible things is the peculiar object of the human intellect. Sense-perception for man is as we have seen, the outpost of his intellectual knowledge; the same sensible being is, in different ways, the object of his sense and his intellect, and what he, the subject of both, knows through the former, he knows through the latter in the higher and different plane of intellectual life.—As the sensible qualities of things, then, are the objects of sense, so is their essence the special object of the intellect. When men ask about something new and strange to them, they are only inquiring for some notion of its essence. They see its external qualities, and their senses have already transmitted these qualities to the fancy for imagery; and now, through these, the mind wants to know *that* in the thing which makes it to be what it is, or, if we prefer to say, to know that in it which determines its existence in this or that species, and which is called its substantial form. Hence, as all experience shows, men distinguish objects from one another, not only by their appearances, but chiefly by their essences; they know that a man differs from a horse not only in outward form but likewise primarily in essence, or nature, or substance; and so too, that an animal differs essentially from a plant, and a plant from a mineral. Let it be maintained that we know not the reality of things, but at most only their appearances, and its very basis is taken from science, since this is derived from what is at least hypothetically unchangeable and necessary, while these are grounded on the essences of things. Geology, some physicists tell us, is hardly a science, because it has no fixed principles, while, on the other hand, mathematics and astronomy are admitted to be sciences,—the former, because it rests on invariable postulates, the latter, because it is based on laws demonstratively true. But in one and the other case, it is the unconditioned or the conditioned unchangeableness of the essence of things that is the foundation of science. It is this essence as a universal that the mind, at its first look, perceives. It first knows a horse to be such; but that it is a particular, individual one, as distinguished from all others of its species, it knows by reflecting on the horse's special qualities as presented to it by sense, or vitalized by sensation. Sometimes, indeed, as experience shows, we cannot know, even imperfectly, the specific essence of an object; but then, falling back on the primary transcendental ideas, we know it as 'being,' as 'something,' as 'one,' etc. Experience being our guide, we perceive our own feelings, our thoughts, our volitions; not relatively or as relations, but, absolutely, as they exist in ourselves or in our substantial spiritual nature, which is an absolute reality.

These are some of the natural, spontaneous operations that the mind goes through in acquiring knowledge. Moment after moment it is engaged in them, sometimes with more, sometimes with less reflection, in view of the nature or importance of the subject. From not duly considering the part that the human faculties take in those operations, the data of knowledge have become quite a puzzle for some writers. They seem to forget that in this mortal life of ours human knowledge is not made by the mind alone nor by the body alone, but by both combined in one nature in man. It is he alone who knows. In it's own subordinate position, the body furnishes through the senses the stuff out of which intellectual knowledge is formed; by them the material object is first mirrored, and, after having been touched by the imagination, comes in the form of phantasms under the active intellect. These phantasms, though sensitive, include the essence of the object, and the essence as such is supersensible. From the phantasms the intellect forms the intelligible species or seeds of thought; then generates in itself the idea, the word of the mind, (*verbum mentis*) and instantaneously, by reflection and judgment, produces the complete act of knowledge. The mere apprehension or the idea, as being only a transcript of the object, does not make for the mind formal conceptual truth, since this is an equation between the idea and the object, and it is only by a judgment that the intellect forms that equation. It not only apprehends the object, but it is also conscious that it directly perceives the external object as really existing and independent of its perception of it. The idea which the mind directly forms is not, however, the object of its knowledge, as Berkley supposed, but is the medium through which it reaches that object. The act by which we judge that the object corresponds to our idea is the complete act of knowledge; but it is not barely ideas that we know, but things. An idea is a true, intellectual representation of the object, as the phantasm is a sensible representation of the same, both like lenses presenting the object in a different light; but to say that in this apparatus furnished by nature it is the lens that we see and not the object,—is as much as to say that, when we look into a mirror, it is the mirror we see and not ourselves. Berkley may have borrowed his false theory partly from Locke, and, again, Hume may have taken his scepticism from both Locke and Berkley; but be that as it may, it is the teaching of these three writers that underlies much of the materialism, idealism, and agnosticism of our time. It has been shown that Kant and his followers borrowed from the views of Berkley and Hume and also that it was from the writings of Bacon and Locke that Condillac and the French materialistic school mainly derived their false principles.

All through this process of acquiring knowledge, the principal power which the mind uses is what philosophers call abstraction, and with it, comparison. It is a power that is natural to the human mind and is used by everybody. It is that by which one makes the visible knowable or renders the object intelligible, or it is an intellectual light, whereby the mind considers, far above sense and apart from all material qualities, the essence of the object pictured by sense-impressions. Abstraction, also, is a power wherewith the intellect can take up for thought one feature or property of an object to the exclusion of its other qualities;—with it, it can consider, for instance, what a tree or an animal has in common with all other trees or animals, no account being taken of what is peculiar to the former. Just as the visual power of the eye sets before us the physical features of an object, so the abstractive powers of the intellect make us acquainted with the nature or essence of the same.

From overlooking or denying this power of abstraction, innate to the mind, agnostics, although using it all the while, mix up the mental with the sensible and the phenomenal with the real or substantial in things. They say they know only what they see or hear. And still practically, in the intercourse of daily life, they contradict their own theory. They converse with their friends and hear their words and know their thoughts; with memory they can go back in thought for many years, and there, in the world of the past, look into and know objective truths. The conversation they engage in thus brings into play the sense of hearing, while it also engages the mind to find objectively the intelligible, or thought in sensible expressions. Instinctively, as it were, the mind seizes the meaning that underlies words and gestures, considers the relations they bear to each other and the judgments they convey. Thus thought, which is the essence of language, becomes food for the mind, while sensible signs and words are food for the senses.

The same exercise of mental and sensitive powers finds a ready illustration in the written or printed page. On it the eye sees words printed or written in parallel lines and gathers at a glance the sensible symbols that make phrase after phrase. Meanwhile the mind is reading the thoughts that are in these symbols and by memory is holding them together, according as they form, as it may be a process of reasoning, or a narration, or a description. The intelligible in the words occupies the mind, while the words themselves are matter only for sense. Those illustrations I use only to show that in acquiring intellectual knowledge there is a two-fold operation, that of sense and that of mind, and that the former only furnishes to the latter the sensible signs out of which it abstracts the intelligible. On this subject it is singular that agnostics have not taken into account the nature of language itself. For, viewed apart from its very first origin, what is language but thought put into words,—the work of the mind assisted by observation—the essence of things idealized and stamped in expressions,—or the natures, or substantial forms or reasons of things, set under sensible type by the abstractive power of the human intellect. For the most part, men talk in *universals*, and what are these but notions derived from things or realized by mental intuition as necessary truths.

Besides the organization of the faculties of sense and mind in man for the acquisition of knowledge, there are also self-evident truths rooted in the kingdom of nature which shine in upon his soul. From them demonstration proceeds and on them it rests; in their luminousness they cannot be rationally resisted, nor thrust aside, nor rejected. They are the "seminal reasons," as well as the staff of knowledge. The truths formulated thus—" a thing cannot be and not be at the same time," or, "the whole is greater than its part," are so clear in the very statement of them, and so draw the mind to themselves, that it must adhere to them. They fall on the eye of the soul with a distinctness like unto that with which the rays of the sun fall on the eye of the body, filling the mind with the light that is in them and leaving no room for doubt or hesitation. They make their own evidence. Deny, for instance, the propositions just stated, and you do away with the resources of all knowledge and with every kind of certainty. You cannot discourse or converse, since this supposes certain judgments as to what is or is not, or as to what is probable or is not; you cannot say for certain that any person or anything is, since, according to the supposition, the contradictions of these propositions can be actually true.

There are also self-evident truths, which hold the mind to themselves, not, however, immediately, by their own native light, but mediately, or through a spontaneous process of reasoning. When perceived, their hold on the intellect is as great as if they were immediately cognized by it, and the convictions which they generate are laws for thinking rightly. That everything, whether substance or accident, that begins to exist, or that every series of forces correlated or co-ordained for an end, has a cause, is a truth that discloses itself to every thinking mind. We know it from the consciousness of our own power of action, as well as from the observation of the physical world around us. The sequence of things, as a gentleman remarked in our first meeting, or the succession of one physical fact to another, is indeed all that the eye sees; but the dependence of one fact on another for its existence is what the mind beholds. It sees that there is a causal relation between them, and that one exists only in virtue of the influx of the other. Thus, instinctively as it were, the mind glances from the painting to the painter, from the plant to the seed, or from boiling water to the action of glowing heat. This inferential power of tracing events to their causes is inherent in the untutored and tutored mind; it reveals itself even in the opening faculties of children, who are so curious to know the reasons or causes of things;—to all minds the idea of a thing which begins to exist correlates the idea of that which gave it existence. So connatural and far reaching, indeed, is this idea of causality among men, that upon it all true science is based; with it, the physicist scrutinizes the sublimest heights of nature, and the philosopher, unravelling the tissue of complex causes, reduces by degrees causal influences to more and more simple elements, until he reaches the one, ultimate, absolute Cause of all things. As a working principle, too, the law of causality supports the very fabric of society; on it are grounded commercial speculations, mechanical skill, and agricultural interests: in the daily routine of life, it underlies the thoughts and the labors of men. It is true that some sceptics have called in question the existence of this principle; but still they act upon it; their rational nature has been stronger than their denial; they have been unable to undo the natural make and texture of their minds, even when they strove to trace their descent from the quadrumana or even from the mollusca. Thus the principle of causality, as a self-evident, necessary truth, declares itself practically to the mind, even when an effort is made to deny it in words.

Another of these intuitive truths that fill the mind with their light, is the reality of the external world. It encircles us, so to speak, enters through all our senses, and demands, on rational grounds, entire adhesion to it. Sense-perceptions, derived as they are from external objects, clearly point to this truth. It is this which explains the make and aim of our faculties, since we act with the full assurance that things exist outside us, and that we are dealing with external realities. By the sensations or phenomena within us, we know our own being, our own substantial reality; by the sensations or phenomena coming to us from external objects, we also know their substantial actual existence. Fancies or mere memory-pictures we can change at our will, but ideas, resulting from actual observation of things in the outer world, we cannot avoid having. Independent of sensation, they have an objective reality of their own, and they, as it were, assert it. Fancies of what was once painful to us may float around our minds, but do not produce any actual sensitive pain; they are as idle dreams; but things from without us, by giving us actual pain, prove to us their own reality. The fire that burns one's fingers teaches him that it is something real. "But yet," writes Locke, "if, after all this, any one will be so sceptical as to distrust his senses and to affirm that all we see and hear, feel and taste, think and do, during our whole being, is but the series and deluding appearances of a long dream whereof there is no reality, and therefore will question the existence of all things, or our knowledge of any thing, I must desire him to consider that, if all be a dream, then he doth but dream that he makes the question, and so it is not much matter that a waking man should answer him. But, yet, if he pleases, he may dream that I make him this answer, that the certainty of things existing *in rerum natura*, when we have the testimony of our senses for it, is not only as great as our frame can attain to, but as our condition needs."[1]

The evidence which the existence of the external world gives to the mind in reality makes the denial of it to be an absurdity. To maintain idealism is to run counter to the common sense of mankind, to undo the practical working of life, and to contradict all experience. To say that all things are like views in a kaleidoscope, or that there is no substantial reality in things, is like saying that your neighbor is a ghost and that gold is merely color. The truth or fact, therefore, of the world around us, since it is a fact, bears its own evidence in upon our souls. The fact might not have been,—and the same is to be affirmed of the evidence of causality,—but as it is, it is its own demonstration. It is a postulate of

[1] Essays, p. 417, § 8.

thought, which the constitution of men's nature forbids them to reject, and which enforces its truth by the interests, needs, and intercourse of every-day life.

Not only is physical nature thus continually supplying the mind with certain matter for truth, but the moral world also is furnishing it with data that cannot be rationally questioned. That the city of Paris or Pekin exists is for the mind of the untravelled a reality which it cannot reasonably reject. The testimony on which it rests is its evidence; either of these cities or both might not have existed, but the fact that they do exist declares itself so imperatively to the mind, on the moral grounds of human faith, that it must be accepted. The assent, indeed, which is given to facts furnished by the physical and moral world is conditional, it postulates the facts that give evidence; but the assent given to metaphysical truths is unconditioned, absolute. "That a thing cannot be and not be at the same time," is a truth that is independent of every condition and measurement in time.

From the data already given, whereby man can acquire natural knowledge, we can infer how from them he can ascend to a higher grade of knowledge, even to the knowledge of God. Sense being bound down to matter is so restricted in its powers that it can know only individual objects; it cannot universalize things and then compare them; but mind, as being immaterial and spiritual, has, though united to the body, operations of its own and apprehends in an immaterial manner the objects which sense offers to it. By universal ideas and judgments it knows the essences of things, and from qualities that are visible it comes, by its own abstractive and reasoning power, to a knowledge of things that are not visible. Through the sensible it has a knowledge of the hidden essence, the substance, and the nature of things. The invisibility of God is then not a reason why the mind could not know Him. Infinite by nature, and a pure spirit, He cannot, of course, be the immediate object of the human intellect; or in other words, by itself, in this life, without any intervening medium, the intellect cannot have an immediate intuition of God. But this, surely, is not to say that the intellect cannot know God from His works, or from His attributes reflected in them. The shadows of His greatness He hast cast upon the world, and these reveal Him to mortal men, just as "to those who suffer from weak eyes," to borrow a thought of St. Gregory Nazianzen, "the images of the sun in water show forth the sun." Our knowledge, to be sure, in this instance is imperfect, since, though true, it is not adequate; we rise from the knowledge of things to the knowledge of their Maker, whereas in perfect knowledge, the object itself being presented to the mind, we know it by itself, through its very essence.

Intellectually, we know created things by that in them which determines their existence, or by their substantial forms. In this way we distinguish one object from another; we know gold to be gold and silver to be silver. Intellectually, also, we form concepts of the perfections of creatures; we affirm, for example, in the concrete, that a person is just or wise, or in the abstract we speak of justice, or wisdom. In the former case, we represent to ourselves a subject in which justice or wisdom resides, in the latter we contemplate the form which needs a subject to adhere to. These modes of speech are exact when applied to creatures, but are altogether inapplicable when applied to God. He is not as a subject that is perfected, and neither is He an abstract form, but He is the all-actual, self-subsisting, substantial Being, Himself the author of all matter and forms. He is wisdom itself, " which is at the same time every other perfection in its greatest simplicity," and consequently, by His very essence, is most approachable to the purely simple and intellectual powers.

In the premises we have seen that in this life the sensible is that which as an object is proportioned to our faculties. Things themselves, we have also seen, we know by their substantial forms as given to us by the mind's natural abstractive faculty. It is only these forms, as being immaterial, that the intellect can grasp. God, therefore, as being by His essence a spiritual, self-subsisting being and form, is in His own nature most knowable.[1] In Him essence, being, and existence are one. In Him is nothing of the potential or possible, but in the plenitude of His infinite nature all is actual, living, and active.

Circumstanced then as we are, while living in this body, the starting point of our ascent to the knowledge of God must be from the sensible. In it, as in an effect, we can trace some vestiges of

[1] " Essentia igitur Dei, quæ est actus purus et perfectus, est simpliciter et perfecte secundum seipsam intelligibilis."—St. Thomæ Sum. Theol., p. 1, 9. 87, art. 1.

God's power, and divinity, and glory, and with these we have matter on which to base knowledge. But the great faculty which enables us to make this ascent to God is our intellect. Endowed with reasoning power, it is boundless in its capacity for knowledge. Put the world, if that could be, into the memory, and the mind would reach forward beyond the world; put the single object before it, and forthwith it goes forth to the universal. By itself, it has virtually an infinite scope, or, as St. Thomas has it, "quantum est de se ad infinita individua se extendit." With this great faculty, then, at our command, we come to know not only that God is, but also, in somewise, to know who He is, or to know His nature, though imperfectly and by analogy. Looking into the visible world, we find that it symbolizes perfections of different kinds: that, for instance, the structure of the world implies power; that the firmament speaks of glory; and that in the vast expanse of the fields of nature there is a glimmering of divine wisdom, and beauty, and goodness. These perfections we can conceive to be greater and greater, indefinitely. Existing in the creature, they necessarily imply that, in some pre-eminent manner, they exist in their Author. In Him they are as if in their eternal prototypes, and with Him also, as being the first cause of the order and harmony of the universe, they enter into the plan of His creative wisdom. To His infinite essence, as their primal reason or foundation, all finite essences are to be referred. But between Him and them lies that limitless distance that exists between the finite and the infinite. He is not Himself the universal, necessary essence of the finite, but the independent absolute cause of all its properties and perfections.

But, however great or indefinite these may be conceived, they must correlate in their supreme Author that which is greater than the indefinite, since in God nothing is limited and nothing indefinite. The possible indefinite perfection of the creature, therefore, supposes the infinite perfection or power of the creator. Following the same method and taking the natural perfections of man as the object-matter of our reasoning from analogy, we rise by gradations to the knowledge of those perfections as they exist, formally, or virtually, or eminently, in God as their supreme, uncreated Exemplar. Thus, to use a finite illustration, the massive dignity and grandeur, the intellectual power of features, the inspired look and countenance of the statue of Moses were in the mind of Michæl Angelo before he embodied them in marble, and so too, after a manner, the sensible, the spiritual, the intellectual, and moral qualities of man were somehow, everlastingly, in their archetypal ideas, in the divine mind, which is also the divine essence. From the book of nature, which, to use St. Chrysostom's metaphor, is in the natural order man's bible, man can, therefore, read of God. Rich or poor, learned or unlearned, barbarian or civilized, bondman or free, he can read that lesson. And not only that, but in this world within him, through the internal senses, by the sensations, impulses, and acts of his soul, he can learn of the properties of spiritual being, and by reflection rise in thought to a knowledge of their efficient first Cause, who is in Himself the life, the light, and the truth. "If there is one divine attribute rather than another," writes Cardinal Newman, "which forces itself upon the mind from the contemplation of the material world, it is the glory, harmony, and beauty of the Creator. This lies on the surface of the world, like light on a countenance, and addresses itself to all. To few men indeed is it given to penetrate into the world's system and order so deeply as to perceive the wonderful skill and goodness of the divine artificer, and even that order itself which an investigation brings to view is admirable for its beauty; but the grace and excellence which beams from the very face of the visible creation is cognizable by all, rich and poor, learned and ignorant. It is, indeed, so beautiful, that those same philosophers who devote themselves to its study come to love it idolatrously, and to think it too perfect to allow of infringement or alteration, or to tolerate even the idea. Not looking up to the infinite Creator, who could make a thousand fairer worlds, and who has made the fairest portion of this the most perishable, blooming, as it does, to-day, and to-morrow burning in the oven,—loving, I say, the creature more than the Creator, they have taken on them in all ages to disbelieve the possibility of interruptions of physical order, and have denied the miracles of revelation. They have denied the miracles of Apostles and Prophets, on the ground of their marring and spoiling what is so perfect and harmonious, as if it were some work of human art, too exquisite to be wantonly dashed on the ground. But He, my brethren, the Eternal Maker of time and space, and matter and sense, as if to pour contempt upon the forward and minute speculations of His ignorant creatures about His works and His will, in order to a fuller and richer harmony, and a higher and nobler order, confuses the laws of this physical universe and untunes the music of the spheres. Nay, He has done more, He has gone further still; out of the infinitude of His greatness, He has defaced His own glory, and wounded and deformed His own beauty,—not indeed as it is in itself, for He is ever the same, transcendently perfect and unchangeable, but in the contemplation of His creatures,—by the unutterable condescension of the incarnation."[1]

But our knowledge of God being only mediate, we see His perfections in His works only through the mirror of nature. In it we distinguish them, one from the other, and we call Him just, or merciful, or good, in accordance with our contemplation of Him at the time. Our concepts so formed of Him, though different, are grounded on His nature; it is by them that we are enabled, in the natural order, to catch even a glimpse of His infinite grandness. When the perfections which we view are all pure in themselves, coupled with no imperfection of the creature, we follow them up, (the law of causation aiding) even to the bosom of the Deity; but when in nature we find them scarcely shadowed, or only denoted by the imperfect, we eliminate it by an abstractive process, by separating the precious from the vile, until we arrive at the unalloyed, infinite

---

[1] "Discourses addressed to Mixed Congregations," p. 235.

purity of the First Great Cause. By the former method we come to know that God is endowed with intelligence, will, and power, and that essentially He is the infinitely true and the infinitely good; by the latter, we clearly recognize Him to be a Being in essence most simple, to be eternal, inimitable, infinite, immense, incomprehensible. And still these rays of divine light which we thus catch from viewing the visible world, when focused in their source, are really and objectively but one. As manifested and as we conceive them, the divine attributes are formally distinct; what is said of the intellect, to our thinking, cannot be said of the will; it is not the divine intellect that wills, nor is it the divine will that thinks. In the animal, if we may take an illustration from the finite, life and sensibility are not distinct from each other as two distinct elements, as we conceive them, though our concepts are grounded on the animal's nature, which, though one and indivisible, is at the same time the principle of its vegetative and sensitive life. Our concepts of the essence and attributes of God are formally distinct from each other, but they refer to the same divine substance, which in itself is most simple and still possesses the plenitude of all perfections. These, indeed, as they exist in God, are peculiar to Him alone, both as to nature and subsisting mode. They are infinite, one with His essence, unchangeable, while man's perfections are finite, changeable, and only accessory to his nature. Man can, however, manifest, in his own way, his perfections; he can at the same time be just and wise, good and forcible in his different acts, though it be but the one, same, individual will from which those different acts proceed. And thus, arguing from analogy, in himself, as in a finite image and bounded on all sides by the finite, he can outline, though obscurely and altogether imperfectly, the nature of his Creator, the depths of whose wisdom are unfathomable and the ways of whose Providence are unsearchable.

The knowledge, then, of the perfections of the creature leads us to some knowledge of the nature and perfections of the Creator. This latter knowledge is indeed at the end of all our thoughts and is the ultimate necessary basis of all scientific and intellectual systems of truth. Every science rightly so-called proceeds from postulates that cannot be questioned. On these it builds up its demonstrations, and holding to them it stretches forward, striving by its deductions to reach other truths. Some of these postulates are intrinsically true; they are independent of all time and space, and no matter what may happen, they must remain unchangeable. The ontological truths that they embody shine in upon the mind by their evidence as "universal judgments." Most simple as axioms and belonging to the metaphysical order of things, we conceive them to be eternally true and to be referable to an immutable, eternal principle which, though altogether distinct from them, is both the foundation and reason of their evidence. Now this principle can be no other than the eternal truth, which is God. Other postulates there are which have been formulated by great scientists from their observation of the working of natural law. The physical world supplied them with physical facts, and from these, by the immaterial abstractive power of mind, they gathered truths which they expressed in unchangeable axioms, universal, though still hypothetical, as being dependent on the existence and invariableness of physical law. And as the very existence and invariableness of physical law and physical nature are from God, on Him all science depends in its ultimate resort.

In this connection St. Francis of Sales, directing his calm, pure gaze towards God, thus writes: "We say that rain is coming on when the sun, having appeared red and fiery at its rising, suddenly loses its brilliant hue; we anticipate the same effect when it looks dim and obscure at setting: but, Theotime, the sun does not really experience any of these vicissitudes; it can neither be red, nor pale, nor green, nor grey; its clear bright light is its only color, and this can never vary except by miracle. The variety of the clouds and vapors, which intercept our view of the sun, is the cause of the change of color which we imagine discernible in that luminary, and which in common talk we ascribe to it.

"The same occurs in speaking of God; we only know His divine majesty by His works, and not as He is in Himself. Hence we speak of Him as if His essence contained a great multitude of divine perfections, and we give Him different titles, according to the various points of view in which we consider Him. When we reflect on Him as the avenger of iniquity, we call Him just; and when we behold Him pardoning sinners and strengthening weak mortals, we term Him merciful; we call Him all-powerful when we see Him performing prodigies, and creating all things; faithful, when we witness the accomplishment of His promises, and wise, when we meditate on the undeviating regularity and order He has established in the universe;—in fine, we attribute to Him as many different perfections as we behold productions of His Divinity.

"Yet there is really no difference or variation in God, because in Himself He is one only, simple perfection. All that is in God being only a part of the divine essence, the variety we attribute to His perfections only exists in our ideas and our method of expressing them. In the Almighty, all is reduced to the most simple and perfect unity.

"In man there is a great number of faculties and different habits, and consequently a great variety of operations, which in their turn produce an almost innumerable diversity of effects...... It is not so with God; He has but one simple and infinite perfection, and this perfection is a single and pure act. To speak more intelligibly, God is one perfection, sovereignly single, and solely sovereign; and this perfection is one pure and very simple act, which, being nothing less than the divine essence, is consequently eternal and permanent. Though convinced of this truth, we speak of the Almighty as if there existed in Him a number and variety of operations. But the weakness of our understanding renders this unavoidable."[1]

[1] "A Treatise on the Love of God," pp. 52-55.

CHAPTER III.

GOD THE CREATOR.

ON the appointed day, the invited guests arrived before ten o'clock at the Brevoort House. Those from the former meeting met as old friends and introduced their companions. Judge Jefferson was in high spirits and welcomed all with a cordiality which made them at once feel quite at home. He had so arranged that one of the parlors should be reserved for their *seance*;—and there it was, that, after some minutes' conversation on the topics of the day, Mr. Jennings opened the discussion as he had promised.

For the benefit of their new associates, he resumed briefly the arguments given at the Fifth Avenue Hotel, laying particular stress on the absurdities that follow from the hypothesis of a self-existing world. First, that, as it was not self-conscious, it could not determine the manifestation of its power and would, if it were a necessary being, as it was claimed, become perhaps conscious of its existence only through contingent facts, namely, the human brain and the changeable features of the world. Secondly, that then there would not be, as everybody, however, knows there are, real, distinct, subsisting beings, but the phenomenal manifestations of one subsisting substance. Thirdly, that then, too, all parts of matter, since matter is extended, would be independent, and still, as forming one whole universe, would be dependent in relation to their end. In opposition to Kant, he insisted that time and space are measurable, the one by periods, the other by numbers; now, what is measurable is of its nature finite; though we may not be able to compass it by actual measurement, we can fancy the number of stars to be greater than it is, and that of the atoms which are said to compose the world to be greater, and what we can add to, is finite. It has even been proved mathematically that the extent and duration of all things are limited. The molecules, for instance, which compose gold and silver are finite in number, since gold and silver are not everywhere; the real duration of things is measured by their movements, as science teaches; it is also measured by numbers, and is therefore not infinite.

Having premised so much, he read the following: "Gentlemen, everything in nature takes us back to God. It is not the heavens alone that proclaim His glory; dull, dead matter, by its wonders, as revealed by the microscope, speaks of Him almost as impressively as the firmament with its golden fire! The limited world proclaims the author of its limits; and all things, by their weight, number, and measure, tell of Him who fashioned them. No matter what revolutions heavenly bodies make or how they may conform to mathematical theorems, there is a law of number or of measure governing all. It did not originate in matter, it is not inherent in my mind; for given that neither matter nor mind existed, that law would exist; not in itself or by itself,—and where then but ideally in God? 'Intelligebat ratio,' writes St. Augustine, 'regnare numeros, reperiebat divinos et sempiternos.'

"To God, then, as the First Great Cause and the source of all truth and justice, reason readily concludes from the finite, but not so readily to Him as a Creator. It easily conceives God as fashioning the universe and as giving to primordial matter its specific initial forms, but the creative act, by which matter itself came to exist, it does not so easily conjecture. Of the pagan philosophers, Aristotle, it is said by some writers, conceived the idea of creation, while others maintain that even he had not the perception of it. But, however that may be, it is evident that the creative act is out of the range of all human experience and above the capacity of every finite agency. Creation is the production of a thing from nothing. 'To create,' writes St. Thomas Aquinas, 'is nothing else than to produce anything without pre-existing matter.'[1] In all other productions, matter is supposed. Nature, always assisted by its Author with the energies which it has, produces changes in things, and decomposition or growth alters their substantial forms or develops new effects in them. By natural causal efficiency, matter is changed from one state or condition to another. Men also can give to matter different forms; angels too, or even demons, can shape it to suit their purposes, but no creature whatever can create matter itself; man, with all his science, and angels with all their power, cannot create a grain of sand or a drop of water.

[1] Sum. contra Gen., 1. 2, ch. 16.

When, therefore, men speak of the creations of genius, or of art, or of nature, they are but using figurative language; they mean to say that there is around man or nature a sort of shadowing of God's creative power, since man originates thought, and nature brings forth new existences. The poet can give to 'airy nothings' 'a local habitation,' and the architect can build according to his conception the stately mansion. But in all this there is nothing like the actuating of being from non-being, or of matter from nothing.

"When I say nothing, I do not mean a subject or term from which the creative act begins; neither do I mean that intrinsic essential conflict between properties which excludes the possibility of existence, such, for instance, as a square circle. All that I wish to state is, that nothing simply implies in itself non-being, or the complete negation of anything existing and finite. Before the creation of the world, if it is taken for the actuating of spiritual as well as material substances,—nothing existed save God. The world was then in His thought, and when, according to divine counsels, the decree of creation was to be carried out, God said: 'Let the heavens and the earth exist,' and they existed; 'let light be,' and there was light; 'let life be,' and life was. In such expressions, indeed, we have to introduce metaphor, in order to bring divine operations to suit the capacity of the human intellect. *We* think, and resolve, and act, but God's creative act in the light of His divine intelligence was immediately the act of His omnipotent will; or, since intellect and will in God are in reality not distinct from His substance, the act of creation proceeded from His own, infinite, ever-active life or substance. Inasmuch, also, as that act was a concept of the divine mind, it was immanent in God; it belonged distinctly to His essence, to His inner life, and though not manifested in the mode in which it existed in Him, since the limitless, as the infinite is, cannot be limited, still, objectively, that act of creation by the divine will produced the limited or the finite. Thus the concept which the architect forms of the church which he plans (to compare things human with divine, and the finite with the infinite) is immanent in him; it has its abiding fulness within his soul, and the putting of that concept into the building of the church is only expressing outwardly his ideal. In God the pattern idea of the universe is eternal, and in His essence, but its actual production is temporal; in Him it is immanent, infinite, actual, but in its realization in time it is finite. In him all things exist in their ideal types, not formally, therefore, as they exist in this world, but eminently; much as, *proportione servata*, the church now built existed in the mind of the architect.[1]

"These data being laid down, the arguments which

---

[1] "All perfections which, without metaphor, are attributed to God, are in Him after a twofold manner,—formally and eminently. *Formally*, if they be viewed in the sense in which they are conceived by God and the Blessed, and the conception thus formed is in itself illimitable. *Eminently*, if they be considered as they are specially conceived by creatures unaided by the light of glory (lumine gloriæ). For although the thing conceived be truly in God, it is not, however, in Him in that manner and with that limitation under which it is conceived......
"All things are in God in a most perfect and most eminent manner (1) as in their *efficient cause*, ... (2) as their *exemplar*, (*causa exemplari*) in virtue of ideas which are the live notions and similitudes of things... (3) as a *final cause*, since, as all things are by their nature from Him, so also are they for Him. (4) Finally, they are in Him, as particular causes are in an universal cause."—"De Perfectionibus Moribusque Divinis," pp. 14-16.—Auctore Leon. Lessid, S. J.

demonstrate that God is the First Great Cause of all things go also to prove that He is their Creator. Secondary causes work from pre-existing matter; they suppose other causes antecedent to themselves; but the first cause is the reason of the existence of all causes, of everything, therefore, that is, since everything in nature can be a cause. This, God's supreme sovereignty necessarily demands; for let it be supposed, what, to be sure, is impossible, that the least particle of matter has been self-caused, and it dethrones God. It claims an existence independent of Him, and a realm that lies beyond His control. Against such a monstrous hypothesis all matter, by its inherent contingency, cries out and says unmistakably that it did not make itself, but was made and fashioned by One without it, its Creator.

"A Being that exists in virtue of His own essence, who has not been limited by any cause, is infinite, absolute, and alone. In Him the ideal and the real are the same; He possesses all perfection and being, and communicates, in the measure which He judges fit, being and perfection to creatures. These, limited and changeable as they are, proclaim that their being is a derived one, or that they have received it, not from themselves, but from without themselves. They did not receive it from chance, since chance does not really exist; nor from fate, since this relates either to the necessity of physical laws or to divine decrees, and thus supposes established order, and refers rather to the government of things, than to their cause; or fate means a certain mysterious something above the world, which, if it exists really, can be no other than the Supreme Deity; if fate exists only as something fanciful and abstract, it is nothing and cannot consequently be the cause of anything.

"Modern pantheism, however, will probably not be satisfied with this brief answer. Born and nurtured in Germany, it has become known to the civilized world. To be sure, it has borrowed largely from the ancient Hindoos, but has been presented under new forms and has availed itself of the light shed by Christian philosophers on the world, in order to confuse thought and make philosophy almost inexplicable. Kant, though not professing pantheism, sowed the seeds of it by denying the objective reality of ideas, and consequently by upholding that all knowledge is merely subjective. Fichte, Kant's disciple, drew out his master's teaching to its logical conclusions. The only reality that exists, he maintained, is the thinking subject, which is nothing else than the absolute Ego, as by reflection it develops itself under various aspects. 'The Ego posits both itself and the non-Ego, and recognizes itself as one with the latter.' Schelling, uniting Fichte's doctrine with that of Spinoza, formed what was called the 'System of Identity.' 'Object and subject,' according to him, 'real and ideal, nature and spirit, are identical in the Absolute.' God alone exists, and to Him all other existing things are equal or with Him are really identical. But this stage has been gained only by the evolution of God from the 'abyss of the Divine nature' to the 'conciliation of the differentiated.' Hegel, applying to Schelling's principle of identity the dialectical ideas of Fichte, produced the system of absolute Idealism. In this view, finite things are not phenomena existing only in consciousness, but phenomena by their very nature, having their being in the universal divine Idea. 'The absolute reason is revealed in nature and spirit (mind), since it not only underlies both as their substance, but also, as rational subject, returns through them, by means of a progressive development from the lowest to the highest stages,—from its state of self-alienation to itself.' According to the philosophy of identity, especially as taught by Hegel, the absolute idea becomes the soul of the world, develops itself in time and space, and takes a thousand different forms. What may seem to the uninitiated to be contradictory in this philosophy is not really so, it is asserted, to the highly speculative mind. To it, the propositions 'God is a Being,' and 'God is nothing,' are equally true. Finally, Von Hartman comes with the 'Philosophy of the Unconscious.' He is not satisfied either with Schelling or Hegel, and brings in the 'will' to make Hegel's 'logical idea' germinate. 'The will,' according to him, 'posits the "That" (das, the real existence) and the "Idea," the "what" (the ideal essence) of the world and of things.' And from these two factors Von Hartman proceeds to unravel the moral order of the world.[1] Now I submit that these pantheistic theories, by their very extravagance, suffice to refute themselves. Against them consciousness, reason, and the testimony of sense rise in revolt and prove pantheism to be not only irrational but contradictory and impious. Its main, central, and almost only dogma is that there exists but one reality or substance ;—but if there be

[1] See Ueberweg, "A History of Philosophy," vol. 11, pp. 136, 205, 213, 231, 336.

any truth that consciousness enforces more than another, it is the distinct, substantial, personal existence of each one. There is no one who has not the unshaken conviction that he himself is distinct from all others; and that he is one thing and the world another, that he is not the modification of a being, but is the source or principle from which his actions emanate. Tell any one that in his sphere he is not an independent being, with an activity and determination all his own, and he will laugh you to scorn, or perhaps his silent glance will tell you that he takes you for one demented. Consciousness tells him that he is a free agent,—the master of his own actions—the subject of different feelings, and that he is identically the same human being that at different times has been affected by these feelings. He can not undo his nature and admit with pantheism that he is a mere bubble on the sea of life—a mere accident in the development of the one great substance. All objects around him speak of the distinction between him and them. He knows, with a conviction that he cannot question, that he is not one with the tree or the mountain, and that gold is not silver, nor silver copper. He knows intuitively that there is an absolute distinction between the morally good and the morally evil, in spite of the negation of such a distinction by pantheists. If all things be but one, argued Aristotle[1] against the pantheists of his time, then things not only contrary but contradictory will be identified, and the same thing will be good and bad, good and not good, will be man and horse; hence one may as justly

[1] Phys., lib. i., ch. 2.

affirm that all things are nothing, as that all things are one.

"The proof of the Stagirite is still available against the pantheistic teaching of our time. As sometimes presented, this teaching in some of its features differs from the crude doctrine of ancient India and of the Greek Eleatic school, but in principle it is the same. At bottom it supposes that God is not distinct from the world, be this, because He is immanent in it as its soul; or because he externates Himself in nature; or because He is the world's combining, permeating force, or the sum total of its parts. Now, in either of these cases, God is one with the world. Pantheists admit that He is an absolute, infinite, necessary Being, that is, a Being whose existence is a necessity of His essence. They also allow that all visible things are contingent, or that the possibility of their non-existence is conceivable, and this too from experience, since things that are, continually cease to be. Thus pantheism supposes that God, who cannot but exist, is one with matter, which, when organized, can cease and does cease to exist; or it makes the imperishable to be at the same time the perishable. Again, God, because existing necessarily, is also necessarily determinate in His mode of existence, and is consequently unchangeable; whereas the world, as all experience shows, is changeable. As geology teaches, it has been changed, and rechanged, and changed again. Say, then, that the world is an emanation of God, or that it is as a body of which He is the soul, and you make the unchangeable, the changeable; the essentially living and actual, to be perishable and potential. Everything in the world is limited or finite, as all perceive, but God, self-existing as He is, is unlimited in perfection, or is infinite; then, according to the pantheistic hypotheses, He is the infinite-finite as well as the unchangeable-changeable. And since the world in the whole is not different from what it is in its parts, it is finite, changeable, contingent, and cannot therefore be the infinite, unchangeable, and self-existing God.

"Against such monstrous absurdities Hegel himself would probably demur and plead that the refutation just given would tell against the gross pantheist Xenophanes, who lived some six hundred years before Christ, but not against himself in this nineteenth century. It is indeed true that modern pantheists deal with the transcendental; they do not speak of the world as an emanation of God, but of God as of being in the abstract, or as energizing the world. But, as in the former case, the same difficulties occur, since the world, after all, will be only an evolution of the soul-god. It is through it that he will obtain his concrete existence, and, since he communicates his being to it, will be one with it, and with it, too, will be multiple and progressive. Infinite as God is, He will never have the fulness of His nature, but will always be becoming. If, then, it be said that, as a soul or an absolute idea, He manifests Himself in nature, He will all the while be nothing but the principle or the force that underlies it. In a word, as the pantheists would have it, the absolute, eternal God is only finite, temporal, changeable nature idealized.

"But here comes another disciple of the school

of Hegel, who holds not to the world-soul or to the idea absolute. His god is being, purely and simply such—being universal, indeterminate, permeating every thing in heaven and on earth,—being without which we cannot conceive an object actual or possible. In this theory we have the most general and the most subtle form of modern pantheism. The notion of being which pantheists abstract from things, they take for deity, much after the manner that positivists abstract humanity from mortal men and then set it up as a divinity. Being, as a universal gathered by abstractive power from things, is a most abstract notion, but is not in itself an existent reality; it is indeterminate, as pantheists themselves admit, therefore, non-existent, since the existent is always determined. In things actually existing, indeed, being is centred, but not as universal being or an emanation from it, but as something in things which the mind can universalize. In objects, then, it is determined and finite; in the abstract, as pantheists conceive it, it is vague, indeterminate, and universal. It can be added to or subtracted from, 'for though it may be *considered* as universal without addition,' writes St. Thomas, 'it is not, however, without the capacity of receiving additions.'[1] From being, as we conceive it in, and abstract it from, created things, we rise by reasoning to the principle and fountain of all beings created or possible, to the self-existing Being Himself, 'from whom are all things.' In Him is nothing vague, or indeterminate, or potential, but the fulness of infinite being in all its intensity. In Him being is life,

[1] Contra Gent., l. 1, c. 26, n. 6.

and essence, and existence, since in Him these too are identical. Eternally actual and active, His being also necessarily excludes all compositions whatever; —most purely simple in perfection, it is most single in its oneness, a most definite object for human thought and affection. 'The Eternal is the sleepless; He pauses not; He suspends not His powers; He is never tired of Himself; He is never wearied of His own infinity. He was, from eternity, ever in action, though ever at rest; ever surely, in rest and peace, profound and ineffable; yet with a living, present mind, self-possessed and all-conscious, comprehending Himself and sustaining the comprehension. He rested ever, but He rested in Himself; His own resources, His own end, His own contemplation, His own blessedness.'[1]

"Refusing to acknowledge the existence of this one, supreme, infinite Being, modern pantheism, since it must have a god, undertakes to make one of its own. For this it has at hand being indeterminate, thought, and phenomena of various kinds. Claiming omnipotence as it does, it proceeds to its work by tearing up, in spite of the protests of the human race, the landmarks set down by common sense and reason, as well as by universal teaching and observation. Its god it will have at any cost. To that end, it pronounces that thoughts and things are the same, and whatever the well founded convictions of men be to the contrary, as it has said the word, things must be as it proposes. It continues to teach that all these phenomena which men feel or perceive in themselves or in objects, are but modifications of the

---

[1] "Discourses, addressed to Mixed Congregations," p. 216.—By Cardinal Newman.

one, great, subjective, absolute Ego. In other words, the pantheist will have men to believe that they are not what they really are, that is, rational beings with the perfectly certain consciousness of their own independent, individual agency and responsibility. He goes on to say: 'When you conceive an universal idea, it is not merely a product of your mind with some relation to the object, but it is the object itself, since the mind is able, as Hegel teaches, not only to perceive objective truth, but to create it.' Still, for all that, though a man can conceive gold as an universal, he will be at a loss, Hegel notwithstanding, to realize his idea universally. Again, he insists that the absolute, by thinking, produces objects by externating itself,—which is astounding,—seeing that sane men never consider themselves or anything in the world to be the absolute or the infinite. But what is more, the pantheist adds that we have an immediate intuition of the absolute, which is almost equivalent to saying that in this life we enjoy the unalterable happiness of the just in heaven.—Wonderful, truly, it is to observe into what abysses of absurdity reason rushes, when it is led by the glare of passion and not by its own clear light. Everywhere, as it has been proved, matter shows that, since it could not have made itself, it had a first, supreme, independent Cause. As an effect it did not exist, of course, in any sense or form prior to its production by God. From being non-existent then, He, by His omnipotence, made it to exist. The fact of creation reason can conclude to, but the act itself, being intrinsically infinite, it cannot fathom. It cannot fathom even its own creative-like power of thought, though it is most certainly conscious of that power. It is through this mysteriousness of the operations of the soul that St. Thomas introduces us to the consideration of God's creative act. 'Since, therefore,' he says, 'by the actuality that is in us, we can, not only produce immanent actions, such as these of understanding and willing, but also exterior actions, by which we produce some things, much more can God, being actuality itself, not only understand and will, but also produce an effect, and thus He can be the cause of their being to others.'[1] He might not have created the world at all, had He so willed it, but as He had decreed to create it, it lay with Him to determine the manner and moment of creation. God's will, to be sure, is eternal, it is immanent in Him, but this does not mean that in its extrinsic object (*terminus ad extra*) it cannot be temporary. The power that in itself is greatest involves the power of doing what is least; infinite as He is, God surely can create what is finite by nature. He does not do so by anything that implies change, but in virtue of His own immutable determination. Therefore, though the decree of creation is eternal, its effect, since it depends on the choice of God's free will, is temporary; it is not an emanation of His nature, as pantheists say, but the result of a determination freely specified in divine, eternal counsels.

"The act of creation has indeed its own special, peculiar features, but in its sustaining power continues always in the preservation of the world and of the creatures therein: 'Every step which a crea-

[1] Contra Gent., l. II., c. 6, n. 6.

ture takes when he has once been created, increases his dependence upon his Creator. He belonged utterly to God by creation; if words would enable us to say it, he belongs still more utterly to God by preservation. In a word, the creature becomes more completely, more thoroughly, more significantly a creature every moment that his created life is continued to him. This is, in fact, his true blessedness—to be ever more and more enclosed in the hand of God who made him. The Creator's hand is the creature's home.'"[1]

After the reading of these explanations, Mr. Randolph remarked: "To adopt a principle and then by inference to do away with it has always seemed to me to be one of the strongest inconsistencies or weaknesses of human reason. The pantheists (and I speak not of those of ancient Egypt, or Greece, or India, but of those in our midst) hold as their cardinal doctrine the unity of absolute being or substance, or again the one absolute idea that is continually developing or energizing itself in created things and attaining to consciousness in man. This absolute something is not personal, they hold, nor determined to any form or faculty, but impersonal and indeterminate, much like force or instinct, if in reality it be not these. Unity is the first principle in their creed, but strange! that unity is always dissolving itself, since it shares its substance with the stone, the plant, the animal, and man. Spider-like, it weaves the tissues of the world out of itself. But when it has exhausted itself, what then? In the abstract, they say, the absolute idea or substance is

[1] "The Creator and the Creature," p. 50.—By Frederick William Faber.

infinite, but when it is concreted in things it becomes finite, and this process of development always going on, the infinite, it may be supposed, at a certain point must vanish."

"The case of pantheism, as just stated," said Mr. Neufchatel, who had been introduced by Mr. Maxwell, "involves certain difficulties that need explanation, but a pantheist might perhaps retort that the difficulties on the other side are just as formidable. He might say, 'you admit that God is infinite, and therefore hold that He is everywhere through creation. And since the infinite excludes the finite, He alone exists in the world, and all contingent beings, as things distinct, do not exist in it.'"

"The pantheist might indeed retort as you say," answered Mr. Randolph, "but to fancy difficulties for his opponent, you will admit, would not clear up objections that lie in his own way, especially so when those difficulties rest on false premises. The objection just made bears on the immensity of God and not on His infinitude; formally, this latter excludes all limit from the perfection of God's essence; the former, from his substantial presence, not only in things that are, but also in things that might be. The objection also rests on the false grounds that, whereas two material bodies cannot naturally occupy the same place, God, who is essentially a most pure spirit, cannot coexist with material substances. You allow, I presume, sir, that there is in man a thinking, spiritual substance, called the soul. Now this soul exists in and with the body, which is material; it gives to it being, and vitality, and activity. It is in every part of the body, as sensation proves, and is the substantial form of that body, in such a manner that in man body and soul make but one nature, the human. Before matter was created, God was eternally immense, and after creation He is the same; only now an external medium exists wherewith He partially manifests the attribute of His immensity, and He is everywhere present because of that attribute."

"But," resumed Mr. Neufchatel, "after creation God is not the same as He was before."—"Precisely the same," was the reply; "a man, after having built a house, does not cease to be a man. The work of creation was entirely outside the constitution of the divine nature, though the idea of it was eternally present in the divine mind."

"Exactly so," rejoined Mr. Neufchatel; "the idea evolved itself into its external manifestations, and, as everything in God is God, He eternally gave forth his own being, and became the soul and substance of things."—"The idea of a statue which the sculptor forms," answered Mr. Randolph, "does not evolve itself, it waits to be evolved. I said that the idea of creation existed eternally in God; my friend takes up my words and concludes that the idea evolved itself, just as if an idea had in itself a determining and constructive power, and could exist apart from a thinking substance. But the idea is God, he says, and then reaches his conclusion. I would be loath to say that the idea which a man for the time entertains makes him a man. He is something else and more. The idea of creation was undoubtedly eternally immanent in God, but its object is not God; it supposes His self-existence, His eternal essence, His liberty of action. As God, then, is a free, independent, personal Being, creation proceeds from Him, not as an evolution, but as the effect of the creative act of a free, omnipotent, efficient cause,—as distinct from Him, to use a feeble comparison, as the picture from the painter. The latter, we say figuratively, puts his idea on canvas, but surely no one thinks that the painter turns himself inside out, and puts his very idea itself in paint,—and neither does God project formally the idea of creation outside Himself, but creates finite things, in which that idea is reflected after a finite manner."

"The comparison only confuses the argument," replied Mr. Neufchatel. "In man various conditions are required to determine him to act, but in God the case is different; everything in Him is actual, consequently his creative power is a cause. Now, the complete cause of anything being postulated, the effect must necessarily follow, that is, creation has been necessarily evolved from God."

"I admit," said Mr. Randolph, "that in many material respects, man as a cause differs from God, but in this they agree, namely, that both are free agents. There are many effects in nature, I acknowledge, which necessarily follow from their causes; the plant comes naturally from the seed duly conditioned, the ice from the freezing cold, and the drought from the excessive heat. It is otherwise with free causes. The time and manner of man's action depend on his free will, and the same surely we can say of God; the act of His will, lit up by His intellect, was the cause of creation, but it was in His power to determine when and how creation should take place. And hence, though His will is eternal, the determination of that will was according to God's choice.'

As Mr. Neufchatel did not answer, Mr. Jennings remarked that, " at the present time, the philosophy of a certain school is returning to the old doctrine of the Stoics. In the literature of the day, one sometimes meets the phrase 'God is immanent in the world,' a thought which was expressed more plainly by the Stoic maxim, that 'God is the soul of the world.' Taken literally, this idea implies the worst form of pantheism, since according to it the material world and everything in it,—the good, the bad, and the indifferent, would belong to God's nature; then, too, He would not be complete, since He would continually grow and change, as men and things do. But taken figuratively, ' the soul,' according to the views of some writers, stands for the world's forces;—these are the directing power, the very life of things, the source of their development,—that is, through all her domains nature proclaims atheism. This reasoning supposes that the forces of physical nature are the ultimate data of inquiry, and that to know their source we are not to go back of them; we are not to seek how they were generated,—how it happened that they were united to matter, to direct and develop it, and that according to a fixed plan and due proportions. Now, to answer these difficulties, I claim that men will strive,—no matter what may be the reckless assertions or denials of atheism, —and by their inquiry will be led to conclude to the existence of God, the Creator."

"I cannot imagine," observed Mr. Babbington, "how a cause which is of one nature can produce an effect which is of a different one."

"Experience, however," retorted Mr. Burke, "teaches that every efficient cause is entirely distinct from its effects, and that the spiritual or immaterial in this world is continually producing material results. It has, I think, been clearly shown in what relation the world exists towards God,—that it did not exist in Him formally, or as it is now materially constituted, but virtually; that is, He had the power, if He so willed it, of producing possible things. I cannot, it is true, imagine God's creative act in itself, since it is beyond the order of natural causes, but I can conceive it, because I know the poles on which it turns, namely—non-existence and existence, with the copula of God's infinite, creative power. Moreover, I know that it is of the nature of finite things 'to be or not to be,' and that in their dependence we can see, though in a dark manner, a faint inkling of the divine creative action. The soul, which is spiritual, produces in the body movements which are material; man can plan a steam-engine and construct it, though there is nothing in common between his mind and iron, and gravitation, it is admitted, draws bodies to the earth's surface, although gravitation itself is not matter."

"This whole thing," said Mr. Maxwell gruffly, "is unintelligible to me. We were told that creation is the making of the world out of nothing, and that nothing meant non-existence; and, still, we are assured that the world existed in the mind of God, and was therefore something before it was created."

"I am glad," replied Mr. Jennings, "that the words of the gentleman give me the occasion of offering an explanation. The fact of creation implies the real, actual existence of the world; the idea of creation simply means its ideal existence. Between both lies the difference that is between the existent and the possible, between something and nothing. To create, therefore, that is, to make that to exist, in its objective reality, which was before only an idea, is to draw it from nothing. The sculptor chisels out the statue, the idea of which he had conceived; in his mind it was something, but as far as real existence was concerned, it was nothing. Let me suppose that he creates not only the form but the matter of the statue, and he gives existence to that which before was absolutely nothing. It is exactly so with God; He creates by the act of His will the matter and form of the world, which, though ideally existing, as it was eternally in His mind, was nothing in relation to its objective actual existence."

"But from your own teaching I infer," rejoined Mr. Maxwell, " that God could have created an eternal world, and as He could, there is no repugnance in saying that the world is eternal."

"He could," answered Mr. Jennings, "but he did not. A great philosophic authority holds that there is nothing intrinsically repugnant in the idea of the creation of an eternal world.[1] But that is quite a

---

[1] Petavius (de Deo, l. iii., c. 6, n. 1.) declares it to be the universal patristic doctrine, used constantly in controversy with the Arians, that the notion of an eternal creature is cognizable by reason as intrinsically repugnant."—The Philosophy of Theism, vol. i., p. 319.

different thing from saying that the world is eternal because it is self-existing. In the supposition of a world created everlastingly, God would not have been prior to the world by priority of time but by priority of nature. He would have been then the Supreme Cause of the world as an effect, since absolutely the world might not have been, not having in itself the necessity of its existence. Contingent as it is, it necessarily supposes the existence of a cause prior to itself; in the whole it is no other than what it is in its parts. In it every new existence implies a cause which precedes it not only in the order of nature but also in the order of time."

"From my reading these past days," remarked Judge Jefferson, "I have learned that pantheists insist that their theory best explains the activity of the divine intelligence, since it supposes that God has always matter for investigation or development. 'What,' they ask, 'can be the activity of a mind which knows all things; to which, therefore, there is neither secret nor mystery?'"—"Yes," said Mr. Jennings, "that is a view which they give; they do not know, or they ignore, the fact that the activity of the mind is twofold; there is an activity which comes from a struggle to master truth, and there is an activity which consists in the enjoyment of truth known:—the former, based on labor, tends to exhaust the mind, the latter, resulting from certainty, deepens and broadens it; the one is occupied in the search for the reasons of things, the other in the contemplation of these reasons and their relations. Newton exercised the first when he was working out his *Principia*; he applied the second when he had finished his work. In this latter sense, making due allowance for the difference between things human and divine, we predicate activity of the divine intelligence. Man knows things only successively; God knows all things at the same time; man knows things by means of the intelligible species; God knows them in His own essence, and as there is nothing potential in God, His mind is all activity in the knowledge and contemplation of His own infinite being."

"In a controversy which I once had with a tourist," remarked Mr. Harrison, "he maintained that a complete knowledge of all things would be the paralysis of the intellect."—"I judge," added Mr. Clayburne, "that, without any risk of such a paralysis, the tourist might have added to his store of knowledge; he would have people believe forsooth, that the more Aristotle and St. Thomas knew, the more stupid they became, and would ask us probably to look up to the *Grand-Être*—defined by M. Comte to be 'the continuous resultant of all the forces capable of voluntarily concurring in the universal perfectioning of the world, not forgetting our worthy auxiliaries, the animals.'—"Still," resumed Judge Jefferson, "admitting all that has been said, may it not be maintained, in view of God's essential activity and immensity, that the world is a mode of God, or that every finite object is a separate part of the infinite, as each wave is a part of the ocean?"—"I think," replied Mr. Jennings, "that what has been already put in proof gives sufficient evidence of the falsity of this pantheistic objection. We have seen that God is one, independent, absolute Being, that the finite is of His creation and adds nothing to Him. He existed eternally in the plenitude of His infinite nature and did not, of course, become greater, when he created the world. In it He is every-where present, and supports it in all its forces and laws. But He is not one with it, nor is He a mode of it, any more than the clock, to take an illustration from the temporary, is one with the clock-maker, or a mode of him. The wave of the ocean is of its nature and a part of it, but the world and all things in it are, in their very nature, entirely distinct from God.[1]

"The illustration, I admit," remarked Judge Jefferson, "was not an apt one, but here is another and perhaps a happier one. Individual reason, philosophers tell us, is a participation of the universal reason, since no one claims or can claim a monopoly of it, and thus the finite mind, dependent on the universal, partakes of it and manifests it."—"This illustration also," answered Mr. Jennings, "is faulty in this, that it supposes the universal to have a real, independent existence, whereas it exists only in the abstract, with a relation to the object from which it has been abstracted. There is no such thing with a separate existence in the world of finite beings as universal reason. It is God alone who in Himself is universal reason, because He is omniscience itself, and is the true light which enlighteneth every man that cometh in the world."

[1] Professor Joseph Le Conte, though protesting against pantheism, uses, however, the following words: "We are compelled to acknowledge an infinite immanent Deity behind phenomena, but manifested to us on the outside as an all-pervasive energy. But some portion of this all-pervasive energy again individuates itself more and more, and therefore acquires more and more a kind of independent self-activity which reaches its completeness in man, as self-consciousness and free-will."—"Evolution and its Relation to Religious Thought," p. 326.

As Judge Jefferson did not reply, and as no one at the time seemed willing to take a part in the discussion, Mr. Taunton said: " Gentlemen, by way of episode in our debate, I shall read, with your leave, some considerations that partly bear on the question at issue, and which I have cast into a controversial form. The scene of the discussion I imagine to be a fashionable watering-place, and the debaters a Californian and an university professor, in the midst of a group of attentive listeners. After some general remarks on the beauty and grandeur of nature, the professor undertook to explain the origin of the world, and quoted in support of his views the axiom, that 'nothing is made from nothing.'"—"I deny your inference, sir," said the Californian boldly, " you seem to take nothing to be the stuff out of which God has made the world, whereas He only made the non-existent to be existent.' The professor, startled a little by this blunt answer, added in a rather patronizing tone: ' There is another axiom accepted by the schools, which states " that beings are not to be multiplied without necessity ;" this axiom is ascribed to Occam and is known in philosophical parlance as Occam's razor. The world explains itself, and the key to the production of all things is evolution.'

"' Occam, the irrefragable doctor,' said the Californian, 'holds exactly my thesis; he teaches most emphatically that God created the world from nothing.'—' I did not appeal to Occam's teaching,' suggested the professor, 'but wished simply to say that he furnished an instrument of disturbance for those who use bad logic.'—'I am glad, sir,' was the reply, 'that you have specified so precisely Occam's invention; let us now see to the application of it. The world, you say, explains itself;—that may mean, either that the world is its own cause, or that its cause is within it. The first hypothesis is self-contradictory; everybody knows that no being can be its own cause, or that the effect is not identical with the cause,—to assert this would be tantamount to saying that a steam-engine or the ship on the ocean before us made itself;—the second implies that it is internal force which makes the world;—this hypothesis is only the former a little attenuated, since it supposes that the force made itself, and together with that, it assumes that force has engrafted in it the faculty of "natural selection," that this faculty has united the rival or conflicting elements of the world into one harmonious whole,—that it has engendered the laws of gravitation, of chemical affinity, etc.,—also that it has initiated life, and nutrition, and thought, and finally, that it has covered the gardens with flowers of different hues and has made man to know the true, the good, and the beautiful. Now I submit that to ascribe such a faculty as this to force is to argue against common sense and to maintain what on the face of it is absurd.'

"'You do not seem to perceive,' said the professor, 'that law begets law, and that the primary law of force springing from a self-existing material substance calls out, in the process of its development, other laws, which fall in naturally and contribute to the harmony of the universe.'

"'That I do not perceive, I confess,' answered the Californian; 'but what I do perceive in the statement just made is that it is a manifold assumption. First, you take for granted a self-existing material substance, whereas that is exactly the point in question; secondly, you suppose that that substance has a primary law of force engrafted in it, thirdly, you take it for demonstrated that this law has in it a regulating power, as if it were a rational faculty; and fourth, matter in its development, in your opinion, draws on the first force for means wherewith to govern itself.'

"'But you omit in your enumeration,' said the professor, 'that it is "the Absolute Being" who unconsciously, through this force, evolves the universe.'

"'I omitted "the Absolute Being" in my enumeration,' was the answer, 'because He did not enter into your argument. But now, that you have introduced Him, you make Him at the same time unintelligible. He is "absolute," which implies that he possesses all perfection; and he is unconscious, you say, that is, he is devoid of rational purpose. Of this sort of reasoning Lord Beaconsfield has well said : "nothing can surely be more monstrous than to represent a Creator as unconscious of creation."'

"As the controversy went on, the attention of the listeners became closer; with bated breath they watched the combatants in this intellectual tournament; I noticed how their features changed with every change in the discussion, and how their gaze was fixed or relaxed, according as one or other of the combatants struck out with the weapons of keen logic, or parried, with intellectual dexterity, the blows dealt at him.

"'In all this argument, you forget, sir,' continued

the professor, 'that, in arguing against an uncaused world, you are also arguing against an uncaused God.'—'No, sir,' was the sharp reply; 'the subjects of the argument are essentially different. The world, by its very nature, shows that it was caused; God, by His very nature, proves that He is self-existent. The world in all its phases and parts appeals to Him as the First Cause, as a supreme, intelligent Being, who is the measure of every finite creature and has in Himself the reason of His existence. He is uncaused because He is self-existent.'

"'How a being can be self-existent is more than I can understand," added the professor.—'Neither can I,' said the Californian. 'In order to know that God exists, it is not necessary to know *how* He exists. I know that I live, but *how* I live, or what is the nature of life in its last analysis, that I do not know.'—'In arguing from yourself to the world,' was the answer, 'you argue from what is real to what is real. But in arguing from the world to God, you derive only the abstract,—God in that case is only an abstraction.'

"'Excuse me, sir,' resumed the Californian, 'the argument in both cases is the same, namely, that from effect to cause. When I reason from the motion of matter naturally inert, or from the limited nature of things, I argue to him who gave to matter its first motion and who gave to nature its limits; thus, also, from design in nature I reason to the designer, or from contingent things to a necessary being; thus, too, I argue when, from my power of thinking, of judging, or of abstracting, I infer that I have a distinct, spiritual substance within me, the soul. When, from examining a watch, I infer that it had for its author an intelligent being, I do not, I presume, sir, arrive at an abstraction.'

"'Your training, I see, sir,' said the professor, as he stroked his beard rather nervously, 'has been on the old lines. Formerly, metaphysics was the study; now it is scientific culture; then, recourse was had to subtle distinctions and to invisible causes to solve the problems of nature; now, for the same purpose, men resort to experiment and the argument of induction.'

"'Allow me, first, sir, to remark,' answered the Californian with a deferential air, 'that it matters not much on what lines my education has run, provided these lines be the true ones; if you wish to suppose them old, I have no objection to your doing so,—truth is old. But in doing so, you set up scientific culture as incompatible with, nay, even antagonistic to metaphysics, and thus you let it be inferred that the causes which science cannot touch are mere nothings. Is this really so? Scientific culture, as commonly understood, I take to be natural knowledge derived from physical nature. Facts are observed and compared, and from these the scientific mind deduces the law that governs them. Into this process two factors enter: the one, the analysis of facts; the second, the deduction from these of the law which produces, governs them. That is, the principle of causation derived from metaphysical study furnishes the basis on which scientific culture rests. Furthermore, I would say, sir, that, though you discard metaphysics, in speech you are continually applying it; the words that you use are for the most part abstract terms, and abstraction is a metaphysical operation. Nay, it is on metaphysics that science itself must rely, in order to settle ultimately the constitution of the elements of matter, as well as to define substance, and essence, and property. Even within its own domain science postulates invisible causes. When scientists wish to explain the phenomena of light, heat, and electricity, they have recourse to an imponderable fluid, diffused, they say, through the universe. They cannot analyze, nor weigh, nor see it, but from its effects they conclude to its existence; they can also analyze light and measure its velocity, but its cause they cannot touch by any sense, and must only conjecture by reason what it is. It is also from effects that they conclude to the existence of the forces with which matter is endowed, and again to the existence of life in plants or animals.'

"'On this subject, sir,' said the professor, 'you overlook the fact that "it is not laws that cause phenomena, but phenomena that cause the idea of law in our minds." This view has become a prominent feature in the teaching of the schools since the time of Kant, who proved that knowledge is altogether from within and not from without one.'

"'Well,' said the Californian, 'I am at a loss to see what force those remarks lend to the argument. Phenomena, you say, give us an idea of the law; —what if they do? The law existed before the phenomena were observed; the law of gravitation did not begin to exist when Newton perceived it, nor did light then first show forth its "aberration" when Bradley observed it. Or, to take a parallel case, it is not robbery that teaches the law against theft, nor murder that against murder. If our knowledge of physical law be limited to the showing forth of phenomena, then we renounce all science, since we give up its basis, which is fixed, definite principle, or law. As to Kant, he did indeed admit that our knowledge is merely subjective, or that the mind knows things only in their ideas, and not in themselves,—or in the forms which the mind furnishes, and not in the objective reality of the things which it perceives. But from nature and from authority I have learned that things or objective realities are formative elements of my knowledge. I have been taught (and in this matter my own conscience has been a teacher) that I can know things within me as well as things without me. I have a full, perfect certainty that I have the honor of knowing you, gentlemen, individually, as living human beings, and not the mere relations you bear to one another. Yonder ship, that rides so proudly on the waves, is present to my mind in her objective reality with a vividness that no theorizing can do away with. And when Kant tells me that my knowledge of her is not derived from any idea which I conceive of her, but from a form which I draw out of the store of my own mind; when he assures me that it is not the object which I know, but my own mind projected on the object, I fall back on the testimony of my own inmost sense and appeal to the practical conduct of the human race. What think you, gentlemen, of Kant's philosophy?' All around were heard, in undertones, expressions condemnatory of it. And a gentleman remarked: 'The common sense of mankind, it has been well said, recognizes the fact that the human mind has been fashioned, not to create objects but to know them.'

"The professor, a little disconcerted, said in an offhand manner: 'Gentlemen, one of the privileges of the modern school of philosophy is that it furnishes different opinions, both in science and religion, for men of different casts of mind;—"liberty" is its watchword.'—'I beg pardon, sir,' replied the Californian hastily, as he sat up erect on his chair, 'there can be no true liberty as against truth. When demonstrated by reason, or declared by unerring authority, truth claims the undivided allegiance of the human soul. In matters of opinion, liberty is the law, but in things necessary on the evidence of reason or of faith, unity is the standard. —"In necessariis unitas, in dubiis libertas," was the golden rule laid down by the great Bishop of Hippo.'"

After this answer, several gentlemen discussed the meaning of the words "religious liberty" and concluded that they mean only freedom of religious worship before the civil law, and not freedom to worship God according to one's good-pleasure. This latter view involves blasphemy, since it supposes that God may be honored by what is false and superstitious as well as by what is true and divine, by Buddhism or Mahometanism as well as by Christianity. Error based on what is objectively false is in itself always wrong. In certain cases, those who with settled convictions hold to error for the time being are exempt from guilt for so doing, not by reason of their error, but by reason of their invincible ignorance, not because they believe what is false, but because they think they believe what is true. They do not make what is false to be true, but because of the state of their conscience at the time they are not held accountable for the false as for a guilt. In this connection, to speak of the 'innocence of honest error,' is to lapse into a flagrant paralogism. In itself error is never honest, but conscience, in the circumstances mentioned above, is honest in embracing it.

"From what has been hitherto said," remarked Mr. Maxwell gravely, "I infer that there is above nature a First Cause, an absolute, supreme, creative Power. But what is the precise nature of that Power, what is the object of His faculties, and how these are exercised, I cannot exactly make out. He is self-existing, I am told, and infinite, and unchangeable, and from these data I conclude that what He thinks, or wills, or loves is infinite, necesary, one with Himself; and thus the world, on this showing, will be eternal and necessary, an emanation of God in nature."

"It is strange, gentlemen," said Mr. Burke, "how differently arguments impress different minds. It seems to me that, from what we have heard here to-day, the great outlines of God's character may be easily drawn. In the first place, on the grounds of reason, it has been shown, in many ways, that the emanation theory is not to be thought of; it is utterly at variance with the divine nature, and involves the grossest absurdities; secondly, the great primal truth of God's self-existence has been clearly set forth, and from it the conclusion has been reached that God is all actuality, possessing in Himself that wealth of knowledge and of love which is the source of His supreme beatitude. His thought is not transient as is man's thought, but is eternally and essentially permanent; it is not manifold as ours is, but one, all-embracing, eternal, and infinite. Within our own sphere, in the formation of knowledge, we need many thoughts; God, by one act of His intellect, knows all things, past, present, and future. In us, thought is an accident of our souls; in God, thought, or His mental Word, is necessarily His substance. Within Himself, therefore, He has the object of His infinite mind, since His own infinite essence alone can be the adequate object of His infinite thought; He knows Himself by Himself, and in that vision of His essence, as if in a mirror, He knows whatever is knowable in time."

"If I understand the gentleman rightly," said Mr. Neufchatel, "in maintaining that the internal Word of God is His substance, he does not seem to perceive that he thereby introduces a duality into the divine nature, and even something more; for if God's mental act be His substance, the act of His will or His love ought also to be His substance, and thus we shall have three Gods instead of one."

"I acknowledge," said Mr. Burke, "that the gentleman has understood me rightly, but the inference with which he concludes is not mine but his own. I said that the mental word of God is His substance, and I shall now add, to suit the gentleman's reasoning, that the act of God's will, or His love, is also His substance. Or, to express the truth in a more definite form, I hold that God is only one in nature, and that He subsists in three distinct Persons. This mysterious truth, I admit, man's reason by itself could never reach; but, enlightened by divine revelation, it accepts it on God's infallible authority. And thus it is that man is enabled to look, so to say, into the bosom of the Deity, and to read, as it were, the relations of the Divine Persons to each other, who, because they have numerically one and the same nature, are but one God. Reason, then, elevated and broadened by revealed doctrine, postulates, for a true knowledge of the Godhead, the Trinity of the Divine Persons. Without that belief Christ would not be God, and were that conclusion accepted, there could be no true Christianity.

"This subject, I am aware, does not come within the scope of our present thesis, but since it has been started, I shall ask your indulgence while I venture to offer a few explanations of it.

"In man, to be is quite another thing from to understand, and to understand is a different thing from to love. In his own nature he is one, independent, subsisting substance: the thought that he conceives he assimilates to his being, so that the thing thus conceived exists, as it were, in the womb of the intellect. Man's thoughts and desires come and go; what he now conceives or desires of external things is not essential to his nature, but is the contingent or accidental product of his soul. What visible phenomena are to things, that, after a manner, man's thoughts and desires are to his individual rational nature. In themselves they have no independent substantial subsistence.

"To be sure, all this is but the faintest shadowing of the divine nature, or the slightest vestige of the Divine mind and will; since the perfect likeness of God can exist only in the nature of God,—His only begotten Son alone being His perfect image,—in man this image exists somehow as the likeness of a king on the silver coin. But in God, since He is all actuality itself, His intellect and will are also His essence. Within His infinite spiritual nature, therefore, there is the twofold operation of the intellect and will, and as it is admitted that every act of the intellect and will has a principle from which it springs, and an object to which it proceeds, the divine Word of God is distinct from the Principle which produces Him, while the divine Love, proceeding from the mutual love of the eternal Father and His Word, as from one principle, is distinct from both. Now, as in God there is nothing in the way of accident, or quality, or faculty, but all in Him is His substance, hence His intellect and His will are His very essence. With us, our acts of mind or will are mere products of our faculties; in God, the acts of His intellect and will are consubstantial with Him, His eternally subsisting Word and Love. We elicit various mental and voluntary acts, but the infinite act of the divine mind, wherewith God knows Himself and all things in Himself, is necessarily one,—His eternally begotten Word; and the infinite act of the divine will wherewith God loves Himself is similarly one,—the Holy Spirit. Thus the divine essence is necessarily existing in three self-subsisting modes, or in three distinct Persons, who, though having numerically the same identical nature, are, by reason of their origin, really distinct from each other. Men are numerically distinct from each other, not only in person but also in nature; the individual nature, for instance, of Peter is neither that of John nor that of James, although the human nature of the three is specifically the same. In no real sense whatever could it be said that they are one. But in the Godhead the divine nature or substance is one and the same, while the Persons in which that substance subsists are three; that is, there exists one God in three Divine Persons.

"I feel, gentlemen, that any explanation of these sublime truths far transcends my reasoning powers, assisted even by the light of revelation. I shall trespass therefore on your patience, while I bring to my aid an extract from the sublime writings of Bossuet." He then read the following from his notes:—

"'Let us return to ourselves,' wrote the great orator; 'we are, we understand, we will.... Thus, in our imperfect manner, we represent an incomprehensible mystery. A created trinity, which God has made in our souls, represents the uncreated Trinity which He alone could have revealed to us and has mingled with our souls, something of the incomprehensible. We have seen that to understand and to will, to know and to love, are very different acts, but not as if they were things differing in substance, since knowing is nothing else than the substance of the soul affected in a certain manner, and willing is the same substance affected in a different manner..... In changing my thoughts, I do not change my substance, which remains one, while my thoughts come and go, and while my wishes become distinct from my soul, whence they continually proceed... Behold, already, in myself, an inconceivable prodigy... O God, before whom I consider myself and am to myself a great enigma, I have beheld in myself three things,—being, understanding, will.... If I were of a nature incapable of being affected by any accident, or in which all were substance (actuality), my knowledge and my love would be substantial and subsisting, and I should be three persons subsisting in one sole substance, that is, I should be God. But as it is not so, I am made only to the image and likeness of God,—an imperfect sketch of that sole substance which is at the same time Father, Son, and Holy Ghost, to whom is due the same worship, the same adoration, the same love.'" (Elévations sur les Mystères, vol., I. pp. 45, 46.)

"Then," said Mr. Neufchatel, "you would say that one is three and that three are one."—" I would not," was the answer; "neither did I say it in my argument. It is a rule of logic, gentlemen, that in a self-contradictory or absurd proposition the predicate is clearly a negation of, or is evidently incompatible with, the subject. Thus, if I say the human soul is three, meaning thereby that it is three souls, I express an arithmetical absurdity, since one cannot be three. But if I say the human soul, though one in nature, exists with three faculties, the predicate, though implying a threefold power, is quite compatible with the subject, which is one by nature. Now, were I to say that God, one in nature, is three in nature, my proposition would be of course self-contradictory, since the predicate would be a negation of the subject; but when I say God, one in His divine nature, subsists in three distinct Persons, there is no conflict whatever between the predicate and subject, and my proposition is perfectly legitimate and logical."

"I think, sir," said Mr. Neufchatel, "you have been all along unwittingly arguing against yourself. You want to prove that God subsists even in three Persons; now, as personality implies a limitation of nature, you place not one but three limitations in God."—"I was well aware, sir," replied Mr. Burke, "of the scope of my argument; your difficulty arises from a misconception of the notion of person. Personality does not, as you suppose, limit the divine substance. Whether created or uncreated, personality supposes for its subject a spiritual substance, since an accident, it is clear, cannot be a person; now, this substance personality so determines, as to make it singular and entire, or 'a complete substantial whole.' That is, personality implies that one has dominion over his own acts (*sui juris*), that he is entire in himself, and, though undivided, is divided from all others. Personality, however, though determining substance, is really distinct from it. Nature is common to many individual beings, and can be communicated from one to the other, for instance, from father to son. But personality cannot be communicated. In the Godhead, the Father communicates His nature to the Son, and the Father and Son, as from one principle, communicate their nature to the Holy Ghost, but the personality of the Father is not communicated, since it is incommunicable. From this incommunicability of divine personality arises the distinction between the Three Divine Persons. Their nature is, not specifically, but numerically, one, whereas, in men, their nature, although specifically one, is numerically manifold. In God, then, personality is in all the completeness of its meaning, while in creatures it exists only by a certain analogy and participation. He is infinitely perfect, self-subsisting, independent, most free, the eternal, immutable fountain-head of right.[1]

"Speaking to the main subject," remarked Mr. Clayburne, "I notice that to the minds of the antitheists creation seems to clash with the idea of the Absolute. 'The Absolute,' they say, 'excludes the relative, and creation and cause, both imply relation.'"

"Assuredly," Mr. Burke, replied, "there has been a great deal of word-sowing and much paradox on this subject, but when things are taken for what they mean all cavilling disappears. The Absolute, of course, is not the relative, any more than a whole is its part, or black white; in itself it cannot denote any real relationship to any thing else, since it contains all being. When God, therefore, who is the Absolute Being, created, He established a term of relationship between the things created and Himself. By His work He was in no real sense modi-

---

[1] Persona significat id, quod est perfectissimum in tota natura, scilicet subsistens in rationali natura."—S. Thomæ Sum., p. 1, q. 29, a. 3.

In Deo naturam concipimus ut id, quod definitioni Deitatis respondet, et tribus commune est, personam autem veluti totum ex natura et proprietate personali constans.—De Deo ipso, p. 441.—Auctore Josepho Kleutgen, S. J.

fied; no more than man, to argue from analogy however imperfect, is modified by the house which he has built. What God is now, to speak after a human fashion, that He has been from eternity. All creatures, as the effects of His power, bear a real relationship to Him as their cause, but He is the self-same eternal Being in whom is eminently and virtually contained all that is and all that will be."

"Those trivial objections," said Mr. Webber, "I consider to be a sign of a losing cause; there is a sophistry in them which marks the insincere or diffident mind, and shows that the vaunted materialism of a few years past is now on the wane."—"And the best sign of all is," rejoined Mr. Clayburne, "that its advocates are quarrelling among themselves. Mr. Harrison is pitted against Mr. Herbert Spencer and calls 'the unknowable an ever present conundrum, that is to be everlastingly given up,' while Mr. Spencer, with biting sarcasm, rails at 'the Godhead' of humanity; and when they are thus belaboring one another, lo, Mr. Justice Stephens steps in and attacks both; after having dealt unceremoniously with 'the unknowable,' he turns to Mr. Harrison and calls humanity, 'a stupid, ignorant, half-beast of a creature;' 'and he would as soon worship the ugliest Hindoo idol before which the natives chop off the heads of goats.' But that is not all; Mr. Tyndall and his confrères have for more than a quarter of a century been constructing a new universe. They had hinged it securely, they said, since they professed to know mechanics thoroughly; they had looked into the home of light, and far back into the primordial world, and could say how atoms and force, and gases and air go to make the world and to form a new firmament. And now, behold, there comes an American writer,[1] who walks into the edifice, and having laid hold of post and pillar gives them such a violent shaking that nearly the whole structure, to the dismay of scientific experts, threatens to give way. In other words, the undulatory theory of light, the nebular hypothesis, the atomic and gaseous theories have been proved, according to a competent critic, Mr. St. George Mivart, to be mere 'philosophical superstitions.'"[2]

At this moment, the bell having rung for luncheon, on the invitation of Judge Jefferson the meeting adjourned.

---

[1] Modern Physics.—By J. B. Stallo.

[2] "But if the nebular hypothesis, the atomic theory, the kinetic theory of gases, and the undulatory theory of light, are to be regarded as hasty and imperfect fancies, useful in their season, and for certain purposes, but with no pretensions to truth, what are we to think of the great mechanical conceptions of the universe, and of its exuberant and enthusiastic promulgators? What are we to think of its original founders and its latest prophets, who have set it forth as the last revealed and only true gospel in the sounding periods of a glowing, not to say turgid, rhetoric?

"It is the illogical assumptions and conclusions of contemporary scientists that Mr. Stallo victoriously combats, but with them he also upholds the theory of 'relativity of knowledge,' or, as he expresses it, that 'Bodies exist solely in virtue of their mutual action.'—Thus," adds Mr. Mivart, "having, to our full content, satisfactorily disposed of our would be physical philosophers as builders of systems upon foundations they have first carefully undermined, he proceeds to perform hari-hari himself by ascending to the extremest heights of the metaphysical tree with the object of demonstrating that it is impossible to reach even its lowest branches."

"But we know by our good common sense that there is truth in science, and our reasonable confidence therein justifies us in rejecting both that inconsequent theory of relativity which Stallo exposes, and the more extreme and logical doctrine of Stallo himself."—*The British Quarterly Review*, April, 1881. Art. *Mechanical Philosophy*, pp. 270-74.

CHAPTER IV.

"The Vestiges of God in Creation."

[AFTER luncheon in the Brevoort House a merry rivalry arose among the guests as to who should be their host at the next meeting. After much joyful banter, it was at last decided that Mr. Walters should have that honor. His favorite hotel was the Windsor, but as the weather was beautiful, and Central Park was quite near and in the full bloom of Spring, he proposed that, after the example of Plato and his disciples, they should follow up their discussions amid the scenes of nature. The proposition was gladly accepted,—and half-past nine, A. M., on the following Thursday was set down as the hour of meeting,—the place, a slight bluff that rises above the lakes in Central Park, at the extremity of the Mall to the right.

On the day and at the hour appointed nearly the whole party met at the place agreed to; the day was a glorious one; all nature was aglow in the sun's soft radiance; the lakes sparkled under the slanting morning rays, while all around there stretched a wilderness of green, dotted here and there with wild roses or luxuriant lilacs. After a few moments' conversation on the morning's news, Mr. Clayburne read the essay which he had promised at the previous meeting.]

"Gentlemen, at our former meetings it was proved conclusively that the very contingent nature of this physical world postulates a self-existent, necessary cause, and that that cause is a living Being, the Creator of heaven and earth. To-day, I do not undertake to reach, at least explicitly, that conclusion. My object is simply to show that the order which reigns all around us in the universe is a premise from which the mind reasons back infallibly to a supreme ordaining cause, or to a Being who, Himself uncaused, designed the world, by adopting means to ends and setting down laws to matter. Order may be said to be unity in multiform variety, or the fitting of things, like and unlike, equal and unequal, into a plan, according to their proper relations. The parts that constitute a whole may indeed have due relations between their constituent elements, while in their place they also contribute to the proportions of the general design, or they may have order in themselves and enter into the universal order that exists in the world. To be truly real, this order must be constant and uniform, and must rest on certain physical laws given to matter for certain ends. What is order now, and a moment after is chaos, is not and ought not to be called order.

"A glance at the universe suffices to convince one that there exists in it an order, the most complex and still the most uniform,—an order which is the result of the combinations of elements, and operations, and relations the most diverse, as well as of means the most varied. In architectural art, we see how, in the construction of a building, it combines materials, maps out the proportions to be observed, calculates the form and strength required in pillar, and arch, and beam, and then sees to it that each part of the building will answer to its purpose, while it contributes to the unity, and solidity, and beauty of the whole. But the grandest mansion of earth is the lowliest miniature of the temple of the universe. In this the materials combined are most massive; the proportions, the grandest and the most exact; the combining force, the most powerful and the most minute; and all brought together and hinged on each other in a way that has always commanded the admiration of mankind. Everywhere through the visible creation there is seen a harmony of parts, a unity of plan, and, as science has proved, an alliance of elements the most opposed and a marshalling of different forces in order to constitute order. The unity that is the result, the tendencies of all nature to the same ultimate plan, the combination of matter and force for the same purpose, clearly show that, as all things go to form one and the same design, they must have proceeded, in the first instance, from one and the same cause. In the primal and supreme ordering of things, diversity of cause would suppose diversity of result. To say that the shaping of the world proceeded from many distinct, independent causes, would be equivalent to saying that the world should not be one but manifold, that there should be a conflict between its parts, and that there should be no co-ordination of particular ends for the reaching of one general result.

"'The stone doth not deliberate whether it shall

descend,' writes Pearson, 'nor the wheat take counsel whether or not it shall grow. Even men do not advise how their hearts shall beat, though without that pulse they cannot live. What then can be more clear than that those natural agents which work constantly, for those ends which they themselves cannot perceive, must be directed by some high and over-ruling wisdom, and who is that but the great Artificer who works in all of them? ..... For, as " every house is builded by some man " and the earth *bears no such creature of itself;* stones do not grow into a wall, or first hew and square, then unite and fasten themselves together; trees sprout not cross, like dry and sapless beams, nor spars and tiles arrange themselves into a roof; as these are the supplies of art, and testimonies to the understanding of man, the great artificer on earth, so is the world itself but a house, the habitation and the handiwork of an Infinite Intelligence, and He who built all things is God.'[1]

"While, then, the unity of nature points to the unity of cause, the same unity, together with the complexity of nature, proves that cause to be intelligent. This has been the universal judgment of the human race. At all times and in all places the visible world has been for the barbarian as well as for the scholar like a vast open page, in which they have read of the mind and wisdom of the Supreme Being who fashioned it. ' He must be blind who, from the most wise and beautiful contrivances of things, cannot see the infinite wisdom and goodness of their Almighty Creator; and he must be mad or senseless,

[1] Pearson: "On the Creed."

"The Vestiges of God in Creation." 141

who refuses to acknowledge them.'[1] Rudely-cut stone-hatchets, or flint-arrow-heads, or Swiss lake-dwellings, or mounds of marine shells on the shores of Denmark, are considered to be tokens of intelligent action, or of the existence of prehistoric man. They are looked upon as the objective vestiges of reason. This same line of argument applied to the physical world leads with incalculably greater force to the like conclusion. Mass balanced against mass in space; matter limited to due proportions; bodies moving in their orbits with the greatest velocity and precision, and held in their places by the bonds of force; the adaptation of creatures in the animal and vegetable worlds to their environments; all these speak to us of intelligence the most supreme, may I not say, unlimited? And in that world on which intelligence is so clearly written there is perpetual change: things live and die, come and go, and still, amid that flux, the same perpetual order remains; proclaiming thereby that its cause is beyond the world and independent of its changeableness. Nature, taken in any of its parts, could not produce order, which is universal; and if taken as a whole, to say that it thus produced it, is to say that it is its own cause, since order is the great constituent law of nature.

"The outlines of the argument from design which I have thus far sketched may be seen by every one who looks into the visible world. They have been continually presenting themselves to minds all along through the ages, as a demonstration of the existence of a supreme intelligent Being. It is not yes-

[1] Coti's preface to the second edition of the "Principia," 1713.

terday only, nor to-day, but forever since their creation, that the heavens tell of the glory of God. Science, it was feared at one time by some persons, would impair, if not wholly destroy, the evidence thus given. But the very contrary has come to pass; science has but confirmed and illustrated the argument from design by its innumerable discoveries. What the savage knew of the Supreme Being from looking at the grand face of nature, that the greatest scientists in ancient and modern times have only confirmed by revealing some of nature's secrets.

"Some of these revealed secrets I shall here attempt to enumerate.

"In the solar system, as being better known to us, traces of design are more distinctly perceptible than in the stellar world. Throughout that system there runs the idea of a plan well proportioned and executed with a grandeur and precision that surpass all finite calculations. Everywhere in its plan there appear choice, discrimination, the beneficial or fitting among innumerable hypotheses, and balancing bodies as to their quantity and movements by laws the most simple and at the same time the most efficient. The central position of the sun is the great binding force of this solar world,—as well as the great source of light and heat for all the planets. Let us suppose the great central orb to be opaque, and one of the planets of the existing solar systems to be ignited or luminous, and we shall be at a loss to account for the equable and sufficient distribution of light and heat through the universe. Then the light of Uranus, for instance, as a luminous body, would scarcely be stronger in the remotest depths of space than that of 'the moon in her waning.' But in the solar system as it is, bodies are co-ordinated for the best possible distribution of heat and light, and show thereby that intelligent choice as well as foresight presided at the primeval formation or evolution of things.

"Another striking feature of the system of the world is the simplicity and precision of the laws by which it is held together. Of these laws the principal is that of gravitation, or that law by which 'bodies attract each other with a force directly as their masses and inversely as the square of the distance which separates them.' That is, the attraction of bodies will vary with their distance from each other; at double the distance, it will have a quarter of its force, at half the distance it will be four times as strong. 'So that, according to this law, the moon, placed at the distance of sixty of the earth's semi-diameters from its centre, is attracted 3,600 times less than bodies that are on the surface of our globe. Now, let this law be changed, or let the attracting force vary according simply to any direct law of the distance, and disturbance of all the planetary movements will immediately ensue. For instance, if the planet Saturn were to pull the harder at the earth because of its distance, it would drag it out of its orbit, and render our life intolerable;— and if at double the distance, the attractive force having become eight times less, the consequence would be that the planets, approaching the sun, would fall into it.' Now I submit that this precision of law, this measuring of force by distance, cannot be reasonably accounted for otherwise than by attributing it to the ruling of a designing mind of the highest capacity. Under the intelligent economy of these laws that govern the world, our planet revolves in its orbit just at that distance from the sun which makes life endurable. Were it nearer to the sun—say in the place of the planet Mercury or even of that of Venus, it would be uninhabitable by reason of the intense heat; were it farther from the sun than it really is, say in the orbit of the planet Mars, again, life would be unendurable by reason of the extreme cold. But as it is, the earth is exactly in the position which makes human life supportable on its surface, and has exactly that force of gravity which gives to the atmosphere a density suited to man's constitution. If that force were reduced to that which exists on the surface of the moon, or if it were as great as that which prevails on the surface of Venus, we could not breathe at all. But, influenced by the double force of gravity and heat, our atmosphere is tempered to suit our nature. To say that such a combination of things is the result of chance, or that atoms whirling in space selected those neatly adjusted physical measures and laws, is like supposing that the letters of the alphabet, by a throw of the dice, produced Homer's Iliad. Maintain that those atoms were governed by law, and you grant that they were directed in their movements by a superintending power, or that the concordance which exists among divergent phenomena can be explained only by supposing a cause that combined such varied elements to a final end. On the other hand, if it be said that the world has come from chaos, or that order has come out of disorder, then there is also postulated a determining cause. If the 'cosmic dust' or 'nebula' be appealed to, the question is only thrown back, since the sceptic will ask whence came the 'nebula' which has a certain definite form, or the 'cosmic dust' which has a certain cohesiveness. It is true that, with this hypothesis, recourse is had to the conservation of energy, and with this theory added to the former, it is sought to span the abyss between the 'cosmic dust' and a clear-cut, symmetrical world. But how this primordial, cosmic, homogeneous mass, diffused through space, could have originated the universe, would still remain a riddle. For, suppose, either that it was at rest or had a settled uniform motion, and in either case, to take a new shape or to acquire a new activity, it needed an impulse from without it. Within itself, it had not the resources of this new form, since, by nature being potential and inert, it was not self-energizing, and being in absolute rest, it could not have produced motion. On the other hand, according to the hypothesis, the 'cosmic dust' was all encircling, had nothing beyond or without it, and should therefore remain, according to the most elementary scientific principles, in the same perpetual rest or motion. In regard to the nebulous universe, it would remain in the same uniform temperature, since the nebulous mass, like the 'cosmic dust,' filling all space, could not be affected by any physical cause extraneous to it.

"But the nebular hypothesis itself, though reconcilable with Theism, has been found to depend on very imperfect, not to say fanciful, premises. The periods which it requires for the orbital rotation of the planets differ enormously, as was shown years ago by M. Babinet, and to add to this, the motions and planes of some of the planetary bodies are the reverse of those supposed by the hypothesis. Thus the orbits of the satellites of Uranus are nearly perpendicular to the ecliptic, while the orbits of all the other planets and their satellites are inclined to it at small angles. Again, the satellites of Uranus move with a retrograde motion, from East to West, while all other planetary bodies, in accordance with the nebular hypothesis, move from West to East. A more serious difficulty still for this theory is the revolution of one of the recently discovered satellites of Mars. According to the theory we examine, the period of the rotation of the satellite in its orbit should be, at least proximately, that of its planet. Yet, in the instance of one of the satellites of Mars, it revolves around that planet 'in less than one third of the time required for the planet's real rotation,'—a fact which strikes at one of the principal postulates of the nebular hypothesis. But those theories being taken for what they are worth, from the very centre of the solar system itself, as we find it, radiates the idea of design,—the sun holding by its attracting power the planets in their orbits,—diffusing light through the world, and giving unity to movements and to forces the most complicated or diverse. Or, if we choose to use the words of Arago, 'by the omnipotence of a mathematical force, the material world is found established on its foundation.' Granting that it is:

"The Vestiges of God in Creation. 147

the question recurs,—how came a mathematical force to be so nicely applied as to become a law? This mathematical law or truth existed only in the abstract, when there was only the 'nebula' or 'dust' in space, according to the hypothesis. The relations which afterwards came to exist between bodies made the mathematical or mechanical laws of the universe actual, but did not create them; they were surely in force before either Hipparchus or Newton discovered them.

"Though 'the heavens show forth the glory of God,' an intimate acquaintance with the constitution of the heavenly bodies and of their relations to each other would add a great deal to the proof of design derived from them. It would show us processes of development towards ends which are now hidden from us, and a co-ordination of parts under a variety of aspects, in order to form the grand whole of the universe. But much of what we miss in this respect for argument in the study of the heavens, we find in the study of the kingdoms of terrestrial nature. All through the phenomena of crystallization, for instance, design is manifest. Molecules come together and form prisms, cones, and pyramids, while each of these molecules has exactly the geometric form of the mass which it contributes to produce. Now, surely, it will not be imagined that they consult about their future product, nor will it be upheld that the material molecule is wedded to one form more than to another, nor, indeed, to any form whatever. The molecules clearly unite in virtue of some physical law, and take this or that regular form by reason of some physical force. The constancy and regularity with which these molecular combinations take place, together with the angular forms of the crystals, in spite of all friction, lead up to the conclusion that in its formation the crystal realizes a plan and is determined to its shape by an attractive power, given to it by an intelligent cause. Nature shapes the crystal, but it does so, not as if in virtue of some innate power of matter and force; neither inert matter nor force, left to itself, could ever construct a tetrahedron. As it is only mind that can frame geometrical laws, so it is only mind that can have projected originally the geometrical forms of the processes of crystallization and given, for that end, its pecular activity to nature. Most fluids, also, by their constituent gases and by the uses for which they serve in nature, bear testimony to the wisdom and power of a supreme intelligent design. Water, for example, the great liquid of our globe, furnishes a most striking proof of purpose in its formation and use. It is composed of two gases, oxygen and hydrogen,—both in themselves highly elastic, but united so closely by chemical affinity, that to decompose a drop of water, according to Faraday, greater intensity of electric force is required, than is necessary to charge a thunder-cloud. The proportion in water's ingredients is one volume of oxygen to two volumes of hydrogen, and unless this proportion be observed those gases will not unite. Another exceptional property of water is that, at about the 7th or 8th degree F° above the freezing point, unlike all other bodies, it expands and continues to do so, until it becomes ice, while at the freezing point its expansion becomes considerable. Hence the specific gravity of ice is much less than the specific gravity of water, and ice consequently swims on the water's surface. Were it otherwise, rivers and lakes would be frozen to their full depth, and all the fish contained in them would consequently perish. Now all this quasi-discriminating capacity in nature for the selection of elements, this balancing of one element against another by chemical affinity, and the exceptional and anomalous quality of water under the action of cold point distinctly to design. 'The anomalous properties of the expansion of water and its consequences, we have always viewed,' says a scientific writer, 'as presenting the most remarkable instance of design in the whole order of nature; an instance of something done expressly and almost (could we indeed conceive such a thing of the Deity) at second thought, to accomplish a particular object.

"The appliances of water in the economy of nature also speak to us of intelligence, beneficence, and forethought. Water, covering three-fourths of the globe, is the great highway of the world; it is also the medium through which nourishment is conveyed to organized bodies, and is the great purifier, washing away the waste tissues and putrid remains of those same bodies decomposed. Changed into vapor by the sun's heat, it is drawn upwards and forms the aqueous atmosphere, so that, by this marvellous provision, the waters of rivers, lakes, and seas float above us in the clouds, and are held suspended, and are duly distributed there by the oxygen and nitrogen of the atmosphere. By these same gases the aqueous atmosphere is so tempered, that, instead of falling with more than the violence of a torrent, it falls 'as the gentle rain from heaven.' 'Were there no air on the globe,' says Prof. Cooke, 'the drops, falling without resistance, would be as destructive in their effects as a volley of leaden shot.' And again, 'every drop of that water has been an incessant wanderer since the dawn of creation, and will soon be merged again in the vast ocean, only to begin anew its familiar journey. If you would gain an idea of the magnitude and extent of this wonderful circulation, you must bring together in imagination all the rivers of the world, the Amazon and the Orinoco, the Nile and the Ganges, the Mississippi and the St. Lawrence, and, adding to these the ten thousands of lesser streams, endeavor to form a conception of the incalculable amount of water which during twenty-four hours they pour into the vast basin of the world, and then remember that during the same period at least four times as much water must have been raised in vapor and scattered in rain over the surface of the land.'[1] All this, one will say, is the result of special laws and enters into the harmony of the universe; certainly it does, but in this complex adaptation of means to ends, in those results which come from the application of special laws, we see design manifested. The fertilizing of the earth by rain, for instance, is an end gained, yet by the adaptation of how many means? The water is first reduced to vapor by heat, then licked up into the atmosphere, held there in the grasp of gaseous elements, transformed into invisible vapor, until, being more and more condensed by cold, it descends to the earth in rain. In this case, it is

[1] "Religion and Chemistry," p. 132.

the number of conditions to be fulfilled, the hinging of facts and forces, one on the other, for certain results, that show forth the wisdom of Him, who, as it is written, 'holdeth the waters in the hollow of His hand.'

"The marks of design that lie on the very face of inorganic nature lead on the inquisitive mind, naturally, to examine whether traces of purpose be not also discoverable in the organic world. And, just on the very threshold of the realm of life, the fact that each kingdom of animated nature has products or creatures exactly suited to it is suggestive of intentional finality. The fish is made only for water, the bird only for air, and man and animals of the brute creation for earth. This very marked distinction, drawn by nature itself, points to an original selective power. Water and air are especially adapted to their respective tenants, and these in turn are specially organized for water and air. The fish has its own motive power complete, being provided with gills through which it breathes and by which its blood is purified; whilst with fins, pectoral, dorsal, ventral and caudal, it swims and balances itself. 'The pectoral and more particularly the ventral fins serve to raise and depress the fish,' writes Paley; 'when the fish desires to have a retrograde motion, a stroke with the pectoral fin effectually produces it; if the fish desire to turn either way, a single blow with the tail the opposite way sends it around at once; if the tail strikes both ways, the motion produced by the double lash is progressive and enables the fish to dart forward with astonishing velocity.... In their mechanical use, the anal fins may be reckoned the keel; the ventral fins outriggers; the pectoral muscles the oars; and if there be any similitude between these parts of a boat and a fish, observe that it is not the resemblance of imitation, but the likeness which arises from applying similar mechanical means to the same purpose."[1] It is to close one's mind to truth, to deny that those peculiarities of the finny tribes do not give evidence of intelligent adaptation, or of the fitting of means to ends by contrivance, the most ingenious and minute.

"The like evidences of design we find in the form and structure of birds. As the fish is fashioned for the element of water, so is the bird for the elements of the atmosphere. Made for swimming through the air, the form of the bird's body is boat-like, with a strong, sharp bone running beneath it like a keel. It's cylindrical bones, made of a shell of firmer texture than its other parts, are more hollow in proportion than the bones of quadrupeds. With the same weight, bones in no other form could be so strong and at the same time so light, their strength as cylinders being proportioned to their diameter. The bird's breast-bone being of a prow-form, is endowed with great strength and braced with strong muscles to resist the pressure of the air; its ribs also have laid over them a small bone, which, like a cross-beam, strengthens them, while the shoulder-blades, which the effort of flying would bring together, are kept apart by two bony braces. In those bodily features of the bird we find again the most marked adaptation of its form for the elements through which it flies.

[1] Paley, "Natural Theology," p. 486.

The wing of the bird has been described by some writers as one of the most striking illustrations of contrivance for the accomplishment of purpose.[1] Its mechanical structure, its different sized feathers, its strong muscles, and its comparative lightness make it a most fitting instrument for its functions. The body of the bird being heavier than the air, it is it, or rather the vital force in it, which, like steam in the engine, works the wings; while these, in order that they may have an almost unlimited range of motion, are 'articulated to the trunk by a somewhat lax universal joint, which permits vertical, horizontal, and intermediate movements.' Their mechanical power is brought out by the elements on which they act and by the laws of nature which they economize. These laws are—(1) the law of gravitation, which draws the bird's body downward, (2) the law of the resistance of the air, and (3) the law of the air's elasticity. By the downward stroke of the wide-spread wings, the bird avails itself of the second law,—and of the third by the rebound of the wings upward, by which it overcomes the law of gravitation. In this operation we see the nicest adjustment of the organic to the inorganic as of a piece of mechanism to the forces of nature. The length and breadth of surface covered by the open wings pressing on the air cause that the upward pressure far surpasses that of gravitation, while the thinness of the wings takes very little from the air's pressure. Again, that the wing may gain a rebound by striking the air, it is made large enough to compress a volume of air proportioned to

---

[1] See the "Reign of Law," by the Duke of Argyle, ch. 3.

the size of the bird,—and that it may be light and at the same time strong enough, it is furnished with feathers. Another contrivance for the execution of purpose, we find in the form and arrangement of the feathers. The elasticity of the air under the downward stroke of the wing enables the bird to rise, but this effect, if the aerial property alone were taken into consideration, would be neutralized by the upward stroke, and thus flight would become impossible. To meet this difficulty, the wing is so shaped that it's under surface is concave while it's upper surface is convex,—so that, when the wing strikes the air, it gathers it in or focuses it and is acted upon by the full force of atmospheric resistance; on the other hand, when it strikes the air with the convex or upper surface, it meets with little resistance, since the convexity of the surface offers scarcely any resistance to the air. Add to this that in giving the up-stroke the bird more or less flexes and contracts the wing and extends it for the contrary motion; and thus the flexion of the wings in the former case opens up the feathers, in the latter, the extension, on the contrary, renders them airtight, underlapping each other as they do. All this, however, will enable the bird to ascend, but will not enable it to fly. How is this to be accomplished? Again, by the combination of the wings' mechanism with natural forces. 'The power of forward motion is given to birds, first, by the direction in which the whole wing feathers are set, and next by the structure given to each feather in itself. The wing-feathers are all set backwards, —that is, in the direction opposite to that in which

"The Vestiges of God in Creation." 155

the bird moves; whilst each feather is at the same time so constructed as to be strong and rigid toward its base and extremely flexible and elastic towards its end. On the other hand, the front of the wing, along the greater part of its length, is a stiff, hard edge, wholly unelastic and unyielding to the air. The anterior and posterior webs of each feather are adjusted on the same principle. The consequence of this disposition of the parts as a whole and of this construction of each of the parts is, that the air which is struck and compressed in the hollow of the wing, being unable to escape through the wing, owing to the closing upwards of the feathers against each other, and being also unable to escape *forwards*, owing to the rigidity of the bones and the quills in that direction, finds its easiest escape *backwards*. In passing backwards it lifts by its force the elastic ends of the feathers, and thus, while effecting this escape, in obedience to the law of action and reaction, it communicates in its passage, along the whole line of both wings, a corresponding push forward to the body of the bird. By this elaborate mechanical contrivance the same volume of air is made to perform the double duty of yielding pressure enough to sustain the bird's weight against the force of gravity, and also communicating to it a forward impulse. The bird, therefore, has nothing to do but to repeat with the requisite velocity and strength its perpendicular blows upon the air, and, by virtue of the structure of its wings, the same blow both sustains and propels it.'

" But were design not discernible in any other creature, or were proof, from other organized beings, of a supreme ordaining cause wanting, 'the glorious mechanism of the human form' would alone be proof sufficient. The nicely-jointed bones; the hundreds of muscles, 'each having its special use, and all working in exquisite harmony;' the nerves, like so many 'glistening, silvery threads,' that carry messages from the mind to the organs and from the organs to the brain; the expression of the human face,—all these show forth contrivance and foresight the most consummate. Man is acknowledged to be the lord of creation; he has subdued matter; he has bound down force; he has caged the lion, tamed the elephant, and slain the monsters of the deep; and in evidence of this pre-eminence he has been endowed with a majesty of bodily structure. 'With an eye like Mars to threaten and command,' he, of all other animals, stands erect. They look to the earth for which they are, he looks to heaven, for which he was destined. In view of this, his head and spine are duly joined and steadied by special muscles; while gorillas and apes of every kind go on all fours, compelled thereto by the receding joint of their head and spine.

"Again, in the animal kingdom, man alone is endowed with intellectual power, and hence it is because he reasons that he has a brain, fitted as an instrument for that end, by its bulk and composition. 'It must not be overlooked,' writes Mr. Huxley, 'that there is a very striking difference in absolute mass and weight between the lowest human brain and that of the highest ape; a difference which is all the more remarkable, when we recollect that a full-grown gorilla is probably pretty nearly twice as heavy as

"The Vestiges of God in Creation." 157

a Bosjesman or as many an European woman. It may be doubted,' he adds, 'whether a healthy human adult brain ever weighed less than 31 or 32 ounces, or that the heaviest gorilla brain has exceeded 20 ounces.'[1] And who, we may ask, made this difference in view of function between the brain of man and that of the gorilla? No other, surely, than He who designed both. In relation to the same supremacy which man holds in the animal kingdom he has been endowed with articulate speech. All inferior animals shriek, or chatter, or roar, man alone speaks; and he does so because he alone thinks: 'Articulate speech,' according to the author just quoted, 'is the grand distinctive character of man... the primary cause of the *immeasurable* and *practically infinite divergence* of the human from the simian stirps.

"In the different members and senses of man writers have distinctly pointed out the most striking traces of design, showing how they are the products of forethought, and that it is not use that made them. Before they were planted in the body, they had existed in design in a mind; so that He who gave the faculty of seeing and of hearing to man must Himself have had virtually and eminently these same faculties. 'He that planted the ear, shall He not hear? or He that made the eye, shall He not see?'[1] To an unbiassed mind this argument is unanswerable; it states the necessary relation between an effect and its cause. To the agnostic, it is inconclusive, since, according to his theory of the process of natural development, it supposes the point at

[1] "Man's Place in Nature," p. 102.

issue. He therefore appeals to evolution, and by it undertakes to explain the planting of both the eye and the ear. Is his appeal admissible? Many eminent scientists refuse to acknowledge such an appeal, while others would only limit it, and some clearly prove that, in some instances, such an appeal is decidedly false. To quote only one instance: the mode of the planting of the eye, according to evolutionists, is negatived, Professor Pritchard tells us, by the very structure of the eye itself. 'From what I know,' he says, 'through my own speciality, both geometry and experiment of the structures of lenses and the human eye, I do not believe that any amount of evolution, extending through any amount of time consistent with the requirements of our astronomical knowledge, could have issued in the production of that most beautiful and complicated instrument, the human eye. There are too many curved surfaces, too many distances, too many densities of the media, each essential to the other, too great a facility of ruin by slight disarrangement, to admit of anything short of the intervention of an intelligent will.'[1] Add to this testimony, that the adjustment between the optic apparatus and the external medium is so fine that the mechanism of the eye measures the vibrations, which, it has been calculated, 'differ from each other by only a few millionths of an inch.'[1] 'The most perfect,' continues Prof. Pritchard, 'and at the same time the most difficult optical contrivance known is the powerful achromatic object-glass of a microscope; its struc-

---

[1] "Address at the Brighton Conference," 1874. (Published afterwards in pamphlet form with the title "Modern Science and Natural Religion.")

ture is the long unhoped for result of the ingenuity of many powerful minds; yet, in complexity and in perfection, it falls infinitely below the structure of the eye. Disarrange any one of the curvatures, the many surfaces, or distances, or densities of the latter; or worse, disarrange its imcomprehensible self-adaptive power, the like of which is possessed by the handiwork of nothing human, and all the opticians in the world could not tell you what correlative is the alteration necessary to repair it, and still less to improve it, as natural selection is presumed to imply.'

" To all that I have been saying, it will be answered, I foresee, that I overlook nature,—ignoring that the order and harmony of the world, or the contrivance or adaptation of means to ends and the manifestation of purpose can be accounted for by the working of a principle immanent in nature, or by natural causes tending to their ends instinctively and necessarily. This, I conceive, is the plea of many anti-theistic writers of our time, and the main argument with which agnostics rest satisfied, although it is clearly based on misapprehension. It is not denied that organized nature has a plastic power given to it, and that it possesses energies wherewith to act and reach definite ends. Living beings have an aptitude, from physical structure and instinct or mind, with which in their kinds they have been endowed, for performing acts or movements conformable to their nature. They fulfil in their respective spheres the commission which nature in general has received, and act, so to say, as the delegated, secondary agents of a supreme primary power. Now, as the fulfilment of duty by a subordinate agent does not negative the source or title of his authority, so neither does the accomplishment of its ends by nature preclude the legation given to it to act according to law in all its realms. An inanimate or irrational nature, to be sure, acts necessarily, whereas rational nature acts freely. So much is easily granted, but furthermore it is contended, that there is immanent in the world a self-adjusting principle or a sufficient reason for the order that reigns every-where. Molecules 'attract each other and repel each other at certain definite points or poles and in certain definite directions.' Granted that they do, that does not constitute the order of things, it does not proportion different bodies to each other, nor number them, nor regulate their motion. It cannot measure their velocity nor hinder their collision, since, as being material, it is not discriminating, and has no knowledge of the end to be reached. Molecules attract or repel each other by the force with which they are endowed, but that they should adjust themselves in such or such geometrical forms points to the controlling power of a superintending intelligence. The self-adjusting valves of the steam-engine bespeak mind; why should not the self-positing molecules of the crystal do the same?

"Matter, physicists admit, being inert by nature, has no discriminating power and cannot, therefore, produce design. But what matter cannot do, perhaps force can. From its manifestation in different bodies, force has got different names, but in itself, some scientists tell us, it is one and the same dynamic power. It does not exist as a distinct, independent unit, but requires a subject in which to inhere; it is 'but one aspect,' writes Clerk Maxwell, 'of that mutual action between two bodies which is called by Newton action and reaction.' It is matter, then, that localizes force; and as matter by itself has no discriminating capacity, neither has force; to contribute to produce design, force needs to be measured and directed. When in nature it acts steadily for certain definite ends it is called a law; hence we have the law of gravitation, the law of capillary attraction, etc. But these laws, any more than force, are not entities distinct from matter, but rather they are the modes through which matter acts; they are called laws by an analogy taken from human law, and they began to exist only when matter and force, as they appear, began to exist. Indiscriminating as these laws are, they act only according to the rule set to them in nature by its Creator.

"There is one kind of force, however, whose dynamic source we know with conscious certainty, and that is vital force, or will-power. Out of the energy of will every one is conscious that he can generate force, while he is also conscious that he can communicate the same to nerve and muscle, can set his whole frame in motion, or endow it with new strength for endurance. The body fitted for action by its structure does not act, however, or move, but under the influence of will, and, in the case of irrational animals, under the impulse of instinct. We have here then the mechanism of the human frame applied to its different functions by the energy of the will, or by force generated by an immaterial substance.

Not only that, but outside himself man can so combine or control force as to make it to be subservient to his purpose. Yonder skiff, as you see, under the stroke of the oarsman flies, through the water like a thing of life. Whence comes its velocity? Primarily, it is evident, from the will-force of the oarsman; it is this live force that brings into play the mechanical power of the arms, while these in their turn use the oars as levers and propel the boat with the water as fulcrum. We have thus the mechanical force of the arms and oars rendered intelligent, as it were, by mind, since the skiff moves with an aim in its progress. By combining and mingling different elements man can also condense force into its most intense form, as we see in gunpowder and dynamite; he can also steal it from the sun's rays and make it minister to photography, or, by uniting steam-power to mechanical frames, can bring force thus generated to execute patterns of the finest kind. And thus it comes to pass that man, by taming brute force, and motion, and matter, can make them subservient to his will and can construct, so to say, his own little cosmos.

"From what we know, then, of the insufficiency of brute force and matter to measure themselves, and, on the other hand, from what they are capable of when under the governing power of mind, we rise to the conception of the force which keeps within bounds the heavenly bodies in their evolutions, or, by the adaptation of means to ends, is working out in nature myriads of designs, which has mind and will behind it, and in reality produces its results only under the pre-ordaining intelligence of the Supreme

Being. Matter, force, motion, and life are instruments by which He governs and directs things to their appointed ends.

"On the face of nature in all her fields, then, design is manifest. Clerk Maxwell has suggested that it is also traceable in the very constitution of matter. To be sure, his argument points directly to God as a Creator, but implicitly it shows that He is also the Supreme Designer of all things.

"'Light,'[1] he writes, 'which is to us the sole evidence of the existence of these distant worlds, tells us also that each of them is built of molecules of the same kind as those which we find on earth. A molecule of hydrogen, for example, whether in Sirius or Arcturus, executes its vibrations in precisely the same time. Each molecule therefore, throughout the universe, bears impressed on it the stamp of a metric system as distinctly as does the metre of the Archives of Paris or the double royal cubit of the temple of Karnac. No theory of evolution can be formed to account for the similarity of molecules: for evolution necessarily implies change, and the molecule is incapable of growth or decay, of generation or destruction. None of the processes of nature, since the time when nature began, have produced the slightest difference in the properties of any molecule. We are therefore unable to ascribe either the existence of the molecules or the identity of their properties to the operation of any of the causes which we call natural. On the other hand, the exact equality of each molecule to all

---

[1] A Lecture on Molecules delivered before the British Association at Bradford, by Prof. Clerk Maxwell, F. R. S. *Nature*, September 25, 1873.

others of the same kind gives it, as Sir John Herschel has well said, the essential character of a manufactured article and precludes the idea of its being eternal and self-existent. Thus we have been led, along a strictly scientific path, very near to the point at which science must stop. Not that science is debarred from studying the internal mechanism of a molecule which she cannot take to pieces, any more than from investigating an organism which she cannot put together. But in tracing back the history of matter, science is arrested when she assures herself on the one hand that the molecule has been made, and, on the other, that it has not been made by any of the processes which we call natural. We have reached the utmost limits of our thinking faculties when we have admitted that, because matter cannot be eternal and self-existent, it must have been created...... They (the molecules) continue to this day as they were created, perfect in number, and measure, and weight, and from the ineffaceable characters impressed on them we may learn that those aspirations after accuracy in measurement, truth in statement, and justice in action, which we reckon among our noblest attributes as men, are ours because they are essential constituents of the image of Him who in the beginning created, not only the heaven and the earth, but the materials of which the heaven and the earth consist.'"

"It was Descartes, I think," remarked Judge Jefferson, "who said that we cannot know God's intentions in creating such and such things, since we cannot know anything of final causes before we know the first cause. Does there not seem to be some weight in that argument?"—"That philosopher," answered Mr. Clayburne, "mistook the point of the proof from design. The reasoning does not proceed on the line of God's intentions, but on the nature of the constitution of things, on the adaptation of means to ends. Even were we not to know *a priori* for what such or such things were, we could know from their very structure that there had been purpose in their creation. Even though I should not know who gave sight and hearing to men, I could know that the eye was made for seeing and the ear for hearing."—"Still," resumed the Judge, " it is contrary to all experience to suppose that anything can be a cause before it exists; every-where and among all men, the actual effect postulates a cause; in the case of unintelligent causes, they have surely no forethought of the effects or ends which they reach."

"In regard to the first statement," said Mr. Clayburne, "it was on it that Lucretius based his argument against final causes,—forgetting all the while that it is not the actual effect which determines the final cause, but the idea or forethought of that effect; the idea of the statue of Moses was certainly alone present to the mind of Michael Angelo before he executed that master-piece; on the second suggestion I remark that causes, unintelligent in themselves, can receive a direction or power for intelligent designs from a primary intellectual cause. Mechanical contrivances of various kinds for working out raw materials into articles for human use, what are they but causes moulded by human skill for intelligent action? And thus, too, natural secondary causes have been wound up, as it were, by their maker, in order that they may produce their special effects in the world. The watch indicates time, we may say, intelligently;—its wheels, and chains, and springs work mechanically for that end, but their motions are governed by the primary ordaining power of the watchmaker."

"Then," said the Judge, "things make themselves; and if they do, they did so always; that, I presume, does away effectually with the argument from design."—"Not at all, sir," answered Mr. Clayburne; "it only varies and extends it. From occupying itself exclusively with the actual structure of organisms for their respective ends, the mind studies design in the very molecules of matter, in order to see their adaptation by cohesion or repulsion in the formation of substances. Instead of observing the uses of water in the economy of nature, it examines the display of design in its composition, in the union according to due proportion of the oxygen and hydrogen that form it. Applied to all other compounds, the argument from design rests on the examination of their simple elements and on the cohesion of these, according to law, for the basis of the material world. The argument, therefore, so far from being done away with by modern science, has but received a greater extension. Men study design now, not only in the form of the wing of the bird, but also in the materials which go to make the wing."

"Still," continued the Judge, "it has been ascertained that the environment in which organisms exist influences or modifies them considerably. Now, such actual modifications give us data wherewith to estimate the gradual formation of these organisms by the action of the medium in which they live and grow."

"It is true," replied Mr. Clayburne, "that climate and the surroundings of an organism will affect it externally. For instance, the luxuriant foliage of the Brazilian forests, we are told, gives a peculiarly green color to the birds and reptiles which it shelters, and bright water gives to the fish therein a peculiar brilliancy. It has also been discovered by travellers that animals and insects under special circumstances mimic nature. The wild duck, to divert attention from her young, will feign being wounded, and a species of moth in certain circumstances will simulate crumpled leaves to avoid detection. But in these instances it is instinct and not environment that is brought into play; it is not so much experience that teaches, but rather the sensitive powers of animal nature that prevail. The wing of the bird has its formation before it is used, and the eye has its constituent organization before it sees."

"But among men," said the Judge, "as we all know, to select means to attain their ends is a sign of their limited power. Now, as God follows the like method, does He not thereby show that He is not omnipotent?"—"This objection," answered Mr. Clayburne, "supposes that in relation to the ends proposed God and man are in the same position. Whereas, on the contrary, God, infinitely perfect as He is, stands in need of nothing whatever; it is not so with man. Moreover, God wills as an end His own eternal glory, but with that He wills the glory of the means, that is, of men who render to Him their reasonable services."

As Judge Jefferson did not care to continue the argument, Mr. Maxwell broke in. "It is exactly here," said he, "that the argument from design fails. You reason from design in the works of art to the authors of them, and your argument is a valid one, since the combination and adaptation of parts in a piece of mechanism or the assortment or blending of colors in a painting point clearly to an intelligent author. But it is quite otherwise in the works of nature. Within her own laboratory she manufactures all that she needs, and that without the aid of any external power; she repairs her exhausted strength, unfolds her patterns by her own energies, and causes matter to form combinations for certain ends. The design, therefore, which I see in her works, leads me only to admire her immanent power, and nothing more. Moreover, to argue from the analogy of human art is not to ground a certain but only a probable proof for design in nature."
—"There is this difference," answered Mr. Clayburne, "between the argument of design taken from the works of man, and that derived from the works of God,—that in the former, design points immediately to man as the author, in the latter, it points to God only mediately through nature; in the one, man himself executes the design; in the other, God uses nature as His instrument for the execution of it. From the painting I conclude directly to the painter, from the flower I conclude directly only to the working of nature. Nature, indeed, paints the flower, but the question remains, who furnishes the

paint? who directs nature's hand and limits her design, and supplies her with patterns? An analysis of nature has shown us that, when resolved into its essential properties, it is incapable of design,—matter is inert, force is blind, life by itself is indeterminate. That they may combine and work for certain ends in organisms, they must be proportioned and specifically determined. The material world, it has been proved, is only the result of the union of simple elements nicely proportioned. Of these, chemistry says, there are sixty-eight, and of these again only twelve or fifteen are used in the formation of organic and inorganic bodies. They make earth, and sea, and air; in their combination, and with the element of life added, they make nature in all her fields. Nature, therefore, is a result, a design, and not a first principle. Down to its first elements it speaks of an ordaining power, and cast partly by the Creator originally into living organisms, it works for the specific ends assigned to them.

"It seems to me," said Mr. Maxwell, "that all I contended for from the beginning has been granted. For, waiving the question of the origin of things, nature now, we are told, weaves its own patterns independently out of its own resources."—"Pardon me, sir," replied Mr. Clayburne, "we do not waive the question of the origin of things; whatever nature has, she received from God, and being dependent and changeable as a creature, needs continually His supporting arm. Were He to withdraw it, forthwith nature would be dissolved and disappear. As it is He who created the world and upholds it when created, all its matter and force, in their working, depend on His co-operation; and the laws of nature are but physical expressions of His Providence. 'It does not follow,' writes Dr. Ward, 'because the laws of nature are fixed, that they proceed independently of God's constant and unremitting premovement.'"[1]

"Then," said Mr. Maxwell, "you unsay what the whole civilized world says when speaking of nature. To her, all men in common discourse attribute independent action. Nature, it is said, designs, paints, weaves, etc."

"Nature," answered Mr. Clayburne, "is one of those words that have been made to blur truth, or pervert it, or to thrust it aside altogether. Formerly used in language as a personification, it was easily interpreted as being a figure of speech, but for some years past it is not merely as a figure that it has been used, but as if it were a living being, endowed with the faculty of teaching, of designing, of governing. Nature has come to be looked upon as a goddess by the agnostic; and still, though beautiful to the eye, it is within often 'full of dead men's bones and of all filthiness.' As it comes out to view, however, it never ceases to mirror 'the invisible things of God;' by it His power is put before the human eye, seeing as it does stupendous results produced by slender causes. There are, for instance, bodies of immeasurable bulk held in their places by the force of gravitation; again elements most fierce and dissimilar united and governed by the laws of chemical affinity; while other elements, similar by nature, are so tied by cohesion that they form

[1] Dr. Ward's Essays, vol. 1., p. 17.

inorganic masses. And thus it comes to pass that by three or four threads of force the Almighty holds the universe together and governs everything."

After a rather embarrassing pause of a few moments, Mr. Walters remarked, "I do not consider that any objections drawn from the mere physical structure of things are of much account as against the argument from design. The great difficulty it has to encounter is taken from the prevalence of evil in the world. There is the evil of sin and the evil of pain; the former, indeed, is the work of man, but the evil of pain, so universal in its sway and so merciless in its exactions, how is it to be reconciled with God's goodness? In travelling I once fell in with a man who, from his own imprudence in cold weather, was suffering excruciating pain, while, in his agony, he blasphemed and denied even the being of God."

"I object," exclaimed Mr. Maxwell, "to having a difficulty dismissed in this flippant manner. As I understand it, the amount of pain in the world of men, the sufferings they have to undergo, do away with much that has been said on the thesis proposed. You insist that God is by nature infinitely good, and by upholding that He has designed all things you virtually make Him the author of the evils to which flesh is heir."

"The gentleman," said Mr. Randolph, "only related an incident and did not dismiss a difficulty for the plain reason that no difficulty had been raised. But now that it has been raised, it does not in the least, to my seeming, impair the conclusiveness of the argument from design, and in nowise conflicts with God's goodness. As to the sufferings which men undergo, I have to remark, in the first place, that much of it is of their own and not of God's making; they violate law, and, as a consequence, have to pay the penalty for their transgressions. They forge their own fetters, while their unbridled passions, their cruelty or tyranny, are often the cause of heart-rending pain and misery to their fellow-men. Secondly, it is to be noted that pain may be imposed when necessary as a means for reaching a beneficent end or for upholding order. A physician judges it necessary to cauterize a wound in view of curing it; he imposes temporary pain, but effects the cure. Or again, the state imposes a penalty on a criminal in order to vindicate public justice. In both cases, mankind have always sanctioned the imposition of pain. Now, in many instances, God's method of acting is similar to that of the physician or the judge. He afflicts in order to cure, or He permits evils to come on a man to remind him of his sinful state, and, should he repent, to lead him on to peace and happiness of soul. To use the words of St. Thomas, 'God, being all-good, would nowise suffer any evil to be in His works, were He not so almighty and good as even to draw good out of evil!'"—" But," asked Mr. Maxwell, " could He not draw good out of good?"—" He could," answered Mr. Randolph, "and He does, but out of evil He draws it (and by evil here I mean pain) by accepting it as an expiation for sin and an exercise of the virtue of patience. 'Patience hath a perfect work,' and patience is impossible without pain."

"It is easy," retorted Mr. Maxwell, " to divide off

the field of pain and set up sign posts and label them as you please."—" It is easier still, sir," replied Mr. Randolph sharply, " to make assertions and not to prove them. My division of the subject is based on the facts of life.

" I say, then, thirdly, that in any just estimate of the sufferings of mankind an account should be taken of the original source from which they spring, as well as of the probationary nature of our present life. Originally God did not design human nature for suffering, but Adam, the head of the human family, by his fall, made suffering to be the lot of humanity. Human nature, centred in Adam as it was, by his trangression was stripped of original justice, and thus sin entered into the world, and by sin death.

" In estimating the extent of human suffering, the next thing to be considered is the condition of our present life. Both reason and revelation teach that this life is not final, but the prelude to a future life, that it is a state of probation, not the ultimate term of existence, that in it men, by the use of the divine aids given to them, can shape their destiny for good or for evil, for eternity. Viewed from this standpoint, suffering is only a discipline by which men fit or unfit themselves, as the case may be, for a future state, or it forms the materials from which men, God helping, can make merit, or from which also, by sinfulness, they can make demerit before Him. Pain endured by the just for God is the seed of their glorious immortality. Death, which is a terror for the wicked, is a relief for them; it ends their probation, since it cleaves man in two. Beyond the grave, until the last great judgment day, he will not exist as man but as soul; he cannot merit, nor, if sin has followed him, can he repent as he could have done in life, but in soul must suffer, temporarily, for venial faults,—everlastingly, for grievous sin. Judgment succeeds the death of each individual; final judgment succeeds the death of the human race and seals their eternal destiny."

"But," said Mr. Maxwell, "could not God have saved men without requiring them to pass through their present ordeal of suffering?"

"The question is not, sir," replied Mr. Randolph "what God could have done, but what God has done. The present sufferings of men we are proving to be compatible with the perfect nature of God. The main-spring of these sufferings, we have seen, is from man himself; he has been his own ruin, and still God in His goodness enables man to build up his greatness and happiness amid the ruin caused by him. He makes man's sufferings to minister to man's merits. Absolutely, God could have chosen another order of things; but as He has decreed that trials are to be man's lot in this world, and that salvation is to be had through sufferings, His divine ordinance must remain. God, to be sure, could lessen man's pains, but then He would lessen his merit and his future glory consequent on that merit. He could have predetermined man to the good, but then He would have done away with man's liberty and the rewards resulting from the due exercise of it. All this tells us how little we know of the mysterious working of divine Providence, and yet we would feign to make ourselves God's counsellors."

"But pain once endured," suggested Mr. Maxwell, "cannot be undone."—"No," was the answer, "but it can be forgotten, or the joy consequent on the triumph to which its leads can efface the remembrance of it. In the future life their sufferings in this world will be a source of glory for the just, while remembrance of the former sinfulness of the wicked will be the great cause of their torments. 'Then,' says the author of the Book of Wisdom, 'shall the just stand with great constancy against those that have afflicted them, and taken away their labors. These, seeing it, shall be troubled with terrible fear and shall be amazed at the suddenness of their unexpected salvation. Saying within themselves, repenting and groaning for anguish of spirit: These are they whom we had sometime in derision, and for a parable of reproach. We fools esteemed their life madness and their end without honor. Behold, how they are numbered among the children of God and their lot is among the saints.'"[1]

"In this connection," said Mr. Ferguson, "the imperfection or waste that exists in nature seems to mar design as much as suffering; while, as, scientists tell us, the human organs and natural things might well be improved, and pain might also be mercifully diminished in the brute creation."

"As to this last point," answered Mr. Randolph, "there is this remark to be made, that the great recipient of pain is the conscious mind alone. Brutes, as it appears, experience dull, distressing sensations under suffering, but having no reflective, conscious power, in which, as in a centre, grief accumulates, they feel not the force or piercing acuteness of pain. The want of consciousness, as modern

[1] Wis. v. 1-5.

pathology proves, neutralizes the effects of the most painful surgical operations."—" But still," said Mr. Ferguson, " brutes suffer in some degree, and that suffices for my thesis."

"You, sir," answered Mr. Randolph abruptly, " would have things according to your views, and I suppose would suggest improvements to a God of infinite justice and wisdom. That seems to be the tone of thought of a certain modern school. Some phases of animal suffering are inexplicable to it, and forthwith, instead of acknowledging its inability to understand, it proceeds to question the justice of the Creator. The logical process should run thus: Whatever a God of infinite justice and wisdom has done, must in itself be wise and just; the inability to see God's wisdom in His works ought to be proof sufficient to man of the error of his reasoning.

"In the case which we examine, the graduated scale of animal-existence outlines the scheme of God's wisdom; inferior animals minister to and support the superior, and these are under the dominion and for the service of man. You, I presume, do not consider it cruel to feed on the flesh of animals slain for your support; why then should you object to animals themselves being by nature carnivorous?"

"I see no unwisdom in that," said Judge Jefferson, " but I should like to have your views on the other difficulties proposed."—" To one who examines the world from an utilitarian stand-point," said Mr. Randolph, " there will undoubtedly appear much waste in nature. Whatever does not contribute to his support or comfort he will look upon as purposeless. But, surely, this is not a true standard for judging in the case, since 'there are more things in heaven and earth than are dreamt of in (our) philosophy.' Even in the appliances and tools of professional labor the untrained eye cannot discover their various uses;—does it follow then that they are purposeless?"

"In small proportions we just beauties see," but God sees order and harmony and beauty in all their proportions, and in view of that has balanced atom against atom, force against force, and substance against substance. Although man has a faculty for appreciating the beautiful, still beauty was not intended only for man's admiration. The universe contemplated in its true light is like unto a mirror, in which the attributes of the Deity are obscurely reflected; viewed thus, everything in nature, the unseen as well as the seen, has its object and fulfils its mission by bearing testimony and giving praise to its Creator. The stars, though unseen by human eye, have spoken since the dawn of creation, through numberless ages, of the glory of God.

"God could, of course, have created a world absolutely better than the present world; but this world in which we live is relatively the best adapted for the manifestation of His power as well as of His glory."—"The argument from design," said Mr. Webber, "is based on the uniformity of physical law, and justly so, but only on the condition that it does not clash with other clearly recognized dispositions of divine Providence. If law be uniform, unchangeable, I should like to know what is the object of praying for relief from temporal woes, and how, in that case, a miracle would be admissible."

"It is clear to me," answered Mr. Harrison, "that

the argument from design contradicts neither the efficacy of prayer nor the possibility of miracles. God gives us many things without our asking for them; others He will give only on the condition of our praying for them. He wishes to teach us our dependence on Him by our wants, and confidence in Him by His beneficence. In this there is no change of physical law, since this was made in view of the law of prayer. Modifications that are introduced in the original draft of a law do not change it, but shape it for some exceptional cases, and neither does prayer change the laws that rule the world; it only modifies them; being, therefore, within 'the domain of law,' prayer, according to God's eternal designs, is also a factor in the government of the world."

"Then," said Mr. Webber, "God changes, since, at the instance of man, He modifies what He has ordained and recalls what he had determined."

"Not at all," answered Mr. Harrisson; "the will changes only when one wills what he did not will before, or when it ceases to will what it had once willed. 'We do not pray,' writes St. Thomas, 'to change the divine disposition, but to obtain what God ordained was to be granted through prayer.' What God wills to do at the instance of prayer is as eternal as what He wills to do by the force of physical law."

"Whence, then, the need of prayer?" asked Mr. Webber.—"From this," replied Mr. Harrison, "that God has eternally willed prayer to be the condition for the fulfilment of some of His designs in time.

"Well, then," said Mr. Webber, "if we do not

pray, we defeat God's purpose, and if we do pray, we are constrained thereto by God's predetermination."

"Infinite as God is," replied Mr. Harrison, "He has thousands of resources at His command. He can, therefore, bring it to pass that infallibly we shall pray, but not necessarily, and, since He works in all things according to their nature, that we shall act freely in prayer while fulfilling His purpose."

"As I understand it, then," said Mr. Webber, "there is no uniformity in the laws of nature, since God is constantly varying them in order to comply with the petitions of suppliants, or, in other words, a miracle is in the order of nature as much as law."

"You mistake, sir," answered Mr. Harrison; "prayer is not beyond but within the 'domain of law,' and though a miracle is not wrought without prayer, all prayer, when accepted by God, by no means implies a miracle. He has all the threads of nature in His hands. He knows most intimately all its secret powers, and can so temper them that, without any derogation from any physical law, the effect prayed for will infallibly take place."

"What, then, is a miracle?" asked Mr. Neufchatel abruptly.

"It is an effect," answered Mr. Harrison, "which, exceeding the capacity of every created cause, can be produced by God alone. In a particular instance it suspends the effect of a law of nature, but does not change the law itself. When St. Peter, as we find it recorded in the ninth chapter of the Acts of the Apostles, raised Tabitha to life, he did not change the law—'that dead once, dead forever,'—

but in this case, in virtue of the superior power of God, he cancelled the working of an inferior law of nature; or when the children in the fiery furnace walked through the flames unscathed, fire in general did not lose its burning power. Miracles, therefore, do not alter nature's laws, but hinder the execution of them in some single instances; they are so many testimonies to God's immediate action in the government of this visible world,—exceptions to general physical law, made for high moral purposes by the all-ordaining infinite will of God."

"But," said Mr. Neufchatel, "how can we know that miracles are what you say they are? I take them to be variations in nature's laws."

"Miracles," answered Mr. Harrison, "are sensible facts, and as such are as much objects of sense as any other visible thing, and therefore as knowable. When St. Peter raised Tabitha to life, the people said it was a miracle. They did not, indeed, know all the laws of nature; it was not necessary that they should; but this one law was clear to them, namely, that it was only divine power that could raise the dead to life. It was not a variation, but a suspension, in a given instance, of an existing law. Change or turn a corpse as much as you may, sir, you cannot make a living body out of it."

"Some time ago, sir, in one of the magazines," said Mr. Babbington, addressing Mr. Clayburne, "it was asserted of the argument from design that the Darwinian theory of natural selection 'in the twinkling of an eye knocked (its) support from under it.'"
—"I fail to see that it did," replied Mr. Clayburne; "I would say even that it has added to its force.

"Let us suppose, for a moment," writes Dr. Browne, "that evolution has been demonstrated, and it will bear only on the matter in which design is wrought, but not on the evidence of design in the world. Instead of design following directly as an effect from the act of creation, it will be 'worked out by a slow process.' In the one case the Creator made the animals at once such as they now are; in the other case, He impressed on certain particles of matter, which, either at the beginning or at some point of the history of His creation He endowed with life, such inherent powers that in the ordinary course of time living creatures, such as the present, were developed. The creative power remains the same in either case, the design with which that creative power was exercised remains the same. He did not make the things, we may say; no, but He made them make themselves."[1]

"With some of the conclusions arrived at," said Mr. Maxwell, "I am not fully satisfied. It has been admitted that evolution now plays its part in the world, and that nature itself, by its innate powers and unconscious purpose, works out its ends and sketches designs. This, I think, is a fair premise for the deduction that, in the eternal past, nature was doing what it does now."

"It is a law of logic," said Mr. Clayburne, "that in sustaining an argument, what has been once demonstrated should not again be called in doubt. It has been proved by an analysis of the properties and elements which make up this physical world, or nature, that it was created, and received consequent-

---

[1] "The Relations between Religion and Science," p. 114.—By Dr. Browne, Bishop of Exeter. The author's first hypothesis, in as far as it relates to the animal species, is most admissible; in the case of man God creates every human soul.

ly all its latent energy and plastic power from Him who gave it existence. Nature taken in the scientific, and not the philosophical sense, is nothing more than the elements that form it. Now these, it has been shown, mark their own beginning. By the succession in the order in which bodies move in space or change in substance, they tell that it is time, and not eternity, that spans their existence. Eternity has neither past nor future, but is the always present. God is in the eternal, the creature in the temporal. On the different strata in the earth's formation, time has written its records, and high above us, in the solar system, has set its dial, whereby men can estimate how old the world grows, and how time itself is split into days, and months, and years. Let the created cease to be, and there is only eternity; let all material things cease to exist, and space exists no more."

"It has been stated," said Mr. Jennings, "that the argument from design proves only the intellectual character of the Being who fashioned the world. But does it not prove more? To me it is unintelligible that a designer who as such possesses all the power attributed to Him should not also be God."

"I said," replied Mr. Clayburne, "that explicitly and directly the argument from design proves that the highest intellectual power was brought into play in the formation of the universe, but constructively or inferentially, I hold that it also proves the existence of a necessary, self-existing Being."

"Would you be so kind, sir," said Mr. Jennings, "as to give the reasons for your opinion?"

"The attributes," proceeded Mr. Clayburne,

"which the argument supposes in the designer, are that He is one, and intelligent, independent, and extramundane. He is above and beyond the world; He holds not from any other being; He is supremely, I would say even (considering the power and reach of man's free thoughts and the wonderful combination of things) infinitely intelligent; He is necessarily one. Now such attributes, I submit, can exist only in a Being, self-existent and infinite, the First Great Cause of all things."

"I did not exactly seize on the scope of the proof," said Mr. Jennings, "made for the extramundane attribute of the designer."

"It is this," was the answer; "if the designing power were in the world, then the world, partially or as a whole, should have designed itself. But it could not have done so partially, since then the argument for the entire world would not conclude; neither could it do it as a whole, since then design would have been its own cause, which is as absurd as to say that a . picture painted itself."—"Pardon me, sir," resumed Mr. Jennings, "I do not clearly see how, on its own merits, the argument validly concludes to God's existence."—"I said," answered Mr. Clayburne, "that it does so inferentially; it relies greatly for its support, writers generally hold, on the arguments from the First Cause and a necessary, self-existent Being. There is, however, this suggestion, which I would offer: the human intellect, according to St. Thomas, is infinite in capacity (*in potentia*) inasmuch as it is never limited by its knowledge; in itself, it has objectively an infinite range. And since there can be nothing designed as infinite in capacity which has not proceeded from the actually infinite, design, as impressed on man's intellectual nature, implies that the author of it is himself infinite. The idea of cause is implied in this case, since every design supposes a cause."

"On the other hand," said Mr. Walters, " would you not consider that the argument, based as it is on analogy drawn from human workmanship, can never rise to the height of a demonstration."—" The ground of the argument, sir," was the answer, " is not analogy, but the principle that the order which reigns in the world must spring from an intelligent cause."

"I deny," said Mr. Neufchatel, "that on the subject there can be any demonstration whatever; we do not know intimately the divine nature, how then can we demonstrate it?"

"Demonstration is twofold," answered Mr. Clayburne, "there is a demonstration which is grounded on the nature of the thing when we know it intimately, and another, which is formed when a thing is not known in itself but from its effects. In this instance, we know first that the effect is and then seek to know its cause. From the arguments given we know that God exists, but what His intimate nature is we deduce from other reasoning."

"I return to evolution," said Mr. Maxwell. "I hold that, by its eternal action on matter and motion, it will explain for us the design that we see around us."

"If you suppose, sir," answered Mr. Clayburne, "motion to be co-eternal with matter, (admitting, for argument's sake, that matter could be eternal) you only double the difficulty, for you have to account for the beginning of motion as well as for that of matter; in addition, you have to explain a contradiction, since, *ex hypothesi*, evolution is eternal, and still goes on, day after day, that is, it is eternal and not eternal at the same time. Again, viewed in another light, evolution turns on the supposition that the world is always advancing to perfection; it was less perfect, it is said, 10,000 years ago than it is to-day, and to-day it is less perfect than it will be 10,000 years hence. Maintain, then, that evolution is eternal, and you hold that a longer period than eternity was necessary to produce a limited perfection, which is absurd. The perfection of the world, being finite, is consequently measurable. In any period, we can compare it with what it was in a former period, and by thus going back in analysis, step by step, we come to the moment when the world had not as yet begun to move, or when evolution had not commenced. Thus the universe, read backward from its present state, through all the grades of its ascent, teaches that its origin is in time and not in eternity."

"Gentlemen," said Mr. Walters, " we have examined thoroughly what nature has done for us. I move that we should now see what we can do for nature."

CHAPTER V.

[At the Windsor Hotel, it had been unanimously resolved to accept the invitation of Mr. Webber to spend a day with him at his villa on Fordham Heights on the first Thursday of the following month.

Before ten o'clock on that day, all his friends greeted their host in his pleasant home. It was a spot well fitted to raise the soul to God. Every plant and flower seemed to glisten with a new freshness under the rays of the vernal sun, while all around every living thing tried, according to its kind, to show forth the life that was in it. Through the thick shrubbery that lined the grounds the eye could notice on one side the waters of the Harlem, and on the other the bold outlines of the rolling lands of Westchester County. It was amid this scene of nature's grandeurs that the gentlemen sat, on chairs duly arranged, to listen to the reading of an essay prepared by Judge Jefferson.

After having welcomed his friends, Mr. Webber returned to his mansion in search of some books indicated to him by the Judge and there met his two guests, Mr. Netterville of Philadelphia and Mr. Mattison of Hartford. "Come, Webber, an instant," said Mr. Mattison, as they looked out on the party, "tell us who is who."—"Quickly, now" said Mr. Webber; "you see these three gentlemen facing us: that large man in the middle is Judge

Jefferson of Cincinnati; on his right is Burke of Chicago; on his left, Neufchatel of Wyoming. Off there on the right, the tall man of commanding appearance is Jennings of New York; he with the slouched hat is Walters of St. Louis; just by him is Taunton of Boston. On the left, the man with long beard is Randolph of Washington, and with him is Babbington, a tourist. The two walking arm in arm are Maxwell of New Haven and Ferguson of Toronto; on the right, under the maple tree, are Clayburne of Baltimore and Harrison of New Orleans. Now, since you know their names, come on, and I'll introduce you. A few moments after, when compliments had been exchanged, the party sat down to listen to Judge Jefferson.]

THE HUMAN RACE BEARING TESTIMONY TO GOD.

THE visible world examined in the light of reason has given us convincing proofs of the existence of God. From the motion that reigns through nature, from the law of causality as seen through the world, from the perishableness of things and the order that pervades the universe, we have ascended by reasoning to Him. To-day, I purpose to take an argument on the same great subject from the world of men, or from the testimony which mankind have always and every-where borne to the existence of a Supreme Being, whose throne is above the stars, and who rewards the good and punishes the wicked.

1. The immediate aim of the argument will be, not to prove the existence of God as He really is, but

rather to show forth the belief in the divinity as it existed among all nations and tribes, and how even the degrading worship of some peoples has in it something which points to a Being to whom they are accountable and who governs the world and its elements. Sometimes, to be sure, in the history of nations, there will be found some persons who, by perversity of opinion or by lascivious indulgence, have darkened the very eye of reason. They are of the earth, earthly, and have fallen below the normal condition of humanity. Their opinions, exceptional as they are, give not a just standard wherewith to judge of the native energies of the human soul. And even such persons making profession of atheism as they do, in moments of impending danger will sometimes, as experience has proved, appeal to God for support and protection. But, whether they do or no, the argument holds good, based as it is on the general testimony of the human race. Of its sort, this testimony is alone; no other truth in the world or outside it, save God's existence, has centred on itself the almost universal consent of mankind, and that with a constancy that has never been shaken by racial changes or by the emigrations or fortunes of peoples. Distorted that testimony has often surely been, overlaid too in many countries by the vilest superstitions, and again misinterpreted and fearfully caricatured by idolatry and polytheism; but, for all that, it has never ceased to be given in some form or other. Grotesque certainly among uncivilized tribes and unintelligible to the stranger the giving of this testimony has not unfrequently been. In their manners and actions the casual observer can see nothing that indicates a belief in theism; but those who live among them, and learn their dialects, and look into the bearing of their personal and social conduct, find that acts which were considered to be merely social have a religious significance, and that words standing for many things have also one meaning which denotes worship. This testimony however, I admit, may have partially originated in tradition and for a time may have been largely upheld by it, but tradition being forgotten or perverted, men for their theistic belief were thrown back on their own natural, rational resources. They could not have got it from education or prejudices, since these continually change, nor could it come to them through some deceit, since this could not be universal, nor could it have arisen from fear caused by natural phenomena, since, these ceasing, fear also ceases; neither could that belief have sprung from ignorance, since, as all history teaches, theism has been confirmed by the advance of true knowledge.

The true and real source, then, of the unshaken belief of the human race in the existence of God is human reason. In its light the savage reads the lesson of God's existence in the motion, change, and order of the visible world; and in the same light, the true scholar does the same, but perhaps with greater precision. The testimony, therefore, of which there is question, is the judgment of the universal reason of mankind; and, as the object of reason is truth, what all men judge to be true must be true. In this case, reason postulates its object; it does not create truth, but objective truth informs it; it does not suppose truth, but, from objective evidence, adheres by the law of its nature to what has been presented to it as true. As gathered from nature, the truth of God's existence shines in upon the eye of the soul, and claims thereto the adhesion of the intellect. In assenting, therefore, to the truth of God's existence, men are but assenting to the law of their nature.

2. After this statement of the nature of the thesis, the main point to be proved I take to be the fact that the human race has always invariably held to a belief in a Supreme Being, the Ruler of the world. Fortunately, one striking proof of the subject has been furnished by the researches of modern scholars. By them we are enabled to read for ourselves in the so called "sacred books of the East," of the nature and beliefs of the religions of antiquity. They put before us what religious sentiments ran through ancient nations during thousands of years, and what was their belief touching the existence of a Supreme Being. After having examined thoroughly the idolatry and worship practised by these nations, Mr. George Rawlinson of Oxford, in his work, "The Religions of the ancient World," sums up his views in the following words: "The historic review which has been here made lends no support to the theory that there is a uniform growth and progress of religion from fetichism to polytheism, from polytheism to monotheism, and from monotheism to positivism, as maintained by the followers of Comte. None of the religions here described shows any signs of having been developed out of fet-

[1] Pp. 242, 243.

ichism, unless it be the Shamanism of the Etruscans. In most of them the monotheistic idea is most prominent *at the first*, and gradually becomes obscured and gives way before a polytheistic corruption. In all there appears to be one element, at least, which appears to be traditional, viz, sacrifice; for it can scarcely have been by the exercise of his reason that man came so generally to believe that the superior powers, whatever they were, would be pleased by the violent death of one or more of their creatures.

Altogether, the theory to which the facts appear on the whole to point, is the existence of a primitive religion, communicated to men from without, whereof monotheism and expiatory sacrifice were parts, and the gradual clouding over of the primitive revelation every-where, unless it were among the Hebrews. Even among them a worship of Seraphim crept in (Gen. xxxi. 19–35.), together with other corruptions (Josh. xxv. 14), and the terrors of Sinai were needed to clear away polytheistic accretions." But sacrifice was not the only remnant of primitive traditions that remained among pagan nations and tribes. Many fragments of a common original belief have been also found in their manifold worship. Defiled by various superstitions, curtailed or distorted in different ways, these fragments, when cleared up and restored partly to their true nature, have shown that they were at first of a piece and belonged to a religion which in the beginning was alone that of the human race. They refer to the doctrines and facts related in the Book of Genesis and taken by the descendants of Noe through the world; borne by them to different countries as saving truths, for want of authoritative teaching, they were quickly stunted in their growth by the rank products of the grossest errors. Thus it was that monotheism, in the very beginning, became the great religious root-doctrine of all peoples and tribes; a doctrine which they learned from tradition, but which they might have also mastered by their reason. Yet, what part reason had in the formation and support of that doctrine, and what part tradition, no learning can now completely determine. Along with the truth of the unity of God were spread the doctrines of the origin of the world, of the fall of Adam, of the promise of a future Saviour, of the existence of angels and the distinction between them as good and bad, of the future life with its rewards and penalties, of the reciprocal relation between man and God, of the fact of the Deluge, of the building of the Tower of Babel, and of the dispersion of the human race. These truths gathered, though obscurely, from the mythologies and traditions of gentile nations, give sufficient grounds for the inference that they had been derived from one common source and had been propagated by the migrations of families or tribes. Of this fully grounded hypothesis a singular proof has been furnished in this century. During it the Pentateuch and other books of the Old Testament have been objected to in a critical spirit which, for impiety and recklessness, had rarely been equalled. The old proof for the authenticity and genuineness of those books, though in reality retaining unimpaired its full force, had been judged to be unequal to the exegetic requirements of "the school of the higher criticism." But just when scientific vanity was at its height, Providence so ordained that out of the bowels of the earth should be dug out a clear refutation of the boasting of impiety. The cuneiform inscriptions on baked bricks found in the excavations made in Assyria and Babylonia amply confirmed the narrative of Genesis and other writings of the Bible. Prominent among the distinguished scholars who deciphered those inscriptions was Mr. George Smith, distinguished for his knowledge of Assyrian and for the interpretation of mythical legends. Of his discoveries he writes:

"In my lecture on the Chaldean account of the Deluge, which I delivered on December 3d, 1872, I stated my conviction that all the earlier narratives of Genesis would receive new light from the inscriptions so long buried in the Chaldean and Assyrian mounds; but I little thought at that time that I was so near to finding most of them... When excavating at Kouyonjik I discovered the missing portion of the first column of the Deluge tablet, ... and in the same trench I subsequently found the fragment which I afterwards recognized as part of the Chaldean story of the Creation. I excavated later on... another portion belonging to this story, far more precious; in fact, I think, to the general public, the most interesting and remarkable cuneiform tablet still discovered. This turns out to contain the story of man's original innocence, of the temptation and of the fall.... I subsequently found several smaller pieces in the old Museum collection, and all join or form parts of a continuous series of legends, giving the history of the world from the Creation down to some period after the Fall of Man. Linked with these I found also other legends on primitive history, including the story of the building of the Tower of Babel, and of the Confusion of Tongues."[1]

Discoveries such as these, dating as they do from hundreds of years before the writing of the Pentateuch, prove that the fundamental truths of religion had been spread among nations through the medium of oral tradition. These truths, interwoven with legends, lost, to be sure, their original significance; still, in their distortion, they showed whence they had been derived, and how they had been transmitted. But of all other truths, there was one which, sustained by the force of reason, appeared, as it were, to claim an ascendancy, and that was a belief in one personal, supreme God. In Egypt He was Ammon Ra; in Assyria, Asshur; in India, Brahma; in Persia, Ahura-Mazda; in Phœnicia, Baal; in Greece, Zeus; in Rome, Jupiter.

Even beyond the range of civilization, the same great truth is noticeable. Savage tribes, wherever found, nearly always cling to the idea of one sovereign, presiding deity. They have no annals, no written history; the great link that binds them to the past is oral tradition. Still, among them, here and there, are reminiscences of the Deluge, while they strive to propitiate supernatural powers by prayer or sacrifice, and believe in a future life of pain or pleasure. Taken in the gross, the belief of most of those poor savage tribes, falling, as they do, far below the normal type of civilized humanity, is in favor of theism, under some form. In America, North, and South, the aborigines, as a rule, look up

---

[1] "The Chaldean Account of Genesis," pp. 11, 12.

The Human Race bears Testimony to God. 195

with reverential awe to the "Great Spirit." In Africa, travellers have found some tribes believing in the supremacy of one God, and others dividing that supremacy among many deities, or worshipping some indefinable power above them. "There is no necessity," says Livingstone, speaking of the Bechuanas, "for beginning to tell the most degraded of these people of the existence of a God, or of the future state, the facts being universally admitted. Everything that cannot be accounted for by common causes is ascribed to the Deity, as creation, sudden death, etc."[1] Of the negroes of the Slave Coast of Africa, the Missionary, the Rev. P. Baudin writes: "The religion of the blacks is an odd mixture of monotheism, polytheism, and idolatry. In these religious systems the idea of a God is fundamental; they believe in the existence of a supreme, primordial being, the Lord of the universe....... in the existence of an Olympus, where dwell the gods and celebrated men who become fetiches, and in an inferior world, the sojourn of the dead, and, finally, in a state of punishment for great criminals."[2] Since Cicero's time, testimonies from a thousand different sources have been taken on the question of the spread of religion. The knowledge, also, of the human family has grown wider and more intimate, so that Mr. Taylor, after having weighed the arguments proposed in support of the theory of the existence of atheistic races, does not hesitate to declare it as his settled opinion in his work on "Primitive Culture," that " there is no evidence sufficient to war-

[1] "Livingstone's Missionary Travels," ch. viii., p. 158.
[2] "Fetichism and Fetich Worshippers," p. 9.

rant the assertion that there exists anywhere any race of human beings without religion of any kind."[1] On this account, Professor Tiele calls religion, "an universal phenomenon of humanity."

The argument thus far adduced for the universality of religion makes it also to be somehow connatural to men. Under all circumstances, the religious sentiment under one form or another envelops them; it enters into their thoughts and affections and prompts their aspirations. Do what they may, they cannot altogether get rid of it. If religion were something adventitious to men, something which they had assumed for comfort, or utility, or through fear, as Sir J. Lubbock supposes, it could be put aside as quickly as it has been taken up. "But religions," writes the Duke of Argyll, "can neither be put on nor cast off like garments, according to their utility, or according to their beauty, or according to their power of comforting."

3. On this subject, another ingenious and, as I think, a conclusive argument has been framed from linguistic studies. For prehistoric times, the evidence of language, according to Professor Max Müller, is "irrefragable"; it gives the thoughts, the beliefs, the traditions of unrecorded peoples, and, when examined according to the inductive method, has enabled scholars to re-construct, in part, the religions, and social and domestic life of races long since forgotten. An analysis of words in various tongues has shown to those scholars that languages form certain families which point to a common

---

[1] "Primitive Culture," vol. I., p. 379.
[2] "Primeval Man," p. 61.

The Human Race bears Testimony to God.

stock, and that this common stock bears affinities to the root-tongues of other linguistic families;—all which discoveries have indicated that once there was only one original tongue, and that this, of course, had a word for religious worship, which took different forms according to the diversity of construction of different languages. On this line of argument, illustrations have been given from modern European nations. Thus, for instance, French, Italian, Spanish, Portuguese, by the variety of their expressions for the same thing, show that they spring from one common type or stock, and though we know this to be Latin, the argument does not, on that account lose its force. "I am," for example,—Italian, "sóno;" Spanish "soy;" Portuguese, "sou;" French, "suis." These different forms clearly suggest one common root—the Latin "sum." So that, were we not to know of the existence of Latin, we should justly conclude that there had existed at one time a language from which those modern dialects were derived.[1] This principle of linguistic affinities being established, we can see how it holds good in the great original families of languages, for instance, in the Indo-European family. Thus, for the word "father," we have in Sanskrit, "pitar;" in Zend, "patar;" in Greek, πατήρ; in Latin, "pater;" in Gothic, "fathar;" in Irish, "athair." For their origin, these different forms point to one common word and to the same idea of paternity. Fitting this law of language to the existence of God as recognized in the prehistoric period, Professor Max. Muller says: "If I were

---

[1] "Chips from a German Workshop," by Max Muller, M. A., vol. ii., p. 18.

asked what I consider the most important discovery which has been made during the nineteenth century with respect to the ancient history of mankind, I should answer by the following short line :—

Sanskrit, Dyaush-pitar=Greek Ζεὺς Πατήρ=Latin Jupiter=Old Norse Tyr. Think what this equation implies.[1] It implies that not only our own ancestors and the ancestors of Homer and Cicero spoke the same language as the people of India,—this is a discovery which, however incredible it sounded at first, has long ceased to cause any surprise—but it implies and proves that they all had once the same faith and worshipped for a time the same Supreme Deity under exactly the same name, a name which meant Heaven Father."[1]

4. The cause of Theism has been also very much promoted in these latter times by the translation into modern tongues of "the canonical books" of the ancient world. Formerly the faith of countless generations of our fellow-beings was either unknown or was often interpreted as being anti-theistic; now we know that, in general, they believed in God and in the rewards or punishments of a future life. But besides those people whose faith is recorded in books, and whose worship can be gathered from written ceremonials still extant, there are hundreds of millions of human beings, in China and in countries adjacent to it, who have neither "sacred books," nor sacred rituals left to them by ancestors. And still we are told by the distinguished sinologue, Professor de Harley of the University of Louvain, that "the primitive religion of the Chinese was and

[1] *The Nineteenth Century*, October 1885.

continued to be the most spiritual, the most perfect monotheism ever known through ancient times outside the pale of Judaism."[1] The Chinese have not "canonical books," but they have their "classics," the four greatest of which are the "Shoo-King," or the Book of History, the "Shi-King," or the Book of Poetry, the "Zi-King," or the Book of Changes, and the "Li-King," or the Book of Rites. The three first of these were compiled by Confucius, in the fifth century, B. C., from Mss. that had existed from time immemorial in the empire. The Li-King, critics assign to another author. Confucius himself professsed to be only "an editor and not an author." "I am one, he said, who is fond of antiquity and earnest in seeking (knowledge) there." In the works attributed to him he ignores the supernatural. In the Hisâo King, a short treatise said to have been written by him, there is not a word about God; but man is supposed to suffice for himself and in his life to have no higher aim than domestic happiness or social interests. His perfection is to turn on four things, which, we are told, formed the staple of Confucius's teaching; these are,—literature, ethics, devotion of soul, and truthfulness,—a programme of studies which might be well adopted by a disciple of Comte or by a teacher in the "Society for Ethical Culture."

It was, then, to this naturally grave, self-centred, rationalizing man, that it was given to put in form or to edit the documentary evidence of Chinese knowledge for, it is said, sixteen centuries before his time. With a temper such as his for his work, it is

[1] *Dublin Review*, vol. 43, p. 100.

certainly not saying too much to suppose with Dr. Legge, that "it is possible that his account of the ancient views and practices took, unconsciously to himself, some color from the peculiar character of his mind."[1] But be that as it may, Confucius was limited in his zeal for naturalism by the Chinese language itself, since it had words for God which had been consecrated by immemorial usage. These, in their objective meaning, had been through all the past in the minds of the people,—informing them of their obligations to the one Supreme Being, the Lord of Heaven and Earth. To efface them from the memory of the nation lay not within the resources of any human power. Uncommon words sometimes become obsolete from want of use or application, but words that stand for man's life-thoughts or are laden with his eternal destiny can never die. They are of his soul and will and cannot be rooted out by the dictate or interpretation of any one. Shang-Ti, according to Professor de Harley, is the word in Chinese for God; it is used frequently, though incidentally, in the "Kings," especially in the "Shoo-King," which is a collection of historical memorials extending over a space of 1,700 years, but on no connected method and with frequent and great gaps between them. In that collection, Shang-Ti means "The Master of the Supreme Heaven," or again, "The Sovereign of Heaven and Earth," or "The King of Heaven;" sometimes it is put for Him by whose command the Chinese emperor lawfully rules and whose disapproval, on

---

[1] "The Chinese Classics." A Translation with Notes by James Legge, D. D. Preface, p. xiv.

the other hand, sanctions the dethronement of an emperor; sometimes also it stands for Him who is to be propitiated by prayer, sacrifice, and penance, whose will is law, who is omniscient, who has given to men a moral sense, by whom kings reign, and who gives wisdom, and happiness, and peace to those who obey Him. The word Tien is also taken for God, since "the expressions Shang-Ti and Tien are constantly interchanged to express the author of the same divine acts, and that not only in different passages but in the same sentence."[1] Thus the emperor Men-Wang (930–907 B. C.) said to the chiefs of Miao:—

"The moans of so many people tortured by a cruel power and guiltless of any crime reached up to Heaven (Tien). The Sovereign of Supreme Heaven (Shang-Ti), seeing what was happening among the people, certified that all sense of virtue was gone... The Sovereign of Heaven, giving judgment on the Migos steeped in iniquity, caused heavy misfortunes to overtake them. Heaven has commissioned me to make the people virtuous.... Heaven is not unjust or inconstant; misfortunes result (from the sins) of men. If Heaven did not inflict the full penalty of the punishments it awards, the people would never enjoy a wise government."[2] In this passage, and in many other passages of the like kind, Heaven (Tien) is taken figuratively for God, as in English we often take it; but illiterate Chinese often took it literally for the material Heaven and fell into idolatry, a circumstance which gave occasion to

[1] "Chinese Classics," "Shoo-King," by Dr. Legge. Introduction p. i.
[2] "Shoo-King," ch. xxvii.

the condemnation of the use of the word as a synonyme for God. On the words just spoken of Dr. Legge writes: " The name Heaven, by which the idea of supreme power in the absolute is vaguely expressed, and when the Chinese would speak of it as a personal name they use the term Ti and Shang-Ti, saying, I believe, what our early Fathers did when they began to use the word God. Ti is the name which has been employed for this concept for fully 5000 years. Our word God fits naturally into every passage where the character occurs in the old Chinese Classics."[1]

" I believe in one God " was therefore the first and greatest dogma of the primitive religion of China, and the first and greatest act of worship of that religion was the offering of sacrifice. A perusal of the " Shoo-King " shows that the Chinese, before their religion was corrupted from foreign sources or was paralyzed by scepticism, had believed also in the Providence by which God overrules the events of life, punishing the wicked and rewarding the good. They had believed, too, in the existence of spirits, good and evil, in the efficacy of prayer and penance, and in the immortality of souls. These doctrines are still read in the " Chinese Classics " as compiled by Confucius, but the written or printed letter cannot in every day life long uphold its sway against the living, spoken word. By his silent atheism and love of mere ceremony, by his merely ethical teaching and his striving to base a religion on filial piety, Confucius himself took the soul out of the primitive religion of his country. In his own

[1] Introduction to the " Shoo-King."

days, his influence on Chinese thought was not noticeable; he died complaining that not a prince of the empire had adopted his principles. And still, two generations had not passed, before his name became the rallying point of a national religious movement which culminated in creating in the popular mind a sort of new religion. Legend had already begun to weave a divine character for Confucius. His grandson Tze-tze, though he does not distinctly make his grandfather a God, makes him, however, to be much more than man. "All-embracing and vast," he writes of him, " he was like Heaven; deep and active as a fountain, he was like the abyss..... Wherever ships and carriages reach, wherever the strength of man penetrates, wherever the heavens overshadow and the earth sustains, wherever the sun and moon shine, wherever frost and dew falls, all who have blood and breath unfeignedly honor and love him. Hence it is said—He is the equal of Heaven."

But, apart from this foolish extravagance of panegyric, Confucius was undoubtedly a man of great political sagacity, with a deep insight into the nature of duty and right, as well as with keen sympathies for the wants of his fellow-men. Self-possessed, seemingly passionless, grave but condescending, he won the esteem of those who came in contact with him. To him goodness seemed to be its own reward and to be its ultimate and highest recompense, while all the conduct of life was by him made to consist in three fundamental laws,—that of subjects towards their sovereign, that of parents towards their offspring and that of husbands towards their wives.

The ground of these laws and the great motive of all human actions, he taught, were simply filial piety. This he considered to be "the root of all virtues, the source of all doctrine." But of God and of a future state he does not, in his scheme of morality, say even a single word, and for the enforcing of the law of duty does not go beyond the circle of the instincts and powers of humanity. "Confucius was a moralist," writes Baron Hubner; "he gave maxims and counsels full of wisdom, but politely declining the discussion of a future state, he sought the source of good and evil in the reason and will of each one."[1] The godless system of ethics which he taught has produced its fruits; under it the Chinese have had the well-springs of their energies dried up, their intellectual powers dwarfed, their moral sense perverted, and their whole humanity degraded by flagrant viciousness.

Confucius, we have said, might be called a disciple of the school of Comte. Laotze, born sixty years before Confucius, has been styled by Chalmers a philosopher of the school of Schelling. Both had been brought up in the ancient faith and religious traditions of their nation, and both used the enlightenment which they had received to corrupt the sources of that enlightenment. Confucius builds on the facts and resources of humanity. Laotze, in his short treatise, "Tao-te-King," strives to peer beyond the world and to unravel the origin of things. According to some writers he was the first virtually to attack the primitive Monotheism of the Chinese and to open the way for Chinese Buddhism. He had the

[1] "A Ramble round the World," p. 493.

idea of God as given in the Chinese classics, but he aims even higher and wants to get at the origin of God. All his speculations turn on the word, Tao, the exact meaning of which has baffled the ingenuity of all sinologues. According to Chalmers, in his translation of Laotze's work, it may mean, " way," or " reason," or " word," but its peculiar application in the treatise seems to restrict its meaning to " reason." In his first chapter he thus attempts to describe it: " The Tao which can be comprehended by the understanding is not the eternal Tao. The name which can be uttered is not the eternal name. Without name, it is the origin of heaven and earth; when named, it is the mother of all things." And in the fourth chapter he writes of it, " in tranquillity it appears ever to remain. I know not whence it is, it seems to me to have been before God. I know not its name, but give it the title of Tao." Reasoning on these and similar passages, Professor de Harley concludes that, according to Laotze, " the origin of all things is the absolute, eternal being: not ideal being, but concrete, real, substantial being." It is not strange that Laotze is obscure in the extreme, for in attempting to go behind God, he attempted the impossible. He imagines something above him, which he strives to reach. It flickers, as it were, occasionally, and then vanishes. He endeavors to tell what it is, multiplies words to denote it, and then, out of the jungle of thoughts and words, cannot free himself.

In the chapters on virtue in the "Tao-te-King," there are profound moral reflections, which prove that Laotze was a keen observer of human character.

Possessed of a philosophical mind and commanding a terse style of expression, he easily won the admiration of a people who were accustomed to think only within the circle of their traditional knowledge. He lived for the most part in solitude, and died in solitude, without any thought of founding a religion. But a life such as his, amid the debased, commonplace lives of those around him, could not remain unnoticed. In the eyes of the people, his life was quite phenomenal and, under the spell of romance, became grander and grander, until at last, if we may use the word, they not only canonized but even deified him. And the " Tao-te-King " came to be adopted as the text-book of a new religion, full of all kinds of superstition, of magic, of spiritism, and necromancy. This religion, called Taoism, tended, with Confucianism, to deaden the spiritual sense of the Chinese. Sunk in moral corruption, haunted or dismayed by fears of spiritual foes, given up to worldly gain and ambition, they have almost lost the power of reading the lessons of God's existence in nature, or of conceiving Him as He is spoken of in their great "Classics." But nature is stronger than speculation; theories, though holding sway for a few generations, as agnosticism, positivism, atheism,—are swallowed up by time, and the truth of God's existence, though obscured by passion, re-asserts itself by the reaction of reason. In this sense, Cicero has finely said: " Opinionum commenta delet dies, naturæ judicia confirmat."

In A. D. 1538, the Chinese emperor offered publicly the following prayer, as quoted by Dr. Legge: " Of old, in the beginning, there was the great chaos without form and dark.... In the midst thereof there presented itself neither form nor sound. Thou, O Spiritual Sovereign, camest forth in Thy presidency and first didst divide the grosser parts from the purer. Thou madest heaven, Thou madest earth, thou madest man. All things got their being with their reproducing power."

In the seventeenth and eighteenth centuries, during the controversy on the Chinese rites, the Chinese emperor and the most learned mandarins of the nation, following the traditional interpretation of the Chinese word Tien, maintained most strenuously that Theism was the traditional faith of the Chinese people. In spite of Confucianism and Taoism, China still, officially, in a most striking manner, makes annually public profession of belief in God. Once a year the Chinese emperor, recognized as the head of the national religion, goes to offer sacrifice to the Shang-Ti in the Temple of Heaven. In this temple, in the national capital, "there is no idol or statue whatever, and nothing to remind one that you are in a house of prayer. It is simply a magnificent and colossal kiosk, worthy of being the meeting-place between the Master of Heaven and the master of earth.[1] In civil life Theism also has its practical influence; "to the Chinese," writes Hubner, "the emperor himself is the representative of God and destiny. The obedience paid to him must therefore be blind and unlimited. He is emperor only because God has willed it so... Success gives legitimacy, because is not success due to the manifest will of God?[2]

[1] "A Ramble round the World," p. 487,
[2] Idem., p. 490,

When God's will is thus recognized by the people as the basis and law of the imperial dynasty, they are following in the ways of the primitive religion of their nation and reverencing, as their fathers did, the Sovereign Lord and Ruler of heaven and earth.

"Gentlemen," added Judge Jefferson, "of late years, a serious argument against my thesis has been taken from Buddhism; as time did not permit me to examine the question, my friend, Mr. Harrison, kindly consented to do so; he will read for you the result of his researches."

"Is it not a fact, Judge," asked Mr. Mattison, "that there have always been atheists in the world?"

"That question, sir," said the Judge, "I am unable to answer. Those known in olden times to profess atheism were few. Cicero, who had, I presume, a tolerably good knowledge of the pagan world, could find in it only three who professed atheism;—they were Protagoros of Abdera, Diagoras of Melos, and Theodoros of Cyrenae.[1] There must have been undoubtedly others who lived as if there were no Deity, but they did not profess atheism. The argument which I have just read has for ground the fact that men will follow the plain dictates of reason and not their prejudices or passions."

"Would you say then," resumed Mr. Mattison, "that reason guided countless generations who universally accepted the Ptolemaic system of the world?"—"I would," answered the Judge; "reason followed the lead of the senses, and these said that

---

[1] Laertius in his work, "De Vita Philosophorum," mentions three others, Bion, Boristhenes, and Epicurus.

the sun revolved around the earth. I presume that there are very reasonable people who think the same now, not having become acquainted with the Copernican theory. But there is not a living human being who cannot read for himself the existence of God in nature's open pages. A knowledge of Copernicanism is derived from study, and is an inference; a knowledge of God in nature comes out of the natural working of reason in view of the physical world. As soon as Copernicanism came to be known as true, the belief in the Ptolemaic system of the universe ceased to be universal."

CHAPTER VI.

BUDDHISM.

IN the year 1824, Mr. Hodgson, an English resident at Nepaul in India, discovered in the Buddhist monasteries there Sanskrit Mss. which contained the greater part of the Buddhist canon. For the world at large this discovery was as much a matter of surprise as the finding by Cardinal Mai of Cicero's treatise De Republica. The fact dated the beginning of the era of the critical study of Buddhism. Up to that time, all the knowledge that the learned had of it was gathered from Buddhist life and usages as seen in China, Thibet, Burmah, Japan, and Tartary. They knew, indeed, that in these countries Buddhism professed to have been derived from India, and from some words used by it, they could see that its parent tongue was the Sanskrit. But the very charter of Buddhism written in that language they hardly hoped to recover. Great then was the joy of scholars when it was announced that the Buddhist bible itself was to be presented for perusal to the learned world. When it came to be studied, it gave special satisfaction to some persons, since they found their own religious tendencies confirmed by it, and they came to know that they were real living Buddhists without being aware of it. In their opinion Buddhism was destined to be the religion of the future. To others, of a sceptical turn of mind, it afforded matter for ironical banter, since it seemed to put human nature at variance with itself and to suggest that, according to the calculations of some writers, nearly half of the human race was different in kind from the other. Buddhism is the creed of Nepaul, of Thibet, of Mongolia, of Tartary, of Chorea, of China in part, of the Japanese archipelago, of Cambodia, of Siam, of the Shan states, of Burmah, of Aracan and of Ceylon. In those countries, the adherents of Buddhism are put down by some writers in round numbers at 455,000,000, by others at 300,000,000, and by others again at 75,000,000. The first number is certainly exaggerated, the second is doubtful; even the third is surely large enough to deserve to be taken into account in an argument for the existence of God drawn from human testimony.

While actual Buddhism thus comes out prominently to view, by its numerous adherents, the student, however, is at a loss to get at anything like a full, clear, definite historical basis for its origin. It is now admitted by nearly all critics that there lived such a person as Gautama, called also Sâkya-Mouni, or again Siddhârta, but emphatically named the Buddha, or the enlightened One, from his mission. He was born at Kapilavastu, a town some hundred miles northeast of Benares in India. His father, one of the petty rulers of the country, was called Suddhodana, his mother's name was Mayadevi, "daughter of the King Suprabuddha." At the age of twenty-nine, Buddha married his cousin, Yasodhara, of whom he had a son called Rahula. But about what year the Buddha was born has not been determined. Professor Wilson "dwells on the fact that there are at least twenty different dates assigned to his birth, varying from the year 2420 to 450 B. C."[1] This space of time, however, has been reduced by a more minute criticism to a period ranging from about the first quarter of the sixth to that of the fourth century before Christ. What seems to be known for certain is that he died at the age of eighty years. "The date, derived from Ceylon, which is usually assigned to that event is 543 B.C.; but those scholars who have devoted most attention to the point hold this calculation to contain a certain error of about sixty years, and a probable error of eighty to a hundred years more, so that the date for the death of Buddha would have to be brought forward to 400 B. C., or a few years later."[2] But this uncertainty about the birth or death of the Buddha becomes still more puzzling when one considers the uncertainty of the Buddhist scriptures. It has been shown by scholars that no written historical Buddhist record extant dates farther back than from about 300 to 500 years after the decease of the Buddha. It is admitted even by Buddhist historians that no Buddhist teaching was committed to writing until between 86–76 B. C. Here, then, during these periods of hundreds of years was certainly a wide field for mental fancy, not restrained by certain, recognized public traditions, to weave stories, and create myths, and conjure up the miraculous in relation to Gautama. And that it did so, is seen by the extravagant and ludicrous stories that

---

[1] "Chips from a German Workshop," vol. I., p 217.
[2] "Encyclopædia Britannica," Art. Buddhism.

are related of him in his " Life or Legend," translated from the Burmese by Bishop Bigandet, Catholic Vicar-Apostolic of Burmah, having for the title of his see " Ava and Pegu." That Buddhism also borrowed from the life of Christ facts and scenes wherewith to adorn its own story has been satisfactorily proved by modern writers. It had come in contact with Christianity even in the Apostolic age, since it is now admitted by all impartial writers that St. Thomas the Apostle preached the Gospel in India. This has been the almost universal tradition of all Christian ages, and is inserted even in the oriental liturgies. The Syriac Chronicle by Gregorius Bar-Hebræsus speaks of it in these terms:—
" Thomas, the Apostle, the first pontiff of the East. We learn by the book of the preaching of the holy Apostles, that in the second year after the Ascension of Our Lord, the Apostle Thomas announced the tidings of the Gospel in the East, and preached to the Indians."[1] Bishop Dorotheus, born in the year 254, A. D., in a fragment preserved in the Paschal Chronicle, says also of St. Thomas:—" The Apostle Thomas, after having preached the Gospel to the Parthians, Medes, Persians, Germanians, Bactrians and Magi, suffered martyrdom at Calamina, a town of India."

St. Jerome and the historian Theodoret confirm the statement of Dorotheus.

Not only St. Thomas, but also the apostle St. Bartholomew preached the Gospel in India, according to the historian Eusebius and St. Jerome.

[1] Chap. i., par. 3.
[2] Calamina is the modern Meliapour, a town at a short distance from Madras.

The proof of it they find in the fact that Pantænus, who nearly a century and a half later went on a mission to India from Alexandria, found there in the hands of the Christians the Gospel of St. Matthew in Hebrew, which St. Bartholomew had brought with him.[1] Taking, then, barely these data into account, as given by the historian Eusebius,[2] we learn that, at least for some century and a half, Buddhism was in contact with Christianity in India. I say, *at least*, since the history of all Christian missions forbids us to say that Christianity then died out of a sudden. There is even some authority for saying, that during some succeeding centuries Christianity was maintained and propagated in India by Christian missionaries.[3]

Later on, in the sixth and seventh centuries, the Nestorian Christians opened missions in India; and even that time was not so late as that Buddhist writers could not have used passages from the life of Christ for the embellishment of the biography of the Buddha. On this issue the "Life of the Buddha," called the "Lalita Vistara," has been oftenest quoted. But the date of its composition is admitted to be altogether uncertain. In its present form, some orientalists, judging from its style and language, would refer it to a much more modern period of Indian literature than that ascribed to it, a critical

---

[1] That it is India proper which is mentioned by Eusebius and St. Jerome is proved with much erudition by the Bollandists. Acta Sanctorum, T. 39 De. S. Bartholomæo, die 24a Augusti.

[2] Lib. iv., cap. 10.

[3] Vide " De Moribus Brahmanorum; "—a work appended to the fourth volume of the writings of St. Ambrose, but which critics reject as not being genuine. It must, however, have been written not long after his time, as it is found in most editions of his works.

view which is quite reconcilable with the opinion which states that the "Lalita Vistara," though in another form, had been translated into Chinese before the Christian era. That the Hindoo mind, when there is question of religion, would not stop at such plagiarism, the story of the god Krishna, the Indian Apollo, is a case in point. " In native legends he is represented as an avatar, or incarnation of the Divinity; at his birth, choirs of Devatas sang hymns of praise, while shepherds surrounded his cradle; it was necessary to conceal his birth from the tyrant Cansa, to whom it had been foretold that the infant should destroy him. The child escaped with his parents, beyond the coasts of Yamouna. For a time he lived in obscurity, but then commenced a public life, distinguished for prowess and beneficence; he slew tyrants and protected the poor; he washed the feet of the Brahmins and preached the most perfect doctrine; but at length the power of his enemies prevailed, he was nailed, according to one account, to a tree by an arrow, and foretold before dying the miseries that would take place in the Cali Yuga, or wicked age of the world, thirty-six years after his death."[1]

The very reading of this story suggests nearly in all its details the account of the infancy and death of Our Lord. Between them there seems to be not only coincidence, but even imitation; the one reads as if it were a copy of the other. In the last century French infidels made merry over this analogy and used it in a vein of irony in their attacks on Chris-

---

[1] " Lectures on Science and Revealed Religion," by Cardinal Wiseman. Vol. ii., p. 27.

tianity. They were aided even by the learning of a few oriental scholars, who capriciously put the date of the Khrishna story many centuries before the Christian era. Answers were given by Sir William Jones, who in his time was considered an authority on Sanskrit literature, and by Mr. Maurice, who was looked up to as a light in the Anglican communion. The former thought that some of the embellishments of the story were borrowed from Christianity, the latter sought to explain the difficulty by the forethought of a future Saviour, which men had gathered from tradition. Both answers, as not being well grounded, were considered inconclusive. Then came the answer of Mr. Bentley, the astronomer, who, by means of his science, pointed out the falsity of the story.—
" It is to the examination of the age in which this god-like hero (Krishna) lived," writes Cardinal Wiseman, " that Mr. Bentley has applied astronomical calculations. For he diligently sought out, in the notices regarding him, some data on which to base an inquiry into the era of his life; and after finding all these too scanty, though it was stated that the celebrated astronomer Garga assisted at his birth, and described the state of the heavens at that interesting moment, he was fortunate enough to procure the *Janampatra* of Krishna, which contains the position of the planets at the time of his birth. From computation, grounded upon European tables, reduced to the meridian of Ujein, it appears that the heavens can only have been as there described on the 7th of August, A. D. 600. Mr. Bentley, therefore, concluded that this legend was an artful imitation of Christianity, framed by the Brahmins

for the express purpose of withholding the natives from embracing the new religion, which had begun to penetrate to the uttermost bounds of the East."[1]

In the case of Buddhism as well as in that of all other false religions, it has been remarked that the effort of error has always been to counterfeit the truth and thus deceive the world. To those, therefore, who believe in the existence, power, and malignity of Satan, it will not seem strange that he strove by his wiles to forestall the spread of the Gospel in the East, and, by borrowing from the life of Christ incidents wherewith to adorn the life of the Buddha, that he desired to put the latter in the eyes of his votaries on a level with the former. Men, he saw, would worship himself in worshipping Buddha. The Buddhas whom the Japanese adored, St. Francis Xavier, in one of his letters, calls demons.

The argument on the other side, if I may speak of it,—namely, that Christianity borrowed from Buddhism,—is simply a specimen of what may be called "the dogmatism of affirmation." From the past, there is no document whatever to show that Buddhism was heard of in Palestine in the time of the Evangelists; no Buddhist had ever taught his doctrine in Judea or was even seen there. No Jewish or early Roman writer spoke of Buddhism; not a word was said about it by the infidel Celsus in his charges against Christianity; and until the time of Clement of Alexandria, the name of the Buddha was not mentioned by any Christian writer, lay or ecclesiastical. There are indeed to be found in the Gospels expressions relative to the nature

[1] "Lectures on Science and Revealed Religion," by Card. Wiseman.—Vol. ii., p. 29.

and practice of moral virtue, expressions which have been also attributed to the Buddha. Their relative position, however, is quite different, in both cases. In the Gospel, they are in keeping with their surrounding, or the virtue spoken of fits in exactly with the fulness of doctrine and of virtue taught in the Gospel's narrations; it is quite otherwise in the Tripitaka, which forms the canon of the Southern Buddhists. In it you find what is true allied to what is false, and what is austere to what is absurdly extravagant. This is not to say, however, that the Buddha, together with many other illustrious heathens, had not a deep insight into the nature and practice of moral virtue. Christianity gives no warrant for the doctrine, which holds that the heathen in his fallen state is totally depraved, and that he cannot love what is true and do what is good. This doctrine, the Catholic Church teaches, is fundamentally false; it runs counter even to all history, since from the heathen mind have come some of the grandest words that have been spoken of virtue, and some of the loftiest thoughts that have been conceived of moral goodness. Nay, things have been done by heathen virtue which even still claim the admiration of the world. In his unregenerate state, then, all man's actions are surely not sins, though, for all that, they are not meritorious of eternal life. As supplementary to this explanation, I will add, that that is not a Christian doctrine which maintains that the graces of Christ do not at all run through heathendom, or that, beyond the pale of the Church, no supernatural aids are given to souls, encouraging or chastening them, as the case may be, and,—when they follow,—leading them onward to the enjoyment of the full illumination of Christian faith. In accordance with the foregoing doctrine, Buddha and a Christian evangelist might have spoken of virtue in the same sublime terms, though in the general teaching of the former there would be, without doubt, some vagueness and deficiency, while in the doctrine of the latter, because he was an evangelist, there would be completeness, consistency, and precision. The fact also remains to be added that much of what Buddha knew and taught, he had learned among the Indian Brahmins.

On this line of argument, or on the contrast between Buddhism and Christianity, it has been further urged that Christianity, as embodied in the Catholic Church, has borrowed largely from Buddhism. For proof of this, reference is made to the Buddhist religious orders of men and women who vowed poverty and chastity, had rules of conventual life and practices of penance, even before the Christian era. St. Francis Xavier tells how in Japan they prayed on beads, and at least in Thibet, missionaries narrate that Buddhists confess their faults, use water and incense in their ceremonies, have a regularly established hierarchy, and in religious functions wear vestments like unto those worn by Catholic priests. That such external observances or practices should have their counterpart in the Church seems at first sight startling; it is apt for a moment to confuse one to find that the Church of God should have anything, even externally, in common with the temple of Satan. But, startling though it seems, it does not, however, furnish the premises for the conclusions which are often drawn from it. To sift the argument, let me suppose the purely hypothetical case, to wit, that the Church borrowed those external practices and observances from Buddhism,—and even then, I say, she did not thereby forfeit her claims to a divine mission, nor did she enter into a league with paganism. Examined in the light of calm reason, those observances are simply external aids for the better furthering of the respective ends of the societies which have adopted them, or they are merely instruments by which men and women strive to attain to the perfection proposed to them by their respective religions. In their application, of course, these instruments will assume essentially different characters by reason of the spirit in which they may be used,—for the Buddhist, they will be means of practising superstition, for the Christian, they will be aids for gaining Christian virtues. The Buddhist's motives for observing the practices alluded to will be his own exaltation and a perfection that will end in nothing; the Christian's motives will be grounded on his duty to God, to his Creator, and to Christ his Redeemer, with the hope of one day enjoying eternal beatitude in heaven. In themselves indifferent, those observances are available for good or for evil: they can be made the means of facilitating the acquisition of true piety, and to this they tend in the Church; or, again, they can be so perverted that they will confirm the mind in superstition, and this they do in Buddhism. It is so with all the material elements; they can be used for God's glory or abused for His dishonor. Within the field of view just taken, sin is that alone which could limit the action of the Church in her economy; she could not utilize for her service any external observance which was of its nature sinful, or which necessarily led to sin,— neither could she have borrowed from a foreign worship these special rites that are wound up with her sacramental system.

The theory which, for the sake of argument, I have been discussing, when considered in the light of the teaching of history, altogether ceases to be at all tenable. The Church never borrowed, and from a historical stand-point, never could have borrowed any religious observances from Buddhism. Before she ever came in contact with it, she had developed and practised all those usages of which there is question. In the beginning, she may have adopted some external forms or signs naturally symbolic of Christian truths, though used by false religions for their own ends; but such signs or forms were of the domain of nature and were not therefore the exclusive inheritance of any religion. Sometimes, to make the way of conversion easy for pagans, she permitted them to retain some merely external ceremonies of their former worship, but she took care, at the same time, to give to these ceremonies a Christian signification. Following up this method of dealing with paganism, when pagan temples came into her possession, she did not, when she could help it, cause them to be erased;—in Rome itself she did not order the pantheon to be destroyed, but, with much pomp of ceremony, consecrated it to St. Mary of the Martyrs.

At Carlee, we are told, in Hindostan, there is a

Buddhist temple, a hundred and twenty-six feet long by forty-five feet wide, hollowed out of the solid rock, with a nave separated from the aisles by two parallel rows of columns, and all leading up to a well formed apse. If, one day, that temple should become the property of the Church, she certainly would not order that it should be blown up with dynamite, but would undoubtedly march into it in procession, with cross and holy-water, with incense and lighted torches, and, having amid the chanting of psalms and prayers sprinkled it with water and incensed it, would set up the cross in the apse, and erect an altar, and then offer the holy sacrifice of the Mass to the omnipotent, eternal God.

But aside from all hypothesis on the subject, the resemblance between these usages in the Church and in Buddhism can be accounted for, as I said, by the spontaneous action of minds seeking perfection. In all men nature is radically the same, and the means for perfecting it in their general features are alike. Buddhists and Japanese Kamis know as well as Christians that mortification is necessary for subduing the passions, and by degrees come "to have the pomp of external worship, processions, litanies, offerings, and images supposed to be miraculous. The fundamental idea of Buddhism required these things quite as little as that of the earlier of the Eastern religions. They grew up around it because they are in reality the expression of the natural instincts of humanity in presence of what it supposes to be divine truth and power."[1]

---

[1] Life and Letters of St. Francis Xavier, by Henry J. Coleridge, S. J., vol II., p. 236.

The most singular feature, however, among these analogies of which I have been speaking, is the perfect resemblance between the ceremonies practised by Buddhism in Thibet, or Lamaism, and those of the Catholic Church. It is on it particularly that the changes have been rung; to it infidels in the last century oftenest referred, and to-day it is a point to which non-Catholic writers sometimes direct special attention. They seem to say, with Professor Max Müller, here was "enough tó frighten priests by seeing themselves anticipated in auricular confession, beads, and tonsure, by the Lamas of Thibet."[1] Naturally enough, indeed, it did seem strange at first sight to Catholic missionaries to find usages of the Catholic Church among Buddhist monks, and to explain at that time how or when such usages could have been introduced was somewhat of a puzzle to them. But now, that the origin of Lamaism has been cleared up on the surest historical grounds, no one can reasonably doubt but that the ceremonies of Lamaism are only a wretched travesty of those of the Church.

The case, as now known on the evidence of history, is this:—During the Middle Ages, especially during the thirteenth century, frequent intercourse took place between Tartary and Western Europe. Tartars might be seen at Rome, Paris, Avignon, Lon-

---

[1] "Chips from a German Workshop," vol. i., p. 189. In a note the Professor gives an extract from "Travels in Thibet," by L'Abbé Huc. In this extract the points of resemblance between certain rites of Lamaism and those of Catholicism are given, and the Professor adds some of his own.—Now, on the next page, he could have found a vindication of Catholicism, but he chose to say nothing about that.

Another instance of the *suppressio veri* on this subject is found in the article on Lamaism in the "Encyclopædia Britannica."

don, and Barcelona, while European travellers or missionaries went through Central Asia, or preached the Gospel. "Twenty embassies," writes L'Abbé Huc, "were sent by the Tartars into Italy, Spain, France, and England, and on the other side, the Christian princes, and especially the Popes, despatched legations and missions to the states of the Grand Khans."[1] Mongols in Europe were free to enter Catholic Churches and to witness the pomp of religious ceremonies, while, at the same time, Catholic missionaries were at liberty to exercise their ministry through Tartary, which then included Thibet. "To try to attract the people to the true faith," writes Joinville, "they carried with them Church ornaments, and altars, and even celebrated Mass in presence of the Tartar court in chapels which they were allowed to have, within the precincts of the palace. Peking was created an archepiscopal see, in 1304, by Clement V., and its first occupant erected a church,[2] to which the faithful were summoned by the sound of three bells, and where they beheld many sacred pictures painted on the walls. At the time, at the Mongol court were not only Christians from Rome, and Syria, but also schismatics from Russia or Armenia, as well as Mussulmen, Buddhists, and Lamas, all able to admire or adopt those rites of the Church which most pleased them. Some members even of the imperial family secretly embraced Christianity. It was in

---

[1] "History of Christianity in China, Tartary and Thibet," vol. ii., p. 8.
"Not only did the Nestorians possess churches in Tartary, but they were spread throughout the Chinese empire, and their disciples were multiplying from day to day, as we learn from their historians and from the testimony of Marco Polo." Ibid., vol. i., p. 249.

[2] Gams, Series Episcoporum Ecclesiæ Catholicæ.

these circumstances and amid such admiration for the Catholic ceremonial that Lamaism was established. Anterior to that time, not a word was said about it by any writer; no proof of its existence had ever been given.

In the year 1261, Tublai Khan, a convert to Buddhism and the grandson of Genghis Khan, after having conquered China, appointed a Buddhist bonze, named Mati, head of the faith in Thibet, and at the same time invested him with the temporal sovereignty of the country. Over its provinces he also placed bonzes for governors, all however subject to the Grand-Lama. The different grades of office and the elections for them were evidently modelled on the organization of the Church. About a hundred years after this, a reform was introduced by Tsong-Kaba, whom L'Abbé Huc, from information gathered in Thibet itself, supposes to have been either an apostate from the faith, or a person only half acquainted with Christian doctrine. But however that may be, he succeeded in engrafting on Lamaism many of the rites and practices of the Catholic Church. The coincidence, then, of time and place, the previous non-existence of Lamaism, the very identity of its religious customs with those used from time immemorial by Christianity, fully demonstrate that Lamaism is only "an attempted imitation," or rather a shocking mimicry of the Catholic religion.

In making out the parallelism which, some writers hold, exists between Buddhism and Christianity, they are fond of drawing the character of the Buddha in the brightest colors, and that by plagiarism, or from legend, or from writings made up of the serious and futile. Their aim, in so doing, is to give weight and worth to his teaching. If they can prove the Buddha's life to be divine-like, they think, they have thereby proved his doctrine to be unimpeachable. This method, in the abstract, is admissible, since he who undertakes to reform or to found a religion ought to give proof in his life that he has a mission to do so. But the standard of the goodness of a life can be differently estimated; some will take that standard to be philantropy, others enthusiasm, some again will have it to be barely ethical culture, and others still intellectual training; and according to the standard which one adopts will be his judgment of the merits of him who teaches. But be the character of the teacher what it may, his doctrine must not be in conflict with what reason, in itself and as realized in the history of the human race, imperatively demands. A teacher of religion or morals, for instance, who denies or altogether ignores the fundamental truth of God's existence, which reason demonstrates, stands, by the very fact, self-condemned. The postulate which his teaching naturally requires he puts aside, and instead of building on the solid ground of truth, proceeds to build without having laid any foundation, or at most with one laid on error or opinions as shifting as the drifting sands. This is what the Buddha did, at least in the teaching attributed to him, in the compositions of his followers there is not a word about a supreme personal God, but in them man is made to be a god to himself, and to have no need of any power above or beyond him, to work out his destiny according to the Buddhist code. On what grounds the Buddha held to this view, whether on those of Herbert Spencer, or M. Comte, matters not, since agnosticism is virtually atheism. Nor does the fact of his giving place in his system to many gods exonerate him from the charge of atheism, since these gods are inferior beings and in rank far beneath the Buddha himself. He is more of a God than any of them, and even thinks himself to be such,—for he is reported to have said, " I do not see any one in the heavenly world, nor in that of Mara, nor among the inhabitants of the Brahma's world, nor among gods or men, whom it would be proper for me to honor."[1] After having examined Buddhist teaching, Professor Max Müller concludes: " Difficult as it seems to us to conceive it, Buddha admits of no real cause of this unreal world. He denies the existence, not only of a creator, but of any absolute being."[2]

In the place of a personal God, Gautama puts, without saying why or how, an impersonal law. To this he himself bows. It runs, he holds, into the life of all men, and winds itself around their actions. Wherever one may go or in whatever position placed, he is followed by the shadows of this law. It has, too, its sanctions, and its violation entails on the offender the penalty of being reborn under some or other form of existence.

When St. Francis Xavier was preaching in Japan, the report prevailed there that the Buddha had been reborn 80,000 times before having reached his final perfection. He had been a human being—

[1] Texts from the Vinaya ; Parajika. S. B. E. Vol. xiii.—Quoted in " The Light of Asia, the Light of the World," p. 178.
[2] Opus. cit., vol. 1., p. 230.

and then in turn say, a rat, a pig, a toad, a kangaroo, a spider, a horse, a crocodile, etc. And thus, by a series of "rebirths," he was purified of imperfections, and merited to be born no longer, or to enter here on earth, though imperfectly, into Nirvana. How a man's individuality could have been preserved during this process of change, or how a law could exist without a law giver, the Buddha did not attempt to say, and indeed in his time he was not asked to do so. He had only borrowed his doctrine of metempsychosis from the Brahmins whom he had abandoned, though he changed its form to suit his own system. They looked upon it as a means of arriving at the absorption of their being into the deity; he considered it to be the way that led to the total annihilation of the human individual. In the theory of the Brahmins it was the soul of man that passed into some other living being, in that of Buddha it was not the soul, (since Buddhism did not admit the soul to be a distinct entity from the body,) but man's "doings" or, as it was called, his "Karma," that is, "the result of his words, thoughts, and deeds." This is the theory; but that in practice the Brahminical view of the transmigration of souls is prevalent among Buddhist populations may be inferred from the letters of Catholic missionaries.[1]

Another law that inexorably rules all men, according to the Buddha, is the law of evil. In his own being, in the lives of others, in the accidents of time and place, he perceived that life itself is a warfare, and that suffering is the lot of human beings. Thence he inferred that existence itself is evil,

[1] "De Halde's History of China." vol. III., pp. 41 et sq.

that not to be is better than to be. With the blank future that he fancied for himself, with no ray of hope to light up the grave, it is not strange that the Buddha took a pessimistic view of life. He had abandoned the faith of the Brahmins, which taught that as "all souls are part of Brahma's spiritual nature, individuated by their connection with bodily forms, but yet having issued from him, they return at last, in their highest state, to him, to be absorbed in his infinite being."[1] In this system there is something like a goal to be reached by the struggles of life; in Buddha's, none; he makes life to be a stage for self-mastery, and when, finally, one should expect to see the prize proclaimed for success, the curtain falls, and that is the end for both soul and body alike. Buddha, however, seems to have seized on, in its true light, one feature of evil, and that is, that it furnishes matter for the gaining of merit, or that it is as an adversary with whom one has to contend and to prove his power of self-control in the struggle. But that which particularly puzzled him, was the wide-spread evil which he saw all around him. Whence did it come? how came it to pass that "the world is out of joint?" He might have known, indeed, from the teaching of tradition that "sin entered the world, and by sin death," and sin, he was aware, from the dictates of conscience, is of man's making. But what a wealth of goodness, what untold-of joy, what resources of happiness underly man's personal existence, the Buddha himself could have somehow experienced, if, as Buddhists assert, he had attained to the fulness of enlightenment.

[1] "The Bhagavad Ghita," translated by John Davies. Introd.

Existence, of which unrestrictedly he predicated evil would have become for him then a source of happiness. Those few points taken from the metaphysics of Buddhism suffice to show its extravagance, but it will be interesting to hear the opinion of one who made the Buddha's teaching his special study. In the "Journal des Savants" Mr. Barthélemy Saint-Hilaire thus summed up, in a review on Buddhism, his views on its system of metaphysics.

"Buddhism has no God; it has not even the confused and vague notion of a universal Spirit in which the human soul, according to the orthodox doctrine of Brahminism and the Sânkhya philosophy, may be absorbed. Nor does it admit nature, in the proper sense of the word, and it ignores that profound division between spirit and matter which forms the system and the glory of Kapila. It confounds man with all that surrounds him, all the while preaching to him the laws of virtue. Buddhism, therefore, cannot unite the soul, which it does not even mention, with a God whom it ignores, nor with nature, which it does not know better. Nothing remains but to annihilate the soul; and in order to be quite sure that the soul may not re-appear under some new form in this world, which has been cursed as the abode of illusion and misery, Buddhism destroys its very elements and never gets tired of glorying in this achievement. What more is wanted? If this is not the absolute nothing, what is Nirvana?"[1]

In view of all this, Professor Max Müller did not state his opinion too strongly, when he wrote of

---

[1] Quoted by Max Müller, opus cit. vol. I., p. 253.

Buddhism:—"such religion, we should say, was made for a madhouse."

However, it is not the dogmatic, but the ethical character of Buddhism that is specially dwelt upon by its admirers. As a system of morals they almost put it on a level with Christianity, and have not terms forcible enough to express their praise of the Buddha. Now we have seen that the metaphysics of Buddhism is but a tissue of the grossest errors, and that this fact is admitted by all scholars of note who have written on the subject. This, one should think, *a priori*, ought to be a strong plea against the soundness of its morality. Morality is a thing not of the will alone nor of the sentiments, but also primarily of the mind, based on sound principles. The world at large does not hold a fool responsible for his actions, nor does it put any estimate on his morals, in view of the loss of his mind. In individual cases invincible ignorance some times comes in as a make-shift for the true rule of moral conduct, and men, though they sin materially, do not do so formally, but let the very sources from which morality springs be swept away, and there remains, as it were, only the artificial form of moral action. If a man's belief be repugnant to nature, it cannot, when followed, make his conduct conformable to it. In the estimation of mankind, morality is the outcome of the whole man, acting as a free agent, by rigid reason, for definite purposes. In the soul it is that morality is formed; there the motives, the ends, and laws of action are blended with thoughts, desires, and aspirations and shaped peremptorily into purposes by the decision of practical reason. But Buddha denies that there is a soul in man—how then can there be morality? The truth is, as we find him in Buddhist literature, Buddha draws out his code of ethics not as a soulless automaton, but as a living, whole-souled man, such as God made him. He uses the instruments of knowledge which nature gave him, and then belies nature in order to broach false theories. As morality implies duty,—and duty, law, —and law, a lawgiver,—one is at a loss to perceive how Buddhism, which recognizes no supreme Lord of all, could have a rational ultimate basis of morals. By crushing also all the aspirations for immortality in the soul, it cuts off all these incentives to virtue, which spring from the hope of a future life. It has, however, commandments, and proclaims "noble truths," and "the noble eighth fold path," and still acknowledges no authority above it, to give commandments, or to proclaim truth, or to point out the path. Man is the measure of everything; he needs no prayer nor help from without him, but by himself can overcome all obstacles, mount higher and higher in perfection and, in his theory, place his throne above the stars. In such a manner it is that the Buddha strives to lay "the foundation of the Kingdom of Righteousness," as he calls it, that is, a foundation whose corner stone is selfishness, and "a kingdom in which there is only an empty throne."

Still, with the object which he had in view, it must be admitted that the Buddha showed a great insight into human nature and character. The rules of asceticism which he laid down for arriving at the high degree of *arâhat*, or the perfect man, bear on them the impress of deep reflection and of a great constructive power of mind. He had learned much, to be sure, from Brahminism, but he also added much of his own. The Brahminical fakir sought to gain perfection by excessive corporal austerity, the Buddhist Bikkus or monk, by a sort of rigid stoicism. For him to subdue passion, to die to himself, was the supreme law of life; and for what? to die eternally, to be blown out like the lamp's flame. Brahminism was a peculiarly exclusive religion; it was looked upon as a close corporation which was to be guarded against all strangers. No Brahmin ever thought of converting his neighbors, but in his pride seemed to have always in mind the words—*odi profanum vulgus et arceo.* Buddha, on the contrary, preached salvation to all, as he understood it. For all, rich and poor, for castes and outcasts, for nobles and peasants, for Brahmins and Sûdras, there lay one and the same way to salvation, provided all the while that they entered on that way through Buddhist monasticism. This equalizing principle and feeling of brotherhood for all men was one cause of the success of Buddhism. Another cause, and perhaps the principal one, was the favor shown to Buddhism by temporal rulers. It became the state religion of India, about the year 250 B. C., under the emperor Asoka, called the Buddhist Constantine. It was his son Mahenda, tradition says, who carried Buddhism into Ceylon; and it was the Indo-Scythian King Kaniska who established it in Tartary, A. D. 65. In the same year, it was officially recognized in China as one of the three state-religions by the emperor Ming-ti. For those rulers there were weighty reasons for their policy. Buddhism was a supple instrument in their hands for the maintenance and exaltation of their authority. It did not speak to them in the name of God and did not therefore put any restrictions on their arbitrary power. It laid down no laws for marriage, did not prohibit polygamy or divorce, nor forbid any superstitions that came in its way. It could bend to human enactments, since it had no dogmatic principle to surrender.

How powerless a system of ethics such as that of Buddhism is to maintain or enforce morality, without the doctrines or sanctions of religion, is seen in the history of Buddhist populations. Of the Buddhist bonzes of Japan, St. Francis Xavier wrote:— "These men are so given up to the most abominable kind of lust, as to make open profession of it. This plague is indeed so common to all here, men and women alike, that the mere custom of it has taken away all their hatred and horror of the crime."[1]

"If the Buddhist moral code has power to influence a people," writes Bishop Bigandet, of the Burhmese, "so far as to render them virtuous and devotional, independently of the element of intellectual superiority, we still lack the evidence of it."[2]

M. l'Abbé Huc writes of the religion and morality of China in the following words: "All the Chinese are at the same time partisans of Confucius, Laotze, and Buddha, or rather they are nothing at all; they reject all faith, all dogma, to live merely by their more or less depraved and corrupted instincts. . . . . . Chinese society has a certain tone of decency and reserve, that may very well impose on

---

[1] "Life and Letters of St. Francis Xavier." By Rev. H. J. Coleridge, S. J., vol. ii, p. 238.

[2] "Life and Legend of Gautama."

those who look only at the surface and judge merely by the momentary impression; but a very short residence among the Chinese is sufficient to show that their virtue is entirely external; their public morality is but a mask worn over the corruption of their manners. We will take care not to lift the unclean veil that hides the putrefaction of this ancient Chinese civilization; the leprosy of vice has spread so completely through this sceptical society, that the varnish of modesty with which it is covered is continually falling off and exposing the hideous wounds which are eating away the vitals of this unbelieving people."[1]

"Infanticide is not confined to the poorer classes; as a proof of the existence of that crime, foundling hospitals are erected in all large towns to receive girls only."[2]

As I suggested in the beginning of this essay, a religious system without God or the hope of a future life in it, and yet embraced by hundreds of millions of human beings, seems at first sight to negative the argument for God's existence drawn from the testimony of the human race. And yet I make bold to say that the argument derives a special force from Buddhism as it has been professed by these millions. Buddhism, as it exists in Buddhist writings, is one thing, and as it is lived out by its votaries in their daily lives is quite another; the one gives us the theory or philosophy of Buddhism; the other, its religion; in the one we have speculation, in the other the working of the human soul in its aspira-

[1] "Travels in the Chinese Empire," vol. ii., pp. 192, 326.
[2] "Martin's China," vol. i., p. 37.

tions towards a Supreme Being. The heart of the Buddhist as well as that of every human being, when left to itself, yearns for God. "It cannot be denied," writes Bishop Bigandet, "that in practice Buddhists in these parts betray often, without perceiving it, that they have some idea of a Supreme Being who has a controlling power in the affairs of this world and the destiny of man. But such an idea does not come from their religious creed; it is the offspring of that innate sentiment adherent to nature, as it is maintained by some philosophers, or is a remnant of a primitive tradition, which error has never been able entirely to obliterate, as asserted by others."[1]

By a strange re-action, Buddha, who, if he did not expressly deny the existence of God, at least ignored Him, is now venerated, even adored, as a God. The letter of the Buddhist canonical books tells us that he has attained Nirvana, and consequently is not even a shadow of himself. His name only remains. But the internal sense of the human soul, feeling for God, will not be down, and rising above all atheistic theories, will not be content until in some way it has found an object for its aspirations. When it has not found the true, living God, it will strive, out of the elements of the world, to make a god for itself. So strong has this yearning for the Deity been among some Buddhist peoples, that in Thibet, for instance, it has led them to believe that the Primal Buddha becomes incarnate in each successive Grand Lama, and they adore him as a god. In China, they venerate, and invoke, and worship the Buddha who is yet to come, as well as the Buddha who has come.

[1] Op. cit. p. 205.

That Buddhism, grotesque in the extreme as a faith, should have so many adherents is certainly a fact most curious and startling. And still it seems to be a more startling fact, that Buddhism, which has rotted populations the most numerous and stunted the growth of nationalities and the affections of the human heart, should be sought after at present by persons in Europe and America. This is a phase of religious innovation that beggars all former apostasies. It is a choosing of darkness for light,— a casting off of the yoke of Christ, the Saviour of the world, in order to take up that of an enthusiast, to whom the future life with its hopes of glory was but blank nothingness. Those people give up seeking after the *summum bonum*, which is God, in order to follow after a *summum nihil*, which is Nirvana. In Edwin Arnold's poem, "The Light of Asia," they have looked at Buddhism done up in false colors, and draped in the charms of poetic diction; they have seen it contrasted with Christianity and that, *horribile dictu*, to the disadvantage of the latter, and they seemed satisfied with the picture drawn and with the evangel of Hindoo paganism. The beauteous features of Christ,—his words full of power, mercy, and goodness, they put from them, and in their place put the form, the words, the acts, and death of the Buddha, as they find these reported or depicted in legend or story.

Here then for reflective minds is a palpable fact at hand which refutes the theory that holds that there is an evolution of religion as there is an evolution in nature. Men and women, with the light of Christianity around them, who themselves were once, perhaps, Christians, fall from their noble estate of Christian life, and from the high plane of a divine religion descend to the low level of one of these godless superstitions that have debased mankind.

When Mr. Harrison finished the reading of his essay, all agreed to take a recess until the afternoon, at three o'clock.

Scarcely had the gentlemen assembled at that hour, when Mr. Maxwell said, "Judge, your argument this morning, was, in my opinion, conclusive, as far as it went; my objection to it is that it did not go far enough. That this or that man, or this or that tribe should not believe in the existence of a Supreme Being, I consider not to be material in the question. It is a moral, not an absolute unanimity of testimony that is sought for. That some men are blind, does not militate against the fact that sight is an attribute of our race. But there are those who cut the very ground from beneath the argument by showing how the idea of the Deity has been begotten, among primitive barbarous tribes, of emotions caused by natural phenomena. Speak to those sceptics of the universal testimony in favor of your thesis, and they will agree with you; but then, they will add in all those cases, the idea of God is merely delusive,—springing from fear, or ignorance, or artificial training."

" The great object of proof, sir," answered Judge Jefferson, " I have always thought to be, to establish the truth of the thing to be proven. A well-grounded proof is to my mind but as a rampart for the defence of truth against assailants. That you consider it in this light, your objection presented in the name of sceptics seems to make evident. But as to the objection itself, let me premise that the thunder-clap, or the roar of the tempest, or the lightning's flash, or the dread quivering of the earthquake, I take for the tremendous trumpet-notes of nature summoning souls to reflection, or to a sense of their origin and of their duty towards their God. To what I said to the point in my essay, I will add: 'Naturally, these phenomena stir the soul with fear, and fear stimulates reason to look for the supreme, first cause of them. When the poor savage looks instinctively through them up to God, he is but reasoning rightly. To say that fear begot the idea of God is to say that fear was its own cause, which is equivalent to saying that a man makes enemies by fearing them, and not that he fears them because they are his enemies. This objection was first broached by Petronius, of whom even the infidel Bayle wrote: " He said, rather by way of witticism than from real conviction, that it was fear which had established belief in God, whereas, on the contrary, it is the fear of chastisement which causes some persons to strive to persuade themselves that there is no God."

"'Besides, the theory would seem to teach that fear always puts out the light of reason, or paralyzes the rational faculties to such a degree that men continue to crouch before the phantoms of their imagination even after all danger or terror has passed. Then, if it was fear that made God and the gods, their characteristics should be wholly awe-inspiring. They should have the attributes of Pluto and of Mars, of Jove and of Hecuba; a supposition which mythology refutes, since it has its Elysium as well as its Erebus.

"Ignorance of many of the laws that govern the universe left undoubtedly to the pagan imagination a vast field to revel in;—though, let me remark, that in this nineteenth century there remains still, through space, a considerable field for the scientific imagination to sport with;—every-where there was change, and justly enough the pagan mind inferred that every change implies a cause, and, then, for want of another reason, made a spirit to preside over every changing scene of the world, and peopled the earth, and the sea, and the firmament with deities. So overpowering was the sense of divinity to pagan thought, that, to meet its needs, it multiplied gods. The thought was gross and false in the extreme; though a poetic conception of what reason and tradition taught concerning divine Providence in the universe, it was a personifying of these laws by which God governs and upholds the world.

"Whence, then, came this universal idea of Deity to our race? Were they schooled into it by designing statesmen? But the belief in the divinity existed before States were formed; it antidates all existing civilization. 'Religion,' says Montesquieu, 'is anterior to the establishment of civil societies and independent of all human conventions.' Besides, this purely fanciful hypothesis has left no record of itself in the past, and, in view of man's unwillingness to have any unwarranted restraints put upon his liberty, becomes impossible. The same is to be said of that other notion, which ascribes the belief in God to sacerdotal influence, a notion which is its own refutation, since the priority of the existence of priests necessarily supposes the belief in God, to whom they minister. Whence, then, gentlemen, this fundamental master-thought of our race in the existence of a Supreme Being? Explain it as some may, I hold that it springs from the constitution of our natural reason, that it is the outcome of looking with the eye of reason into the material world, or along with that, that it is the inherited thought of generation after generation through immemorial traditions."

"My difficulty on this subject," remarked Mr. Ferguson, " comes not so much from what sceptics propose as from what some modern travellers say. Among barbarous tribes, they find, that there exists a universal belief in the existence of certain supernatural intelligent beings, and that these, as among the Tonguans of Polynesia, ' comprise everything spiritual, from a ghost to a god.' The like belief prevails among the aborigines of Australia and America, and, indeed, more or less, among all nations. Contrasting this belief with that of the 'Old Israelites' in the time of Samuel, Mr. Huxley finds that the religious conceptions in both instances were pretty much the same. ' Elohim was, in logical terminology, the genus, of which ghosts, Chemosh, Dagon, Baal, and Jahveh were species.' Thus Elohim was to the 'Old Israelites what ghosts and gods were and are to the gentiles.' Add to this that many religious practices among savage tribes are similar to those of the Israelites of the eleventh or twelfth century before Christ, and you have data for inferring that the idea of one supreme God is only an after-growth, springing from fetichism, or hero-worship, or ghosts."

"I have read," said Judge Jefferson, "Mr. Huxley's essays in the *Nineteenth Century* on the 'Evolution of Theology.' His aim in general, I think, is such as you have described it; he endeavors to prove that the idea of God was evolved by the human mind, in the past and present, out of a belief in the ghost world. In my opinion, the first thing in the argument to be proved is that the 'Old Isrealites' attached, in its ordinary and literal sense, to the word Elohim the meaning which Huxley gives to it. They may have applied it, as indeed they did, figuratively or in a transferred sense, to false gods, to 'supernatural intelligent beings,' or even to men, (all languages allow such liberty) but such use did not do away with the primary sense of the word, especially so, when this was marked out in the Sacred Scriptures, and recalled continually to memory by the tradition and teaching of their race.[1] In the very first verse of the Bible they read, —'In the beginning God (Elohim) created heaven and earth.' Now, if there be any attribute more than another characteristic of God, it is His creative power. To man or to angel He cannot communicate it,—it is exclusively His own; by the unlimited act which it supposes, it indicates His infinite nature; by the production of all things from nothing, it shows that He has nothing in common with His

---

[1] Jehovah was God's proper name, denoting His essential, incommunicable nature, as defined by God Himself in the words—"I am who am." For the Jews, Jehovah was the ineffable name, τετραγράμματον, and could not by analogy be tranferred to beings who, somehow, partook of some of God's attributes, or to whom, through error or superstition, men assigned the same.

creatures. With this meaning in it the word Elohim is repeated in nearly every verse of the first chapter of Genesis. Being in the plural number in Hebrew, it is coupled with a verb in the singular number, —thus intimating a unity of nature in the Godhead together with a Trinity of Persons.[1] In the second chapter of the same book, I find that the name of God, Jehovah, or, as Mr. Huxley prefers, Jahveh, is introduced in conjunction with Elohim. In the seventh verse we read: 'These are the generations of the heaven and the earth, when they were created, in the day that the Lord God, (Jehovah, Elohim) made the heaven and earth.' But in a clearer manner still the real relationship of the meaning of these names comes out in the fifth chapter and sixth verse of Deuteronomy: 'I am the Lord thy God, (Jehovah, Elohim) who brought thee out of Egypt, out of the house of bondage.'[2] In like manner, all through the Book of Genesis and, indeed, through the other books of Holy Scripture, those names are applied almost indiscriminately to God.[3] In the very first Book of Kings or of Samuel, on which Mr. Huxley particularly insists, they are also in the same text predicated of the Deity. 'There is none as the Lord (Jehovah) is,' exclaims

---

[1] Elohim, when applied to the true God, is coupled with a verb in the singular, when denoting a false god it always takes a verb in the plural.—In the former sense it is used some two thousand times, in the latter about five hundred.

[2] "Nota, pro Domino, hebraice est nomen tetragrammaton *Jehova*, quod est proprium divinae essentiae.... Rursum, pro Deo, hebraice, est *Elohim*, quod Deum, qua judicem et gubernatorem omnium significat."—Cornelius A. Lapide, Comm. in Deuter. Ch. 5, v. 6. (See Appendix)

[3] "Know therefore this day that the Lord (Jehovah) He is God (Elohim) in heaven above and in the earth beneath, and there is no other."—Deuter. iv.39.

"The Lord, (Jehovah) is my God (Elohim), the God (Elohim) of my fathers."—Exodus, xv. 2.

Anna in her inspired canticle, 'for there is no other beside Thee, and there is none strong like our God (Elohim).' And the prophet Samuel himself, in his address to the people after the appointment of Saul as their King, says: 'If you will fear the Lord, and serve him, and hearken to His voice, and not provoke the mouth of the Lord; then shall both you and the king who reigneth over you be followers of the Lord your God.' (I. Kings xii. 14).

"Jehovah-Elohim was therefore the Lord God whom not only the Israelites in the time of Samuel worshipped, but also the Israelites, through all the ages, from the very beginning. Sometimes called Jehovah, sometimes Elohim, He was their God, not in an exclusively national sense, but because, as a race, they served Him, and through much adversity and changes of fortune remained the guardians of His promises of salvation for the world.

"It is a remark of St. Chrysostom, 'that God spoke to men in early times; but when the whole human race became estranged from Him, He communicated with them by writing, as to persons afar off.' Any of the elements or any material thing He can use as a tongue, so to say, wherewith to speak to men; from amidst the burning bush on Mount Horeb, and amid thunder and lightning on Sinai, he spoke to Moses; the plagues he used as signs wherewith to warn Pharao; and the manna was as the gentle rain from heaven, by which He daily told of His beneficence to the Israelites. To give the Hebrew people the visible assurance of His presence, He ordered Moses to make an ark, and from above the mercy-seat therein communicated with him. Thence

He gave His orders and spoke through Moses His commands to 'the children of Israel.' The construction of the ark and of the tabernacle as well as the making of priestly vestments are described at great length in the book of Exodus. They were to be made of the richest materials and with great perfection of artistic skill, and this, in order to chasten or to restrict the feelings of the people, to elevate their minds, and impress on them reverence and respect for the divine presence. ' Clothing, emblematical of office, is of more consequence than is generally imagined,' writes Adam Clarke.

"Of these aids to worship and of these ritual observances, reminiscences, though most imperfect and obscure and, at the same time, distorted, are to be found among pagan tribes and peoples. Some of these vestiges of Hebrew worship Mr. Huxley, as we have said, finds among the aborigines of Polynesia and Africa, and from them strives to show that the Israelites of the age referred to, in point of religious culture, were then what the Polynesians and Africans are now. 'We shall find,' he writes, 'not merely that all the features of old Israelitic theology which are shown in the records cited are found among them, but that extant information as to the inner life of these people tends to remove many of the difficulties which those who have not studied anthropology find in the Hebrew narrative.' In other words, that the religion of the Polynesian Islanders is at present what that of the Israelites was some eleven or twelve centuries before Christ. That this supposition is utterly groundless, the remarks already made have, I think, shown conclusively; that they are a clear perversion of historic truth, is what every unbiassed person can see for himself by reading the Books of Judges and of Kings. In no other part of Scripture, perhaps, are we made so much to feel the exercise of God's sovereignty as in these very books. He was then as He always had been, not only the Lord and the God of the Israelites, but besides, He condescended to be their temporal Ruler, and as such provided for their wants and defended them against their enemies. Ungrateful for such care, some among them sinned most grievously against Him as their God and rebelled against Him as their sovereign; but with their lives they had to pay the penalty of their rebellion. Now, though not having studied particularly anthropology, I have no difficulty whatever in seeing that there is no parellel between the religion of the 'Old Israelites' of the time of Samuel, and that of the Polynesian Islanders of the nineteenth century."

"In the views just given, it seems to me," remarked Mr. Netterville, "that Mr. Huxley had been anticipated by Professor Tiele of the university of Leyden. Some years ago the latter published a 'Manual of Religions,' the leading feature of which was *animism*, or the doctrine which holds that the first religion of all primitive peoples was a belief in genii, or supernatural beings who live in every nook of the earth, in the air, and in space among the heavenly bodies. These are souls or spirits wandering through the immense void or else having 'a fixed habitation' in some animate or inanimate bodies."

"That is a fine theory," suggested Mr. Walters.—
"Perhaps it is more," said Mr. Neufchatel; "in my

opinion, it is borne out by what we know of primitive races; the descendants of the aborigines of different countries bear testimony to it."—" That is," answered Mr. Walters, " you suppose that savagery or even the bestial state was the original condition of man—a hypothesis that has been conclusively refuted, over and over again."—" Conclusively, I deny," said Mr. Neufchatel.—" The proofs given warrant the use of the word," answered Mr. Walters; " I shall barely indicate them. First: As far back as any ancient records go, they represent men as civilized, professing belief in one Supreme Being. This has been proved to us by the Judge, for China, and on the authority of Mr. George Rawlinson, for the other great historic peoples of antiquity. Second: In the prehistoric languages, civilization is clearly indicated by the words that are used. This argument has been fully developed by Mr. Adolphe Pictet, in his work; 'Les Origines Indo-Européennes' etc. From the primitive words of the oldest Aryan dialects he shows what must have been the social condition and religious belief of the ancient Aryans. Arguing from the ancient names for God among them he infers that they could not have been polytheists, but in the beginning of their social life must have been monotheists, and with that having the habits and usages of civilized people. Third: The Book of Genesis, in sketching the genealogies of the sons of Noe, gives us also evidence of what was the religious and social condition of various primitive peoples."—" That is, sir," said Mr. Neufchatel, " you assume the Book of Genesis to be authentic and then argue from it."—" No sir," was the reply; "I do not assume, but if you require it, I prove it to be authentic, and that on testimony the like of which cannot be offered for any other book extant,—namely the testimony of the whole Jewish race, generation after generation, for 4,000 years."—" You are aware, sir," said Mr. Neufchatel, " I presume, that forgeries have passed current as genuine during centuries; for instance the collection of 'the False Decretals.' This is quite intelligible in uncritical ages, when one generation receives without any questionings the writings of another."—" Allow me to say, sir," replied Mr. Walters, " your illustration is not a happy one. 'The False Decretals' never passed current in the Church as being authentic. She never gave any sanction to them, never quoted them as an authority in any official document. They were false only in this, that they attributed, without distinction of dates, the acts or decrees of the councils or Popes of one century to those of another.[1] But let it be granted that a literary forgery may have been accepted as authentic for centuries, I hold that this was impossible in the case of the Book of Genesis as one of the five Books of Moses, or as they are called, the Pentateuch. These books were known to the Hebrews as the Law (Thorah). Of it, levites, priests, and magistrates were bound to have copies, and to be versed in the knowledge of it. It was read to the people, explained, and enforced, since it regulated all the affairs of the nation, whether domestic, social, political, or religious. A code thus interwoven with the life of the people and

---

[1] The Pseudo-Isidore forgeries merely attribute to Popes of the first three centuries what was said by councils of the fourth and fifth.—Hergenröther, " Catholic Church and Christian State."—Vol. II., p. 282.

bearing rather heavily on them in some of its enactments could not, I repeat, have been a forgery. Human nature forbids it. To restrict men in their liberty, law must be presented to them on credentials that cannot be questioned. You would admit, sir, I suppose, the impossibility of imposing, in any lapse of time, on the American people, with their present political organization, a spurious constitution containing new burdensome enactments. Alive to the grants of liberty which they possess, they would reject with indignation an unwarranted interference with their just liberties. Now, I say, with much greater reason would the Jewish people have rejected the books of the law with their many regulations for all the concerns, not only of civil, but also of religious life, had they not known on the clearest evidence that these books contained the commands of the Almighty, and were the authentic, inspired writings of their great Prophet and Lawgiver. It is a mistake to say that, in regard to the Pentateuch, those ages were uncritical. When the truth of a book cannot be questioned, there is no room for criticism, and when the book itself is regarded with religious veneration by a whole people, and guarded in the purity of its sacred texts by many duly appointed ministers, it is beyond the reach of any notable corruption. Those by-gone ages among the Hebrews had their training schools for those who were to explain and interpret the Law. In them Hebrew youth were taught the structure and peculiarities of their language, the obligations of the moral code, the meaning of prophecy, the doctrines touching God, and the provisions and · application of civil enactments. You would not consider uncritical the seventy grave Hebrew scholars who gave the Septuagint version of the Old Testament, three centuries before Christ; Josephus and Philo you would not take to be men of no critical acumen; and St. Paul you would certainly not judge to be unfitted to give a settled opinion on the authenticity of the Pentateuch." As there was no answer from Mr. Neufchatel, Mr. Netterville begged leave to add that Professor Tiele admits that *animism* is often found coupled with a belief in the existence of a Supreme Being.

In a conversation that followed, gentlemen described some bass-reliefs that they had seen in some collections of oriental antiquities. Mr. Mattison spoke of one in which the Egyptian god Khoum is forming out of clay, on the potter's wheel, the embryonic egg from which was to spring the universe. The same god is again seen, forming man in a like manner and from the same materials. Mr. Babbington described an Assyrian bass-relief in the British Museum, London, in which a mysterious tree is guarded by two winged figures, having the heads and arms of human beings, and touching with the tips of their fingers the fruits of a tree which attracts them. In the same Museum, a fruit-tree is represented, on the opposite sides of which sit a man and a woman, and each having one hand outstretched to take the fruit. Behind the female figure there rises at full length the form of a serpent, in a sort of seducing attitude. This figure is clearly suggestive of the history of the fall as given in the Book of Genesis.

"It is really curious to see," remarked Mr.

Jennings, "how common among all peoples and tribes was this symbolism of the serpent. In all the mythologies, besides many harmless or propitious serpents, there is one that is supposed to personify evil or to be itself the evil principle. In a bass-relief from the temple of Elfou, in Egypt, the Egyptian god Horus is represented piercing the head of a serpent with a long, light spear. Among the Phenicians, the serpent was taken for the Titan, who with his companions revolted and was cast down into Tartarus by the god Cronos (El). In Mazdeism, or the religion of the Persians, the serpent always represents the evil principle, or the adversary of all good. It was under this form that the god Angromainyous, after having attempted to invade heaven, returned to earth and was conquered by Mitra. The inhabitants of ancient India took the serpent for one of the elements in the contests that seem to take place on the field of nature. Indra, the god of the sunlit heaven, contends with the serpent Ahi, who personifies the storm-cloud. And in the contest, Indra, with a thunder-bolt, tears up Ahi and thus gives fertilizing rain to the inhabitants of earth. For the Mexicans their god Quetzalcoath was 'a feathered serpent.'[1] In Africa the fetich-serpents have temples dedicated to them."

"Aidowedo, this genius," writes the Rev. P. Baudin, "is a large serpent; among the Zoroubas the boa-constrictor, called Ere, is supposed to be the messenger of this serpent-genius."[2]

---

[1] Lenormant. "Histoire Ancienne de l'Orient." T. i., p. 27 et seq.

[2] "One of these subordinate divinities, driven by fire from the bushes where he lived, took up his new abode in a thicket near the house of one of our Christians. The neighboring fetich-priest declared that the serpent was sacred and scattered

These traditions, and those mentioned by the gentlemen, and many others described by different writers, are explicable only by reference to the one common source from which they spring; they are like so many relics of a wreck cast on the shores of every country; by themselves they are often almost meaningless, but when loosed from the rubbish around them, and sorted and put together, they form in part the body of the teaching and revelation that we find in the Book of Genesis."

"It seems to me," said Mr. Ferguson, "that we are now undoing what we did. We proved that reason can demonstrate the existence of God, and now we try to show that we come to that truth by revelation and tradition, since there was no time in which reason was not assisted by revelation." —"I allow," answered Mr. Jennings, "that there was no epoch in which our race did not enjoy the benefit of revelation. Revelations were made to Adam and were by him transmitted to his descendants, and thus became the inheritance of the whole human family. But this fact nowise interferes with what we had determined about the powers of reason. You would surely be willing to grant, to use a familiar illustration, that the use of the telescope does not in any way diminish the power of eyesight, but on the contrary adds to it. What the naked eye

---

palm leaves in front of the thicket, thus proclaiming the thicket sacred also. The neighboring blacks offered hens in sacrifice to the new god: but as these sacrifices were not frequent, the god came out at night and devoured all animals that had not been carefully locked up. All the hens or goats that approached too near the thicket during the day forfeited their lives by their temerity. My Christian dared not rid himself of his neighbor, having a certain superstitious fear of him. I advised him to offer the monster a sacrifice difficult to digest; and by this means he was disposed of." "Fetichism and Fetich Worshippers," p. 47.

cannot reach by any effort it may make, that it can easily do by means of a telescope; it can examine the sun's disk, look into the volcanic craters of the moon, and analyze the orbits and variations of the different stars. Now, what the telescope is to the eye, that, we may say, in its own way and in a different order, is revelation to reason; though above reason, it does not lessen its power but elevates it; it does not narrow its range, but enlarges it; it does not cloud its vision, but opens up for it new fields of view, and presents new truths for its acceptance on the ground of the infallible reason of God. We can, therefore, now test the power of reason in regard to those truths, as we can test the power of eyesight in regard to physical objects. It has been done in every age; it is being done at present. No one, perhaps, has put reason to its highest tests in relation to the truths of God with such force as the Angelic Doctor, St. Thomas Aquinas. Besides, reason may be often left to its own resources, when revelation has ceased to be a source of enlightenment, and tradition, distorted by falsehood, becomes one of the greatest obstacles to truth. And, again, on the other hand, men may profess to be using only reason in the investigation of religious truth, and be all the while using the light that revelation has shed around them."

"From the illustration just given," said Mr. Ferguson, "I infer that revealed truth is beyond the reach of reason; then, since that is so, I should like to know what will be the grounds of our knowledge of it."—" The authority of God revealing," replied Mr. Jennings.—" But here the difficulty recurs, was the answer; "how can that authority which is above reason become cognizable by reason?"—"By means of sensible proof," said Mr. Jennings. "Miracles and prophecies are proofs on which reason can rest its belief for the fact of divine revelations."—But," rejoined Mr. Ferguson, "miracles and prophecies do not exist every day."—"They exist as recorded," said Mr. Jennings, "and witnessed to by unimpeachable witnesses and presented for acceptance by the Church. Miracles and prophecies exist every day, but not for everybody nor frequently, as the public tests of revealed truth. Many a miracle wrought by the saints of God remains unrecorded. In this respect it is with the saints as it is with their divine Master."

"I am to understand, then," resumed Mr. Ferguson, "that natural reason by the help of sensible facts can accept revelation,--or that, having been projected into the spiritual world, it becomes supernaturalized, and thus the supernatural is the natural prolonged."

"Excuse me, sir," replied Mr. Jennings, "your conclusion does not follow from my premises. Natural reason cannot accept revelation as such without the light of divine faith, any more than the naked eye can realize the existence of Sirius without the aid of a perspective glass. Reason can indeed know of revelation from the proofs given of it, but to accept it as such, it needs the light of divine faith and grace."

"Then," said Mr. Ferguson, "since it is by revelation, and not by reason, that we perceive revealed truth, reason remains in abeyance and has no function of its own."

"I beg pardon, sir," answered Mr. Jennings; "if one perceives a mathematical truth in consequence of a demonstration of Newton,—does he thereby forfeit his reason? or does he not rather, by the light of a superior mind, raise his own reason to a higher plane? And much after a similar manner, but in a different order, the revelation of God does not stunt, but only elevates by its supernatural light the natural reason of man."

"In what, then, does the supernatural consist?" asked Mr. Ferguson.—"To answer briefly," said Mr. Jennings, "in regard to man, the supernatural rests on faith and revelation; its end is the beatific vision in the next life, or the seeing of God face to face; and the means in this world for attaining that is divine grace, both habitual and actual. The supernatural, then, differs from the natural, not only in degree but also in kind, and cannot be reached or merited by the unaided faculties of any intelligent creature."

"By what faculties then?" inquired Mr. Ferguson. "I had always thought that man is fully equipped in his natural powers for everything that lies before him, here or hereafter."—"Certainly," answered Mr. Jennings, "fully equipped he is for attaining natural ends and for natural development, but you would not suppose that he could reach what is necessarily above him and is of a different order."

"What order is that? I know only of the order of nature."—"That of which, I spoke," was the reply, "is the order of grace."

"I can understand very well," said Mr. Ferguson, "how, by the natural faculties which I have, I can apprehend the natural, but how, by substantially the same faculties, I can apprehend what is above nature, is beyond my comprehension."

"In the supernatural order," answered Mr. Jennings, "man remains man; grace only elevates and perfects his nature. When he accepts the supernatural and becomes a member of Christ's mystical body, the habits of divine faith, hope, and charity are infused in baptism into his soul. By means of these faculty-like habits, when quickened by actual grace, he can readily apprehend the things of God. Thus it is that even in this life God has given to men, as St. John teaches, 'the power to be made the sons of God.' Man has in his faculties an aptitude for apprehending, within the range of the natural, God and the things of God; he needs only God's elevating power to rise above nature into the world of grace, and act in it according to its laws."

"In all this argumentation," said Mr. Ferguson, "there is this much always supposed, that I must accept the supernatural, since the supernatural exists. I should think that, to claim my rational obedience, the supernatural should present its credentials; I am not inclined to accept even the great supernatural gifts offered to me, until I have clear proof of the authority on which they are offered. Like St. Thomas I must, as it were, see the proof sensibly with my own eyes, and touch it with my own hands."

"Very well, then," answered Mr. Jennings; "and first, allow me to premise, that relying so much on reason as you do, you will undoubtedly have no difficulty in admitting this its imperious dictate—

that the religion which God reveals to men they should unhesitatingly follow, and again, that the manifestation of the supernatural by evident sensible signs should be accepted as a test of its existence and veracity." Mr. Ferguson assenting, Mr. Jennings resumed, "then, sir, you may see the proof of the supernatural and even touch it. Reason, it has been admitted, leads up to the threshold of revelation considered as authentic history. And from this we learn that God Incarnate, while on earth, established a Church, to which He entrusted His own divine mission. 'As My Father sent Me, so I send you,' said He to His apostles, and in their persons, constructively, to their successors. The end of the Church—namely the salvation of souls—is supernatural, the means which it uses for attaining that end are supernatural, and the government which it exercises is supernaturally grounded. It teaches infallibly in virtue of Christ's promise; it has sacraments as channels of divine grace, and the ultimate special aim which it puts before its adherents is the beatific vision of God. Made up of mortal men, this Church then, by reason of the end it has in view and the means which it employs for attaining that end, is supernatural, since it is the end and the means used thereto that specify the nature of a society. In the Church, then, as being of divine institution, you can see for yourself the embodiment of the supernatural."

"There is one point," said Mr. Randolph, "which I wish to hear explained, that is, the fact that in those countries overrun by Buddhism polytheism prevails; now polytheism is equivalent to a negation of all real theism."

"I allow," said Judge Jefferson, "that polytheism is widely spread in the countries referred to, but polytheism is not surely synonymous with atheism; the one sins by foolish excess, the other by blatant negation.—Polytheism errs grossly in its conception of the Godhead, but in our thesis we do not enquire directly into the nature of the Deity, but into the fact of the universal belief in His existence. In atheism, men deny the very existence of a Supreme Being, as Ruler of the universe; in polytheism, though oppressed by a credulity in the existence of many gods, they are always striving by the very logic of natural reason to rise, or they do rise, to the belief in the existence of one, supreme God, the Ruler of the world. This, as you are aware, mythology teaches."

"What has been said of the natural and supernatural," said Mr. Walters, "has suggested the following case to me. A person, I suppose, has observed the natural law, has acknowledged the sovereignty of God, has elicited acts of natural love for Him, and dies in these dispositions. Is he to be deprived forever of God's presence?"

"I think, sir," answered Mr. Jennings, "the case you suppose bears with it its own solution. I hold, that a person observing the natural law will infallibly receive the light of supernatural faith; and if need be, according to St. Thomas Aquinas, God will send an angel to enlighten him. But apart from this certain interposition, and considering the case as a mere hypothesis, I say, such a person could not see God, for the simple reason that he possesses not, as revelation teaches, the medium for doing so. God, in the order of grace, cannot be seen but through the medium of the supernatural. You might as well suppose that a blind man could see the light of day, as that the unaided human eye could in the supernatural order see God, who 'inhabiteth light inaccessible, whom no man hath seen nor can see.' On this subject, God's ordinance and not man's view is to be the rule of thought and judgment."[1]

"What then would be the lot of such a one?" asked Mr. Ferguson.—"He would forever," was the reply, "be deprived of the joy of seeing God face to face; this would be his great torture for eternity.

"I cannot understand how," said Mr. Ferguson, "in this world those who profess not to believe in God do not seem on that account to be particularly unhappy."

"They do not *seem* to be unhappy," rejoined Mr. Jennings, "but are they really not? I can easily understand how, amid the excitement of the pleasures of life, they may shut out all gloomy, distressing thoughts; but the soul must have sometimes its serious, reflective moments, in which the present and the future come up before it. The phantom of a dark, eternal exile, for the soul and body alike, is not a visitant, I presume, to make a man happy, even in this world.

"There are, of course, in this life many things calculcated to excite pleasant feelings,—friendship has its charms, and so have all worldly enjoyments, but beyond the grave there will be none of these.

---

[1] "Dicimus : Deus pro loco et tempore confert omnibus adultis gratias saltem remote sufficientes, quibus ita ponitur æterna salus in eorum potestate, ut, si non salventur, ipsis et non Deo id sit tribuendum." Car. Mazzella, "De Gratia Christi," p. 598.

Then every one must stand or fall by his own deeds; then the soul, severed from the pleasures or distractions of sense, will naturally strive with all its force to gain the true, the good, and the beautiful—which is God. And its inability to do so will be its unutterable woe.—In this life, there is hardly any greater torture for a person than the slow process of starvation,—intensely to desire to eat, and not to have wherewith to satisfy one's appetite; to thirst, and to see the water receding from one's lips, is an excruciating pain, and thus, in another world, the ardent wish to see God will be the everlasting hunger of lost souls; they will yearn to eat of the food of the tree of life, which is God, and to drink of those waters of eternal life, which are the joys of the beatific vision, but between them and the object of their longing there will lie a gulf that can never be passed over. From the impossibility of their gaining happiness will spring remorse, and with remorse, despair, and then a racking of the spirit by the contending feelings of pride, of envy, and of anger."

[Mr. Taunton consented to read an essay at their next meeting, which was to be held, on invitation, at the villa of a gentleman of Westchester County. The day of their reunion being determined on, a vote for adjournment was unanimously carried.

On the appointed day the gentlemen met at the villa to which they had been invited. After having conversed for some moments, and admired the surrounding scenery, they took their seats to listen to Mr. Taunton's address.]

CHAPTER VII.

God in the Moral World.

For one who examines the finite under its different aspects, the physical world is not more real than is the moral world. The former we can see and measure, touch or handle; the latter we can estimate by reason and follow even the vastness of its reach, beyond the limits of time, into eternity. In the one, we come immediately in contact with the sensible; in the other, with the real, with the substance or the making of human actions, and with the division of them into good and bad.

In the physical universe, the harmony of its different parts, the co-ordination of its laws, and the adaptation of means to ends, show forth its unity and point to the one, supreme Source from which it derives that unity; in the moral world, its principles, the co-ordination of its powers, the end to which these finally tend, point immediately to man as being the depositary of the primal law of that world, and beyond it they point to Him who is the author of that law. Written on the heart of every human being, this great primal law has been also promulgated in the heart through the light of reason. All positive enactments come to man from without him, and bind him to a certain line of duty; the natural law recorded within man's own breast claims, by its own native force, his submission to its dictates. And further still, it must enter into or be the basis of all just human legislation;—a law that is directly at variance with the natural, moral code is no law at all, has no binding force, and is ruled out of court by man's heaven-given, natural right. The elementary, fundamental principle of this inborn, natural law is, "avoid evil and do good;" a principle that manifests the two great characteristics of law, since it forbids and commands, and when expanded by the interpretation of right reason, counsels and permits, pronounces actions to be right or wrong, lawful or unlawful.

This law, then, is not merely for one man, or for a few men, or for one class, or for some classes of society; it is not given to illumine one generation or one people, but to guide all generations and all peoples. It is the centre of light for man's moral nature,—a reflection on him of the Divine mind,—a participation of that eternal light "that enlighteneth every man who cometh into this world." Looking, then, in that light through the vast domains of the moral world, we can discern an order somehow analogous to that which is seen in physical creation. In both, there appear the like great sweep of providential care, the like great principles of order, and the like great forces of combination and of adjusting power. Through physical nature, storms and floods, and the lurid lightning, and the terrific thunderpeels seem ready to upturn and rend everything; but when the strife of the elements has passed, and forces are again balanced, nature regains its calm, and physical laws, freed from the strain put on them, continue to work harmoniously. In the moral world, the great disturbing element is man's free-will, influenced by passion. From it come manifold strife, and moral corruption, and rebellion against man and God, under every form. Sometimes it would seem as if the whole moral world was about to be utterly wrecked or blotted out altogether, and again, after evil has done it worst, things, under some superintending influence, re-adjust themselves, and the great landmarks of morality remain unchanged. Now, as in the former instance one legitimately infers that there must be a supreme, independent Lord of the universe, from whom its order springs, so in the latter, from the stability and harmony of moral laws working to their ends, the just conclusion is reached, that back of that moral order there must be a sovereign, all-wise Lawgiver, who, by just rules and in measure, governs this moral world of ours.

From the self-evident facts of that world also the same conclusion is clearly reached. In the general moral course of human life there is nothing that comes out to view so strikingly as the distinction that exists between some actions as essentially good and others as essentially bad. This distinction is by its nature objective and intrinsic, universal and immutable. Being outside the human faculties, it is not dependent on them, or made by them, but springs from the very essence of things, and is the same every-where and at all times. In the physical world, we conclude from the limits of finite things to the existence of Him who imposed those limits, and here again, in the moral order, we are certainly justified in reasoning after a like manner from the limitations set immovably to the qualities of human actions. The worship of the Deity, filial duty, justice, temperance, fortitude, prudence, have been held to be laudable in themselves by all men, and at all times, and in all places; whereas blasphemy, impiety, injustice, intemperance, etc., have been regarded as vicious always and every-where. There is, therefore, between the morally good and the morally bad a fundamental distinction,—not changeable by any notions or efforts of men, and not suppressed by any viciousness or cruel legislation. It is this distinction which makes morals to be morals. Let it be capricious or changeable, and then what is essentially good to-day can be evil to-morrow; injustice in one will be justice in another; blasphemy now can be afterwards an act of virtue, and thus, the whole moral order being reversed, moral scepticism becomes a rule for human thought. Since nature itself rises in revolt against such impiety, the question occurs,—whence sprang that order, and how came it that some actions are essentially bad, and others essentially good? or who laid the foundations of this moral world, and who " hath laid the measures thereof... or who hath stretched the lines upon it "? To these questions no other answer can be given than that contained in the Book of Job. That order of things whence directly springs the morality of human actions must ultimately be referred to the divine wisdom and goodness, or to God dictating the nature and relation of things, mirrored, as it were, in the divine essence.

Still, in that direction efforts have been made, both by the way of hypothesis and by the invention of definitions. The needs of the happiness of the social organism will account, it has been said, satisfactorily enough for the aforesaid distinction. In a paragraph quoted by Mr. Mallock, Mr. Huxley writes: "If it can be shown by observation or experiment, that theft, murder, and adultery do not tend to diminish the happiness of society, then, in the absence of any but natural knowledge, they are not social immoralities."[1] "If," though a convenient word for one who is at a loss for an argument, often proves false to him. Taken by the writer to qualify the antecedent of his conditional syllogism, it is provisionally made to cover crimes which are such by their very name. Theft is theft, and murder is murder, (to speak only of these), every-where, the relevant circumstances remaining unchanged—and no observation whatever, or experiment, can show the contrary. As the antecedent, then, is altogether false, the consequence, according to the laws of logic, is altogether wrong, while the whole reasoning is well calculated to spread, to use the words of Mr. Huxley, "social immoralities."

Following out his views on evolution, Mr. Herbert Spencer considers moral well-being to be only a development of animal activity. To show this he skilfully classifies, in his "Data of Ethics," that activity, whether of man or of beast, under the same general term, "conduct." And conduct he defines to be "acts adjusted to ends."[2] In its most rudimentary forms, conduct, he says, is observable in the lowest types of animal organisms. The *infusoria* have hardly a shred of it, so little do they adjust acts to

[1] "Is Life worth Living," p. 47. [2] "Data of Ethics," ch. 1-2.

ends; the rotifer, a higher developed aquatic creature, conducts itself better, and the floating ascidian better than the rotifer, and the cephalopod better than the ascidian, so that conduct is proportioned to organism, and the more artful the creature is to use means to secure its ends, the better it conducts itself. Mr. Spencer would have his definition of conduct cover only animal-actions, but in spite of him it has a wider range. Machinery of various kinds is often said even to act and has, as it were, an organization wherewith it adjusts acts to ends; so that, consistently with Mr. Spencer's definition, we may speak of the "conduct" of a steam-engine or of a sewing machine.

Mr. Spencer's theory on biology seems to interfere with his theory on ethics. The preservation of animal-life he considers to be the basis and end of the moral code, and the goodness or badness of an act to be taken from its consequences and not from its nature. The conduct of the irrational animal thus differs not in kind but in degree from that of man, so that a dog can be said to have morals as well as his master. This conclusion, in the light of the common sense of our race, is refutation sufficient of its premises. Men as well as irrational animals try undoubtedly to preserve their lives, but the manner in which they do so shows the difference of their natures. In all life-purposes animals are necessitated to act by instinct, and that by fixed, determined means; men, on the contrary, by the knowledge of the reason of the end they have in view, determine themselves to act and select the means for attaining that end. The sensible qualities of the object draw the animal to it; not only these qualities, but much more the ethical character of the thing and of the means thereunto, go to determine the man. These different lines of action of irrational animals and of man, the classification of those animals into distinct species, as well as the direction and limitation of their organic functions, supply us with data, I think, wherefrom to conclude to the existence of a supreme, ethical, ordaining Cause.

At the same conclusions one arrives, when, in the moral world, he looks for an ultimate, absolute standard for moral action, for a *norma* wherewith he can unmistakably distinguish the good from the bad, the right from the wrong. Pleasure, according to one school, is this standard or *norma*. To be sure, pleasure is taken in a gross sense by some, and in an utilitarian sense by others, and is thus respectively upheld by them as a moral rule of action, but in either sense it certainly cannot be a guide or *norma* for man's moral well-being. In the former sense it is Epicureanism, and this, I need not remark, stands self-condemned in the judgment of all upright and honest people. This system, so far from furnishing a true standard of morality, is a real negation of it. The philosophy of pleasure, according to its advocates, is merely subjective; its measure and joys are only in the soul and, as they maintain, are its highest good, its *summum bonum*. This philosophy is consequently as changeable as are the dispositions of men, and is modified by age, education, and talent. In its working such a *norma* of moral action would be the perversion of all moral notions. If pleasure alone were to be the rule of the good, then religion itself would be commendable only inasmuch as it were pleasurable; and things that in themselves are reeking all over with moral turpitude would be good when pleasurable, and evil only when painful. Then, too, duty's sanction would be pain or pleasure, and conscience should be guided in its rulings only by the disagreeable or delectable. How such a base rule of conduct would work for evil, every-day's experience bears witness to. The pleasurable, unfortunately, is the rule of life which many follow, and to what horrors of degradation it leads them, the world itself is almost ashamed to record. Still, such is the standard of moral worth upheld by such writers as Hume, Bentham, John Stuart Mill, and even Mr. Herbert Spencer, who defines that "the good is universally the pleasurable."[1] These writers, however, protest that they have nothing to do with Epicurus and disclaim all connection with the voluptuous philosophy of Aristippus. Pleasure, they say, to be a fit rule of action, must be limited by the useful, or utilitarianism is the ground and the law of life.

But this latter system is simply a modification, not a rejection of the former; it is merely an effort to find a firm basis for pleasure, as a standard of moral action, and not an abandonment of it. Pleasure, it was found, is not a principle, and therefore to supplement it, or to give it a buttress, utility was adopted. But the same difficulty recurs; utility being as changeable as pleasure, the question is: is utility a principle or a fixed basis for moral guidance? Experience teaches that it is as subjective as pleasure,

[1] "The Data of Ethics," ch. iii., p. 30.

as dependent as it on individual disposition, and as subversive of moral duty and conscience. It is useful, indeed, the utilitarian holds, that "the sanctity of life and property should be preserved;" but if private utility counterbalances these, or if their violation just now does not interfere with the general tenor of social order, the sharper, according to the utilitarian teaching, can steal your watch or your land, and a man can murder his enemy and then commit perjury. "If a man be convinced that nothing which is useful can possibly be criminal, if it be in his power, by perpetrating what is called a crime, to obtain an end of great immediate utility, and if he is able to secure such absolute secrecy as to render it perfectly certain that his act cannot become an example, and cannot, in consequence, exercise any influence on the general standard of morals, it appears demonstrably certain that, on utilitarian principles, he would be justified in performing it. If what we call virtue be only virtuous *because* it is useful, it can only be virtuous *when* it is useful. The question of the morality of a large number of acts must therefore depend on the probability of their detection, and a little adroit hypocrisy must often, not merely in appearance, but in reality, convert a vice into a virtue." [1]

John Stuart Mill felt the force of these difficulties, and hence, to get, if possible, a secure basis for utilitarianism, regarded not the quantity of pleasure but its quality. Gross pleasure, which, when intensely indulged in, is its own surfeit, he would not have to be the motive of action, but would rather take for

---

[1] Lecky, "History of European Morals," vol. i., p. 43.

such motive the feelings derived from fine taste, or from social intercourse, or from refinement and simplicity of manner. Still, the principle of the philosophy of pleasure remains the same. The difference between pleasures must of course spring from the difference of their causes. There must be in the object which produces an ennobling or virtuous pleasure something which is not in the object, which causes mere sensuous delights. Now, what else is this, but to say that there exists in one thing a quality of the good, which does not exist in another; and consequently that there exists in things a real, essential, objective basis for the good and the bad, and that there is a philosophy of law above the philosophy of pleasure. Alluding to the teachers of some of these false ethical methods of our times, Cardinal Manning says: "There are men at this day, who consider themselves intellectual, openly denying the existence of the soul; and who, having denied the existence of the soul, deny the existence of right and wrong. They tell us that right and wrong, and the instincts, dictates, and rebukes of our conscience are arbitrary associations of pleasure and pain, connected with certain actions by the conventional traditions in which they are brought up. If so, then there is no such thing as law, either human or Divine; and if no such thing as law, then no such thing as sin or crime, and therefore no such thing as justice; and if there be no such thing as justice, there is no such thing as injustice; and if there be no such thing as intrinsic right, there is no such thing as intrinsic wrong; and if not, then we are in a world which has no more right, order, sweetness, or beauty, but we are turned back again into the inorganic state of creation, 'void and empty, and darkness rests upon the face of the deep.' "[1]

Another school of modern thought holds that reason alone, without any reference to a Supreme Being, is the sole, ultimate, and objective basis of morality,—that in itself reason is an absolute standard of moral worth, and that reverence for it is the great means of forming and promoting moral principle, of creating "independent morality." There is question, not of the proximate rule of morals, let it be remembered, but of the objective, ultimate basis of the moral order; not of reason as an immediate law of conduct, but of reason as a first objective source of morals. But how reason could form such a basis, or source, is not intelligible; since it is not in keeping with its nature. In itself, reason is within man, not outside him; it is subjective not objective; it is a faculty of his nature, not an external standard above him. As the distinctive endowment of human beings, reason is specifically the same in all men, though numerically it is different, and in its operations and judgments is also often different. Reason in man is not distinct from him. It is not above him as a superior, but as a faculty is, as it were, his instrument. " It is in us, as a principle, not for generating obligations but for knowing it." It often hesitates before judging and often doubts about its act. Nay, on the subject of morals, misguided reason has led men into the grossest errors. With Locke and his school it has sanctioned utilitarianism; with Hobbes and Puffendorf, it has made state-power and the

[1] "The Fourfold Sovereignty of God," p. 43,

civil law the great fountains of moral goodness; and with French infidels it has lent itself to approving self-love, or interest, or animal appetite as the source of morality. In our days men use their reason in striving to divest themselves of their moral attributes and in place thereof to take to themselves the bestial instincts and habits of the gorilla or of the orang-outang. Make reason, or rational nature, to be the ultimate fountain-head of moral goodness, and you have as many standards of that goodness as there are men, as many variable tests of morality, practically, as the judgments of men are often practically variable. In reason there is unquestionably a light that enables it to perceive the distinction between right and wrong, between the good and the bad. But these, while it perceives them, it does not make, any more than the eye makes the sun or the stars that shine in upon it.

In our days, reason, resting on grounds that had been cleared for it by theistic teaching, and relying on principles given to it by Christian civilization, claims to be self-sufficient in the moral world and to want no aid for its development from any source external to it. This is the creed of the school of "ethical culture." It will have nothing to do with God, and at this late day in the world's history, and after having received its first lessons from theism, it will slightingly cast it aside, and will set up and parade ethical articles of its own making. With some reflective power, this school might learn a salutary lesson from the past. If there be any feature more than another which comes out in the lives of peoples, it is the insufficiency of reason to be the one, absolute, independent rule of morals. Under paganism, it is acknowledged, that the great lever for raising the moral tone of a nation was divine authority, even such as it then was. When the authority of the gods fell into contempt with the people, when the falsity of polytheism came out to public view, and impure rites were introduced into the worship of the temples, then also was spread dissolution of morals and practices of obscenity, to read of which strikes one with horror. Reason, looking to no power above itself, cast around, at the time, for some sort of moral standard, and lapsed either into sensualism with Epicurus, or into scepticism with Carneades, or into dark fatalism with Zeno. Every-where through the pagan world, the rankest corruption kept pace with the most blatant atheism—so that men, women, and children, acknowledging no divine superintending power, sank into the lowest degradation. When Horace described the carpenter as doubting whether he should shape the log of wood into a bench or a god—he was but pointing out the contempt into which Roman religion had fallen, and indicating, together with that contempt, the unbridled license of the Epicurianism of the Roman world of his time.

To supplement mere rationalism as an objective criterion of morality, some persons introduce the idea of progress. Taken in the abstract, progress is merely a word; but viewed in the concrete, it possesses only what is put into it. As generally used, the word stands for material or scientific development, and to speak of it in this sense as furnishing the materials of morals would be tantamount to speaking of the morality of a railroad or of the electric telegraph. Sometimes, however, it is made to stand for culture, which, in the minds of its votaries, implies some moral excellence. In its range, it embraces education in all its methods and departments, together with the opinions, and manners, and customs of civilized society. Now, to form one, absolute, unchangeable moral type out of these elements, partial, changeable, and contradictory, is more than even Moses could have done. But does culture by itself imply morality? To have an eye for the beautiful, to be an acute art-critic, to have a graceful literary style, do not, by themselves, necessarily imply any moral excellence; again, in regard to scientific attainments, no one would hold that the *Principia* of Newton are the data of ethics, that the law of gravitation is a moral law, or that the invention of the telescope was in itself a moral act; and furthermore, in general, it will be granted that bare intellectualism does not make morals. It is known to all that simple-minded, illiterate persons have often been found to possess an exalted moral sense, and to lead the purest moral lives, having nothing to guide them but a few points of doctrine and the voice of conscience within them. While, on the other hand, it is notorious that persons of high intellectual culture have been worthless in point of morals. Another truism is, that manners do not make morals, and neither do mere circumstances. Morality enlists in its making all the powers of the soul and God's law, and indeed manifests itself in conduct; manners by themselves are only the tinsel of an etiquette which one has put on, and can be with or without morals. Every-day's history teaches that, as far as manners go, persons may pass for ladies and gentlemen, and on the score of morality be most disreputable. To say that circumstances alone make morals, is altogether to ignore or to misinterpret man's nature and the formation of morality.

As an inference from these truths I assert that morality is not only subjective, but also objective; that its basis is not solely reason, and that a good will, as Kant would have it, is not the one thing which is unequivocally good in the world. Principles there are, and human qualities, which are, by their nature, good, independently of the use that is made of them. Alms-giving in itself will always be good, even though it should sometimes be used to cover hypocrisy, and courage as a virtue will be always something laudable, though it may sometimes be found in a villain. Examine, then, as one may, the structure of the moral world, and the relations of the distinction between good and evil in things, and he must finally come to the uncaused, absolute source of all ethical life, the supreme, self-existing Being, who is God.

But Mr. Herbert Spencer will here object, saying, "then, were there no knowledge of the divine will, the acts now known as wrong would not be known as wrong."[1] Some would; since their wrongness is inherent in them. Some things are forbidden because in themselves they are wrong, other things are wrong because they are forbidden. Blasphemy would be known by reason to be wrong, even though it were not known that it had been forbidden by a

[1] "Data of Ethics," p. 50.

commandment. To argue from an effect to a cause, I am not supposed to know the cause in order to know the effect. I can know the inherent goodness or badness of an action in itself, without any reference to precept or prohibition. Two things are, therefore, to be considered in this connection: one is, that the essence of morality is objectively grounded on the rational order of things; the other, that the obligation of moral actions ultimately arises from the divine will. What is wrong in itself, God undoubtedly always forbids, what is good in itself, He may not always command. "The morality of human actions, then, *immediately* depends on the objective order of things as apprehended by reason, but *mediately* on the order of the divine wisdom or goodness, or on the eternal law."[1]

In this great, universal system of the moral world of which we speak, the visible centre of its activity is man in the exercise of the faculties wherewith he has been endowed. To him are subjected all the domains of nature, and for his use or pleasure all inferior things in their respective spheres work to their ends. He is the lord of all, and being possessed of free will, he alone is master of his actions, and consequently he alone can perform a moral act and be accountable for it. Such, too, is his nature, that he cannot act deliberately without acting for an end. He must have a purpose in his action, or a good as an object to be gained. This end, though the last to be actually reached by him, is still the first as his motive power. It is this which gives him the first impulse to act, which determines his will,

[1] "Liberatore, Ethicæ Institutiones," p. 46.

and holds it to its determination amid difficulties. The profession, for instance, which one intends to embrace will be for him the goal to be gained. As a particular end, it will be the last thing he will realize, but as a motive it will be the first thing that he will act from. It will be the thought that will directly underlie his studies and will support him in his fatigue. The end of his action has this energizing and bracing power for man, because he judges it to be imperative as a duty, or desirable as a good. It is something definite, something which he considers as suited to his nature, something, therefore, which he regards as his good. In other words, the end for which he acts is also the good which he purposes.[1]

Through life, the particular ends which man may have in view are as numerous as are his purposes. They come from the duties of station or profession, from the claims of religion and society, from the wants of sustenance and from the thousand circumstances or accidents of daily labor. Subordinated to some main object to be gained, they are as means towards it. In this subordination the end that is last in order of time is the cause of that which preceded it in the order of execution. For instance, the cure of his patient is the cause of the remedies which the physician applies, or of the ends which he has in view. "Since nothing is moved," writes St. Thomas Aquinas, "to attain its proximate end, but by the final end."[2] To realize its ends or purposes is life's great work. Men, no matter in what rank or position placed, are continually trying to reach their particular ends, and when they have mastered

[1] See Appendix.   [2] "Summa Contra Gentiles," lib. iii., ch. 17.

these, other aims or ends they seek to gain and, though they do not reflect on it, are virtually reaching forward to something beyond all these goals of human exertion. Of their nature, finite ends being only limited, finite goods, they have not in them wherewith to satisfy the boundless reach of the human faculties. Let them be rolled back to their first great motive power, and this will be found to be no other than the highest good, the *summum bonum* or the ultimate end of all, which is God. It is with finite moral ends much as it is with finite physical causes. The one as well as the other postulates an ultimate efficient cause. The ultimate end is as necessary to give life and subordination to finite moral purposes, as the first great cause is to give a beginning and support to limited, temporal agents. "In (moral) ends," writes St. Thomas, "there is a twofold order, namely, that of the intention and that of the execution. . . . The principle of the first is the ultimate end, that of the second is the first of these things that lead to that end. And in either case an infinite series of developement is impossible."[1] Particular projects man can indeed continue to propose to himself, and by this means bar the aspirations of nature, but his life flows on, project succeeding project as the wavelets of the ocean, until at last, having spent all their active force, they break on the shores of eternity.

In the argument just stated we have been led up to God by following the direction of human intentions; let us now see whether, by following the tendency of human desire, we shall not be able to reach the

[1] "Summa Theologia," 1, 2. q. 1 a 4.

same goal. Everybody's experience tells him that the great master-trait of man's nature is its inborn desire for happiness, or its longing to possess an object that by its qualities will completely content the human heart. This desire is rooted in man's rational nature; directly it emanates from the will, but its basis is laid in the operations of the intellect. Of this the special object is truth, and since the true differs from the good only in relation, the universally true will also be equivalently the universally good. What the intellect apprehends as true, is the measure of what the will embraces as good. Moment after moment those two faculties are grappling with the matter of morals,—examining it in view of law, sorting, changing, or assimilating it, and then spontaneously, as it were, weaving it into the woof of human actions. In this process, the intellect goes before as the herald of the will, casts its light on the object or the end of the action, and presents it to the will for its acceptance. In virtue of the freedom which it possesses, the will can reject this or that good presented to it, since its object is the good in general, considered apart from any subject, finite or infinite, in which it may be supposed to inhere. Being then engrafted on man's rational nature, the desire for happiness is manifested by him in various ways. Whether he plays, or reads, or walks, whether he tries to escape disease, or ignominy, or confinement, it is happiness that he seeks for. To this he naturally strives to make all things contribute; and though the desire of it, sometimes satiated by indulgence, may cause him in particular instances disgust, it will not, for all that, be thoroughly satiated. Now a desire so radically interwoven with man's nature, and so supreme and unconquerable in its tendency, must necessarily have an object to satisfy it. Claim that its end is void, that it is a feint set within man for his deception, and forthwith you open the way for universal scepticism. If the will has no real object for the full contentment of its desires, why should the intellect have one for the real ground of its thoughts? And if it has not, then the true no more exists objectively than does the good; so that here in life we are only striving to catch after shadows, and are living in a sort of dream-land. Besides these absurdities which the hypothesis involves, it is altogether at variance with design in nature. Through all her domains there is not a created being that has not an object proportioned to its capacity; there exists not an irrational animal that has not means and objects, given to it for the satisfying of its animal instincts. In this point of view, then, the brute creation would be superior to man if he had not the means or an object wherewith to fully satisfy the irrepressible propensity of his nature for happiness.

By happiness, I may here remark, is meant the possession of all that good which goes to satisfy that rational desire of man. There must not, of course, be the least particle of evil in it, it must be permanent, forming a perfect state, and must be "absolutely final." "And," writes Aristotle, "of this nature happiness is always thought to be; for this we choose always for its own sake and never with a view to anything further; whereas, honor, pleasure, intellect, in fact, every excellence, we choose for their own sakes, it is true (because we would choose each of these even if no result were to follow), but we choose them also with a view to happiness, conceiving that through their instrumentality we shall be happy: but no man chooses happiness with a view to them, nor, in fact, with a view to any other thing whatever."[1] As, then, happiness is proportioned to the good as its object, the greatest good, the *summum bonum*, must be the object and reason of the greatest happiness.

Where then is this object, the greatest good or the *summum bonum*, to be found? Many think they can find it within the compass of the objects of earth, and try to live entirely for worldly pleasure. But in their sober moments they confess that they have not found happiness. The happiness-giving object, I remarked, must of its nature content all the longings of the human heart, not for a time or partially, but completely and forever. It must consequently contain all good, be immutable, and always enjoyable, and shield the soul from even the danger of evil. In the objects which the world presents, these qualities, it is clear, cannot be found. Whatever earth offers to man for his enjoyment must necessarily be limited by nature; and being thus limited it cannot be the source of all good, nor give to man an unfailing warrant of security against all impending evils. Finite it is and finite it must be in its effects. It is changeable; it can be added to and subtracted from, and when men say that it gives them complete contentment, they are only striving to check the yearnings of their souls in order to be consistent

---

[1] "The Nicomachean Ethics," b. i., ch., 3.

in adhering to their prejudices. Finite goods are the external goods of fortune,—such as riches, glory, honor, power; interior bodily goods, such as sensible pleasure, health, strength, beauty; or the adornments of mind, such as science, art, æsthetics, moral virtue. Now it is evident, that not one of these qualities or goods contains the rest in any way whatever, which, however, would be required, were it to be the source of every good and of all happiness to man. There is not one of these goods, moreover, which a man may not possess, though he be at the same time weighted with the greatest evils: not one of them which cannot be increased or diminished, while many of them, such as those of fortune and of bodily well-being, are transitory and changeable. And what these qualities are, when taken separately, that they also are taken collectively. Even if one were in possession of all the goods of earth, he would not be contentedly nor perfectly happy. The King of old has left us his experience on this subject. After having tasted of all the pleasures of life, and enjoyed the goods which earth could give, he records that in all he found but vanity.

Since, then, nothing finite can be an adequate object of happiness for man, it follows that it is only the infinite good, which is God, that can perfectly satisfy his desires for happiness. Therefore, I conclude, man's inborn desire of happiness implies the existence and possession of a Being infinitely good. "To possess God," writes St Augustine, "is happiness itself. Consecutio Dei est ipsa beatitudo."[1]

[1] "De Moribus Eccles.," chap. 13.

The supreme Good being objectively determined, a further inquiry is, how is it that man is to make that Good his own? or how is that happiness to be subjectively realized by him? From what has been said, it is evident that man can possess the great object of his happiness only by means of the faculties by which he knows and loves it. By his intellect and will alone he can reach God, who by nature is essentially spiritual, and consequently it is only by means of the same faculties that he can enjoy Him as the great object of his contentment. The senses, indeed, contribute remotely to the knowledge of God, but it is the intellect that comes, as it were, in contact with Him; it is it which acquires a knowledge of Him as the ultimate end, and through that knowledge the will may love Him and be delighted in the enjoyment of Him. The knowledge and love of God, then, are the two great elements of man's ultimate future happiness, though in this life that knowledge can exist without love, but love cannot exist without knowledge. Allied exclusively to no state or condition of life, the humble husbandman may possess the knowledge and love of God in a higher degree than the learned scholar or statesman. But the happiness produced by knowledge and love, however great, will in this life be continually broken in upon by trials or temptations, by the worry of cares, by the relations with the neighbor, or by bodily infirmities. In another world, for the just, no such obstacles will exist, but, elevated and strengthened in intellect and will by divine light and love, they shall be in the enjoyment of perfect happiness and see God as He is. To gain this crowning glory they needed continually the aids of supernatural grace. Born in the supernatural order, as all the children of Adam are, the unjust had also been destined in God's eternal counsels for unfailing happiness, if only with His grace they observed His law and died in His friendship. By sin they fell from the state of grace; the end for which they had been destined they forfeited through their own fault, and banished themselves for ever from His presence by frustrating His beneficent designs. Having passed the boundary line of human existence, they must eternally lie where they have fallen. Rebels against God in death, rebels, from the nature of the case, they must remain for eternity.

From what I have hitherto said, I infer that the moral order, universal as it is and immutable, imperative too in its obligations, has been imposed on free rational beings by a superior power, to the end that order may reign in their free actions, just as physical law has been imposed on the universe, that order and unity might exist in its movements. And as from the harmony, beauty, and arrangement of the visible world, reason concludes to the invisible things of God, so too, from the stability, unity, and excellence of the moral order, it concludes to the authority of Him who established it. Rationally we infer from the adaptation of parts to parts and to the whole in the material world the existence of its intelligent author, but in the moral world it is not mere brute matter that is co-ordinated in its relations, but the free, intelligent actions of rational beings. They freely think, and will, and desire, and resolve, and still on the whole they feel that they are under the constraining power of a law that is around them and in them. No man can escape that law;—universal in its scope, it bears on all men at all times; in the time of Cain it was what it is to-day. "It is not one thing at Rome," writes Cicero, "and another at Athens, one thing now and another afterwards; in all nations and at all times, this one, eternal and immutable law must have sway."[1] Now the order which thus rests on an universal law must have for its author an intelligent, ethical Being of universal sovereignty. It is an order, too, which, as it is based on the essential distinction between moral actions and on the fundamental relations of men to their destiny, must be grounded on law eternal and unconditioned. Consequently this law of right and wrong, of truth and justice, must always remain unchanged, thereby proclaiming, since it is necessary and determinate, its author to be also a necessary and determinate Being—God.

"Many objections, I foresee, gentlemen," said Mr. Taunton, after he had finished reading, "will be raised against the grounds which I have taken in this essay; you will allow me to forestall some of them, while I give in outline a discussion which I once had on the subject of morality with a friend of mine, whom I shall here call Montagne. We had been arguing on the nature of moral action, when suddenly stopping and turning towards me he said: 'Taunton, do you know what it is, to do the right is all I care for.'—'Certainly,' I replied, 'that too is my only care, but the question is—what is the right?'

---

[1] "De Republica," l. iii., ch. 22.

'That is right,' he answered, 'which, as a citizen in a human commonwealth, I judge to be so.'—'But,' I resumed, 'another may think quite the contrary.' —'Of course,' was the reply, 'allowance is to be made for diversity of opinions, but a person swayed by the new conception of virtue will scarcely differ from me.'—'I am curious to know,' said I, 'what this new conception is.'—'Well,' he answered, 'the old conception of virtue was based on the relation of an immaterial soul to an immaterial God; the new conception is based on usefulness to others as its object, and on devotedness to the "social organism" as its motive, or, if you like, on sympathy for humanity. Altruism is the great moral science of the age.' —'Allow me to say, Montagne, that you have given me a tangled skein; in a phrase you have put together half-truths, wrong motives, and false assertion. Let us begin with the motive of this new virtue. Sympathy you call it, and this sympathy, I suppose, for the afflictions which weigh on humanity.'—'Yes,' said he, 'that is my meaning.'— 'Now,' I continued, 'I have no difficulty in admitting that sympathy for distress is in itself a worthy motive of action, but I fail to see that it gives a basis broad enough for universal moral conduct. There are thousands of actions in every-day life which fall not under that sympathy. If you go to the Exchange and purchase stock, you are not, I presume, influenced by sympathy for humanity, nor do you think exactly of the "social organism;" and if you take a drive, or eat a hearty dinner, or drink champagne, you are not moved to do so, I ween, by the afflictions of the human race. Besides, that sympathy, though not broad enough for conduct in many respects, is too restrictive in another relation: it implies that love for my friend must spring from my devotedness to the "social organism," or from my love of the human race, and that the good of the social body is to be of more moment to me than my own personal wrong, or affliction, or sin; in fact, that only is sinful, which is socially wrong. At whatever cost it may be, I must suffer myself to be ground to powder under the wheels of this modern juggernaut, the "social organism." In another way sympathy is an uncertain rule for moral science, since what may excite the sympathy of one may excite but the aversion of another.'—'You argue exclusively,' said Montagne, 'from a subjective point of view. I think, the question ought to be considered also from its objective bearing; the "social organism" has claims on individuals.'—'Certainly,' I replied, "but if in itself a rule of morals be subjectively false, it cannot in its application be objectively true. The "social organism" has claims on individuals, but not such as take the manhood out of them. To surrender oneself totally, if required, to the promotion of the welfare of the "social organism," is to act contrary to what one's personal nature and happiness demand. Man's happiness is, first of all, essentially personal: it must be for him, must be by his own co-operation, and not the product of any social prosperity, no matter how great or extensive.'—'I only say,' replied Montagne, 'that to labor for the social good, for the happiness of the greater number, is the directive law of life.'—'Much misapprehension on this subject,' I answered, ' has come from confounding two things in themselves distinct—the social good, and personal moral worth ;—the one relates to the external order or decorum of a people, the other to the private virtue of individuals. Now, either of these can exist without the other. In a State the best order might exist, since this largely depends on police-regulations,—and still, in the same State, the most hideous moral corruption might extensively prevail, since this can be hindered only by the sense and sanctions of the higher law. The cities of the Plain, I conceive, may have been altogether decorous to the human eye,—men and women may have attended well enough to social requirements, and yet, in those cities, beneath the glitter of fashionable life, lay a sink of iniquity—reeking all over with all that is foul in bestial crime. People, therefore, can work for the welfare of the "social organism" and pay little or no attention to their own moral culture; they can be philanthropists in public, and sybarites in private. Morality is a personal matter and is the substance of the happiness of each one, while this in its turn leads on to the social happiness of all.'

"'Yes,' said Montagne, 'in the formation of ethics, you begin with yourself, whereas we begin with others ; in the old routine, selfishness is the basis of morals, in the new system, devotedness is their basis.'—' You mistake, Montagne,' I replied; ' altruism is not a new conception ; on the contrary, it is, I may say, as old as the rocks. " Thou shalt love thy neighbor as thyself," is surely not an invention of the modern ethical-culture school. Even nature dictates that a duly ordained love of self must precede a justly regulated love of the neighbor.

Man must naturally support and care for his own life, in order to be able to do good to the lives of others.'

"'You are an admirer of Mr. Herbert Spencer; here is his work on the "Data of Ethics;" in it he is inclined to favor your views, but truth forces him to make the following statements: "Of self-evident truths so dealt with, the one which here concerns us is, that a creature must live before it can act. From this, it is a corollary that the acts by which each maintains his own life must, speaking generally, precede in imperativeness all other acts of which he is capable. For if it be asserted that these other acts must precede in imperativeness the acts which maintain life, and if this, accepted as a general law of conduct, is conformed to by all, then, by postponing the acts which maintain life to the other acts which life makes possible, all must lose their lives. That is to say, ethics has to recognize the truth, recognized in unethical thought, that egoism comes before altruism. The acts required for continued self-preservation, including the enjoyment of benefits achieved by such acts, are the first requisites for universal welfare. Unless each duly cares for himself, his care for all others is ended by death; and if each thus dies, there remain no others to be cared for." . . . . And again—" In one further way is the undue subordination of egoism to altruism injurious. Both directly and indirectly, unselfishness pushed to excess generates selfishness. . . . . Every one can remember circles in which the daily surrender of benefits by the generous to the greedy has caused increase of greediness, until there has been produced an unscrupulous egoism, intolerable to all around. There are obvious social effects of kindred nature. Most thinking people now recognize the demoralization caused by indiscriminate charity. They see how in the mendicant there is, besides destruction of the normal relation between labor expended and benefit obtained, a genesis of the expectation that others shall minister to his needs; showing itself sometimes in the venting of curses on those who refuse.'"[1]

"'Of course,' said Montagne, 'all human conduct is to be regulated by prudence. What I maintain, is, that to work for selfish motives is immoral—and to look for a recompense as a payment for work done takes all the worth out of it.'—'Then,' I answered, 'you should not pay your tailor's bill.'—'Why?' he asked.—'Because,' said I, 'you will be contributing to immorality, since, if to work for pay demoralizes an action, your tailor ought to work for you gratuitously and then . . . . starve.'—'Well,' he replied, 'you hold then that to work for pay offers one a higher motive than to work for the pure pleasure of devotedness.'—'In many circumstances it does,' I replied, 'inasmuch as a man's pay may be necessary for his own support and that of his family; besides, due payment for work is one of the bonds of social order. Here, then, is a twofold duty,—and duty comes before pleasure. Your difficulty, Montagne, I think, comes from this, that you suppose that man in his actions must be limited to the one motive for which he directly acts. I can work for the benefit of my neighbor,—this is my immediate motive, but that is subordinate to the

[1] Pp. 187-196.

higher motive of pleasing God and, in consequence, of securing my own salvation.'

"'All that, Taunton,' said he, 'is a matter of opinion; both of us struggle for righteousness through different methods, you through the motive of the highest good which is beyond humanity, I, through the motive of the highest good that is in humanity; you, that you may probably live always in beatitude in heaven; I, that I may live forever in the memory of men, and gladden and be gladdened by them.'—' You mistake,' I replied; ' the righteousness we seek is not the same, no more than the shadow of a thing is the same as its substance, or a counterfeit is the same as a true coin. The righteousness I look for is grounded on God's eternal will; His authority is its law, and His glory its determining cause. My motive is for the highest good in humanity as well as for the infinite good beyond it. I am as much alive, I claim, to sympathy with humanity as any man: I feel keenly for its woes, but I allow not my sympathies to outrun my reason, nor do I suffer utopias to take the place of God's providence or of man's final destiny. You tell me that you work for the happiness of others, and your motives for so doing are the lovableness of that happiness, and the breath of it in the world of the future. Now I should like you to test these motives on one of the hardy sons of toil that throng our thoroughfares. From early morn till late at night he has to earn, in the sweat of his brow, a pittance for the support of himself and his family. Present to him your motives for action and your theory of happiness; he probably will stare at you in silence, or if he answer you, will say: "My dear sir, that sort of thing may suit some well-to-do ladies and gentlemen, but as for me, my happiness lies in conforming to God's will, and accordingly in performing my duties; I find none of that loveliness that you speak of in work—for me life is a warfare, but there is a future, sir, and there the scales in which man's worth is weighed are different from those which this world holds; 'I know that my Redeemer liveth'."'

"'What others might think or say on the subject,' said Montagne, 'does not concern me; I find in humanity motives sufficient for action; be these motives immediate or mediate.'—'And who is humanity?' I asked.—'Rather,' said he, 'you should have asked, what is humanity? To this, I answer, it is the sum of human goodness and greatness under every form; the deeds

> "Of those immortal dead, who live again
> In lives made better by their presence."'

"'Come, Montagne,' said I, 'let us put aside poetry and sentiment. Tell me, is humanity something living, actual, individual?'—'Certainly,' he answered; 'it lives in living, individual men.'—'Then' I resumed, 'it is not humanity in the abstract that supplies you with motives, but men as we know them, good, bad, and indifferent.'—'Yes,' he answered. 'Then,' I added, 'man, as he is given to us by nature, and not as Christian civilization has made him, is the great reason of your motives; you live for him, you look up to him, and in consequence of your devotedness you must pay him some religious cult; man is your God.'—'I do not go so far,' he answered; 'but as man is the noblest work of life, to

him I give my highest respect, my sincere devotedness, and, inasmuch as he is to be of "the choir invisible," who by the memories they leave behind them gladden the world, I reverence him.'—
'Really,' I replied, 'considering the qualities of goodness and greatness that are required for membership in that choir, very few, I judge, will belong to it; but this choir is, after all, only a figurative expression, and men will exist in the future only in metaphor; you tell me that all that remains of men after death is their memories, or, as the Buddhists say, their Karma, and, "like a streak of morning cloud you shall have melted into the infinite azure of the past." Is it possible, Montagne,' said I, 'that you do not believe in the spirituality and immortality of the soul?'—'No,' he answered sternly, 'and I challenge you to prove either.'

"'I would not venture,' I answered, 'to extemporize on such a subject, but I will send you my proof in writing.'"

"I am not quite sure," said Mr. Ferguson, "that there was not some truth in Montagne's reasoning. I don't see why the practice of benevolence cannot suffice for man's contentment. Everybody knows how virtuous deeds spread joy over the soul, and how the satisfaction of being of benefit to others is a laudable end of human actions."

"Certainly," answered Mr. Taunton, "I do not deny that virtuous deeds give a passing joy to the heart, or that the relief of human suffering is not a laudable motive for conduct; the question, however, is not about the effects of virtuous acts or of the immediate object of beneficence, but about the very fundamental principles of morality itself. We want to know what are the true primary data of ethics. The emotional nature of man can be soothed indeed by momentary pleasure, but we should falsify his character, were we to judge him from his emotions. It is intellect and will, I need not tell you, that make him a man and form his immediate rule of action; his emotions and imagination can stimulate his will to act, though sometimes they stand in its way by clouding its real object, yet even then the desire of the soul for the true and good always remains and, seeking something greater and greater, rises above present enjoyments. To be sure, in particular objects the mind perceives what is true, and the will enjoys what is good, but the mind and the will are always reaching beyond these to their objects, — namely, the illimitably true and the illimitably good. Nothing else, as apprehended even in this life, can perfectly satisfy the longings of the soul. Find me the man who amid his present earthly enjoyments is perfectly contented, who wishes for nothing more, and who has no distress of heart, even when he boasts that the aim of life is to eat, drink, and be merry. Besides, sir, particular pleasures produce only particular joys, but that the soul may be fully at rest, it must have an object that will completely satisfy it, and this it finds only in the highest good, that is in God."

"Let us be more definite," said Mr. Ferguson; "I admit much of what has been said, but I still hold that within the resources of his being man has wherewith to perfect his moral nature and to realize his destiny."

"The perfecting of his nature must imply," said Mr. Taunton, " that he can discern right from wrong, good from evil, or that he has an intuition of what is evil and false, as well as of what is good and true in principle."—" So I understand it," subjoined Mr. Ferguson. " That intuition, then," continued Mr. Taunton, " means that man perceives directly not only what is permitted but also what is forbidden, or that, somehow, he cognizes in his being a law in its double character of sanctioning or forbidding human actions, and as law supposes a law-giver, that he consequently reasons to the supreme authority of God, to whom he owes allegiance."

" All that may be true," rejoined Mr. Ferguson, " and still in the practical order man may not be led by it. The data of his ethics he can find in the directing power of nature."

"With a witty French writer I am inclined to ask," said Mr. Taunton, "' Nature, who and what is this woman?' But in the present hypothesis at least, I dare say, sir, you would consider the power of nature as impersonal."—"Yes," was the answer.—"Then you maintain that an impersonal power, or in plainer words, that a material force can impose on man a law of right and wrong."

" Humph," muttered Judge Jefferson, as he frowned and made a note of the point.

" I meant to say," replied Mr. Ferguson, " that nature prescribes that things are to be considered good for a person, because they are desirable, or that they have that in them which will give him contentment and pleasure. Thus I estimate the excellence of things by their capacity for imparting pleasure."

"In your theory, then, sir," replied Mr. Taunton, "the excellence of things will be in proportion to their power of imparting pleasure; and hence, religion, science, law, will be less excellent because immediately less pleasurable than sensual indulgence, or riches, or bodily comfort. But the universally admitted fact that men consider the former as more worthy of being desired and more excellent proves that they possess an excellence incomparably superior to the latter. The desire of a good does not make it, but simply indicates it."

"Still," resumed Mr. Ferguson, "it is I who make for myself the good or the bad; it is admitted that it is from the heart that virtue as well as vice proceeds."—"Certainly," answered Mr. Taunton; "morality is also subjective as well as objective; conscience is the immediate rule of man's actions; it is by it that he shall be judged. But the question we discuss just now does not turn on the immediate rule of human acts, but on the ultimate law or basis of morality, or on the power that draws the objective line of distinction between good and evil. Conscience, as the eye of reason, perceives that distinction, but does not make it; it applies the law and as a rule of moral conduct holds man responsible for his acts. Thus the heart of man becomes the source whence come forth both good and evil."—"Then," said Mr. Ferguson, "you make duty, or obedience to law, and not good, the basis of morality."

"Excuse me, sir," answered Mr. Taunton; "I said that there are things which in themselves we conceive to be good anterior to law; maternal love, for instance, is good in itself, and is founded on the very order of nature established by divine wisdom. Hence maternal love, being intrinsically good, and anterior to all positive law, is also the ground of maternal duties; it is a law to itself."

Mr. Ferguson not having resumed the discussion, Mr. Walters remarked that there were some historical facts which, he thought, could hardly be reconciled with the unchangeableness of the moral code. On the other hand, Mr. Burke argued that the first principles of morality are unchangeable, while the application of them is various according to different circumstances. The principle of justice is always the same, but the application of that principle in courts of law is manifold. "Let us, then," said Mr. Walters, "test the case by a historical fact. During many centuries, magic and sorcery were accounted heinous sins, and for them men and women in thousands were put to death; at present, those sins are looked upon as mere delusions and the bugbears of dark ages. Would you not consider that to be a change in a principle of morality?"—"Before answering your question, sir," answered Mr. Burke, "allow me to ask whether you believe in the existence of evil spirits."—"Certainly," was the answer.— "Well, then I cannot understand how you can deny the existence of magic or sorcery, since it is of the malignity of Satan to tempt to evil, and when souls consent to his temptations, to use both soul and body for various purposes. In his fall, he has not lost his original angelic nature. Endowed with a most subtle intellect, he knows all the hidden resources of matter and can combine diverse material elements in such a wonderful way as even to counterfeit the miracles of God. In such cases it is only by his trail that Satan can be discovered. What he did in past ages, he can do, and does to-day, though often under different forms. Magic and sorcery, then, as diabolical practices, have not become obsolete."—"So then," rejoined Mr. Walters, "you believe in all the witch-stories of the past."—"No sir," replied Mr. Burke; "no more than I believe in all the witch-stories of the present. There were shocking exaggerations of the influence of sorcery in former ages, I admit; at times, in some countries, a belief in the extent of magical practices became a sort of moral epidemic; under it, men and women were ruthlessly murdered. But that then there were true cases of magical practices, or of witchcraft, even rationalistic writers are forced to admit. While striving to disapprove it, Mr. Lecky, by the cumulative evidence in the case, has been compelled to write the following passage, just pointed out to me. 'It is, I think,' he writes, 'difficult to examine the subject with impartiality, without coming to the conclusion that the historical evidence establishing the reality of witchcraft is so vast and so varied, that it is impossible to disbelieve it without what, on other subjects, we should deem the most extraordinary rashness... The evidence is essentially cumulative.... In our day, it may be said with confidence that it would be altogether impossible for such an amount of evidence to accumulate round a conception which had no substantial basis in fact.'[1]

"But suppose," said Mr. Mattison, "that I were to deny the existence of evil spirits,—what then?"—

---

[1] "Rationalism in Europe," vol. i., p. 38.

"Then," answered Mr. Burke, "I should prove it to you; from the Bible, if you admit its divine authority; if you do not, then from it as a most ancient,—perhaps the most ancient—authentic record, in its opening books, of any historical documents extant. Either that, or I should have recourse to the universal testimony of the human race. But still, it is most probable, I would not appeal even to that, since from contemporary facts I might prove the thesis."— "I should like to hear you do so," said Mr. Mattison. —"Spiritism, you are aware, gentlemen," continued Mr. Burke, "has tried to organize itself into a religion in our time; it holds its meetings regularly and by means of *mediums*, holds converse with spirits, and receives answers from them. Gradually developed from the superstitious practice of animal magnetism, it differs from it principally in this,—that in the latter the evil spirit acted in man through the influence of the magnetic trance; in spiritism he acts chiefly from without man; through material things or material elements, spirits nowadays clothe themselves frequently in matter and appear visibly; when evoked, they answer to names, pagan, Jewish, Mohammedan, infidel, or Christian. They will extol Protestantism at Geneva and Catholicism at Munich, and in *seances* of free-thinkers will brand all revealed religion as sectarianism. Personifying sometimes angels or archangels, or even Christ Himself, they will hold high converse with their votaries, will not stop at blasphemy, or infidelity, or idolatry, or, to suit their audience, will play tricks and indulge in trivial, drivelling gossip. All this, resting, as it does, on well authenticated facts, clearly shows that the spirits of spiritism are demons, and that this whole system of spiritism itself is a stupendous network of diabolical fraud, cast on the souls of men. There is one thing that it unquestionably reveals, and that is the existence of evil spirits."[1]

"Would you not consider, sir," asked Mr. Maxwell, "that many of these phenomena attributed to spiritism may be explained on scientific grounds?"

"I would not, sir," replied Mr. Burke, " when there is question of phenomena which directly point to an intellectual or preternatural cause. No possible material cause can ever so much as answer yes or no to a query. What material power is there in physical nature that can make a table give so many raps in answer to questions proposed; that will write with a pen attached for the purpose to some material object; that will even play on musical instruments; that, without visible contact, will raise from the floor the heaviest tables and hold them suspended in the air; that will even form phrases by putting together the letters of the alphabet cut out separately. Physical science undoubtedly occupies much of the thought of this century, and that laudably. The discoveries and inventions that have been made have given special characteristics

---

[1] "They do not serve religion well, who strive to set down as old women's fables or puerile ravings the facts and phenomena which are related (of spiritism). . . . . . As too great credulity, so also too great incredulity in this matter is to be avoided by a prudent man.

"Among the stupendous facts historically proved (of spiritism) may be mentioned: writing in the inside of tablets firmly closed and pressed ; the introducing of things into apartments, the doors being closed; the apparition of hands, of faces, nay, of the whole human person,—which manifest themselves to the sight and touch as real, live apparitions. Now these and similar facts of themselves proclaim that the devil is not only the prompter of them, but commonly their real author." Lehmkuhl, "Theol. Moralis," vol. i., p. 238.

to civilization. But, sir, it is a singular fact that it is amid physical phenomena especially that the devil has tried to burrow, in our days. It was, indeed, his habit of old, but during the great modern development of physical experiments he has been striving to utilize physiology for his purposes."—"Then," said Mr. Maxwell, "you would bar the progress of science by imputing to it such an alliance."—"Not at all," answered Mr. Burke; "I would only save science from disrepute by breaking up that alliance. The methods of science, when followed out, will always merit praise and will recommend themselves to all intelligent men. By induction and deduction, scientists are able to trace effects to causes in the physical world and to note the relation and proportion that exist between them; but in the phenomena of spiritism it is quite otherwise. In these there is no proportion between physical cause and effect, or between the power of any human faculty and the results of spiritistic operations. And, as we have seen, these results cannot be ascribed to good spirits; they must consequently be the work of demons."

"We do not know," said Mr. Maxwell, "all the powers of nature, and hence we cannot say that phenomena which seem inexplicable may not after all be attributable to natural causes. There are many things connected with animal magnetism which to some would seem miraculous, but to scientists are natural effects proceeding from natural causes."— "It is not necessary, sir," replied Mr. Burke, "to know all the powers of nature, in order to know that any material thing cannot, by itself alone, perform an intellectual act; everybody you meet in the streets has sufficient knowledge to judge, infallibly, that of itself a table cannot write. As to animal magnetism, in its fullest developments, though there are some phenomena connected with it which in themselves can be ascribed to natural causes, there are many others which surpass all the powers of nature, and are even in conflict with its laws. In the first stage of the magnetic trance, the magnetized person is simply under the complete control of the magnetizer, and the phenomena that occur therein do not generally, it is said, surpass nature's powers. But in the second stage, which is called 'the lucid magnetic trance,' the magnetized sometimes sees with his eyes closed, knows the hidden thoughts and wishes of others, sees things absent or distant, speaks in unknown tongues, knows diseases and attempts to prescribe remedies for them, etc. When this system came into vogue at the beginning of this century, it was thought that a new era had dawned upon the medical profession, and that now all diseases, seen at their roots, could be effectually cured. This artifice of the demon deceived many; but sickness went on as before, and, clairvoyance notwithstanding, men, women, and children died after the old fashion. Sober-minded persons immediately perceived that, joined with the phenomena just spoken of, there must be a great deal of jugglery and of deviltry, since there was no physical proportion between the causes and their effects. Of course, much was said of a fluid averred to be transmitted by the operator to the person magnetized or hypnotized, but what that fluid was no one could say. And how a fluid could give a faculty to perform actions such as these just mentioned shocks all common sense to think of. It is no less absurd to suppose that the magnetizer transmits his thoughts and wishes by a mere mental act, since, as philosophy and, indeed, experience teach, intellect does not immediately manifest itself to intellect, nor will to will; whatever is understood or wished by one, the knowledge of it is acquired by another only from sensation, and therefore from words or some other sensible sign. Of the phenomena, therefore, of which there is question, no other cause can be reasonably assigned than a preternatural one. The wanton circumstances that accompany those phenomena absolutely forbid the supposition that either God, or angel, or any beatified or just soul has anything to do with them, and this being so, the only other competent cause that can be assigned for them is the demon.[1]

In an Encyclical Letter issued, in 1856, by the Holy Office of the Inquisition to all the bishops of the Church, on the subject of magnetism, mention is made of a decree of the same Office in 1847. "All error," says this decree, "and sorcery, and explicit or implicit invocation of the demon being removed, the use of magnetism, as a mere act of applying physical means otherwise lawful, is not morally forbidden, provided it does not tend to an unlawful end, or to one anywise illicit. But the application of purely physical principles and means to things and effects truly supernatural, that they may be physically explained, is nothing else than a deception altogether illicit and heretical." The Letter then goes on to

---

[1] Gustavus Lahousse, E. S., "Prælectiones Metaphysicæ Speciales," vol. 2., p. 582.

explain the superstitious practices of magnetism as developed in spiritism and adds: "In all these practices, with whatever art or illusion persons use them, since physical means are applied to produce non-natural effects, there is found a deception altogether unlawful and heretical, and a scandal to good morals."

"The person to be magnetized," writes Lehmkuhl, "or the one that is to be used as a *medium*, must subject himself and his will to the will of the magnetizer, which is impious."[1]

After this, a general conversation ensued on the spread and delusions of spiritism. Mr. Neufchatel, who did not take part in it, was seemingly busy with his own thoughts, and when an occasion presented itself, remarked:—"I do not dispute that it is the mental faculties, with the aid which is given to them, which mould the good into morality, but the question is, what is the good, and where is it to be found? I admit that in the sources to which reference has been made, it is found in some measure, but to a greater extent it is found, I maintain, in scientific knowledge. Make men wiser by scientific training and you make them better; you put them in a position wherefrom they may contemplate the dignity of their nature, and may rise to a sense of their moral greatness."

"Viewed practically," said Mr. Randolph, "the argument just given comes to this—drench a youth with physics and you make him holy; teach him the binomial theory, or chemistry, and you make him temperate; explain to him the laws of biology and

[1] Op. cit., vol. i., p. 226.

of literary style, and you hinder him from becoming a thief,—since, as the gentleman would have it, the data of science are also the data of ethics.

"Besides the glaring fallacy that underlies this argument, it has also this inconvenience, that it is altogether inapplicable. Take the aggregate of the human race, and you will find that the knowledge of the very great majority of them is on a level with that of the honest Corin, all whose philosophy consisted in knowing that, 'the more one sickens, the worse at ease he is; and that he that wants money, means, and content, is without three good friends;— that the property of rain is to wet, and fire to burn; that good pastures makes fat sheep, and that a great cause of the night is lack of the sun.' Hardly greater than this is the knowledge of many men and women in civilized communities. Would you for a moment entertain the thought that they are therefore without morals? Why, sir, on the showing of Mr. Alison, in some provinces of France in his time, the state of morality was in the inverse ratio of their learning; and Ireland, stinted fearfully up to the present in education as well as in many other things, has been put in the comparative national statistics of morals first among the nations.

"The nations of antiquity were intellectually refined, as their literary and artistic remains testify; would you, sir, say that they were virtuous? Purely secular literature or science has never yet made a soul good or converted a sinner. It is not their fault since they were not intended for that,—'in morals as in physics the stream does not rise higher than its source.'

"But the strangest thing of all in this matter is, that the modern state, while it promotes mental culture, has no sanctions for the preserving of it; it has no penalties for bad grammar, or bad writing, or bad logic;—none for false scientific theories, nor for the blundering of zoologists, of chemists, or of astronomers; on the other hand, the same state has a full catalogue of penalties for violations of the moral code, about the teaching of which it has sometimes no concern whatever. It does not allow the fifth commandment of the decalogue to be explained authoritatively to its pupils, and yet it punishes for murder; neither does it permit the heinousness of perjury or the grievousness of theft to be impressed on youthful minds, and still it has penalties for these. It punishes for the violation of the great laws of duty, and still, within its own sphere, it will not permit these laws to be taught. Now, I do not say that, even with moral training under religious sanctions, crimes will not sometimes be committed, since passions never die in the human breast, and the will's liberty has in it a side towards evil, but what I assert is, that bare, natural culture, when not coupled with a reverent and religious feeling, gives no guaranty against viciousness and is apt to lead minds into atheistic theories. It deals only with matter, and of itself, beyond matter it cannot rise."

"Is, then, the state bound to teach morals?" asked Mr. Neufchatel.—"No, sir," was the reply; "it is not bound and ought not to teach morals; it has received no commission for that. The state's duty is to favor those who have been authorized by God to teach the moral law."

"Who are they?" asked Mr. Neufchatel.—"The ministers of the true religion," was the answer.—"Then," said the former, "you hold that religion and morality are the same?"—"The same in principle," said Mr. Randolph.—"It has been demonstrated for us that God is the Creator, the Sovereign Lord and Ruler of this world;—would you admit that?"—"Yes, sir."—"From this truth, then, it follows," argued Mr. Randolph, "that all that we are and have, we owe to God; that justice requires that we should render to Him the homage of our whole being, in the manner in which He has prescribed or revealed, and that we should obey His commands in everything ruled by His divine will. His absolute dominion over us as our Creator grounds His absolute title to our worship and obedience. And since he has made us with a purpose, His will is to be our rule of life, His law the great source of our goodness. We are bound by the very law of nature to offer to Him homage and worship, and that makes religion; we are bound to conform our reason to the Divine reason, and that makes morality. True morality, therefore, cannot be separated from religion, and neither can the practice of true religion be separated from morality."

"To return to the point we were discussing," said Mr. Neufchatel, "the state, you hold, is not commissioned to teach morals, but its special duty is to protect them. Now, this it does by legislation and by punishing the publishers and venders of obscene literature, and thereby fulfils the functions which alone, as you say, belong to it. But if you limit the action of the state on one side, you enlarge it on the other. You maintain that morality is inseparable from religion; since, then, according to the hypothesis, the state must enforce the former, it must also enforce the latter—a doctrine which is at variance with all contemporary legislation; freedom of worship before the civil law having been adopted as a *modus vivendi* of all modern nations."

"I need hardly say," replied Mr. Randolph, "that it is quite one thing to hinder one from doing what is wrong, and quite another to teach him to do what is right. Though maintaining that the state is not commissioned to teach morality, I say it is bound to promote the teaching of it; and here I subjoin that to this it is held even by its own interests. A state not resting on sound moral principles is like a house built upon the sand,—under the pressure of adversity, all historical experience teaches, it will certainly come to ruin.

"The gentleman, however, seems to reproach me with exaggeration, because I teach the dependence of morality upon religion,—religion being here restricted to faith in the existence of God as the Moral Ruler of the world. Of this doctrine convincing proof, if I mistake not, has been given, since it has been shown that to suppose moral worth without the basis of religious thought is like supposing foliage and fruit without a tree to produce them. Accordingly the remarks about freedom of religious worship are beside the question. I grant the gentleman's whole argument; it does not touch my thesis; namely, 'that atheism is incompatible with morality,' or that belief in God as just mentioned is postulated by the moral code. Now, as all modern nations accept this dogma of religion, I am inclined to think that, when the gentleman speaks to us of freedom of worship, like the knight of La Mancha, he is but charging against a windmill."

"Then," said Mr. Neufchatel, "you would by law enforce religion as you have defined it."—"Just after the manner," answered Mr. Randolph, "in which you would enforce morality. The propagation of atheism I consider to be at least as criminal an offence as the propagation of immorality. The state, however, forbids the latter, whilst it does not say a word against the former; that is, it permits the poisoning of the wells and then tries to stop the spreading of the plague. The man who, by writing or discourse, denies the existence of God, or blasphemes His holy Name, or ridicules His divine attributes, is to my mind a greater corrupter of morals than the most obscene of all obscene writers. This is my decided opinion on the subject; I submit it to your consideration, gentlemen."

The points taken by Mr. Randolph were then discussed with some warmth; at last Judge Jefferson, who was often appealed to during the debate, decided, " that the question being considered at its lowest level, a state, purely on social grounds and for its own stability, would be justified in forbidding by law the propagation of atheism by discourse or by writing."

After this, some side issues brought out during the debate were talked over in a tone of light banter. Messrs. Mattison and Babington debated the right of holding a false opinion, the former maintaining that no one has strictly a right to hold what is false any more than he has a right to use counterfeit coin, the latter insisting on man's liberty. To this the retort was, that as man *can* tell a lie, therefore he may do so; that physical power is not the measure of moral right, in other words, " might is not right."— The controversy was now becoming a little exciting, when Mr. Walters interposed and talked at some length on the liberties of our age in contrast with those of past centuries, and concluded by citing the saying of Sydney Smith—that it is always considered as a piece of impertinence in England, if a man of less than four or five hundred pounds sterling a year has any opinion at all upon important subjects. This saying was received with great laughter, and the discussion and meeting were brought to a close.

CHAPTER VIII.

[This paper, sent to Mr. Montagne by Mr. Taunton, though read at the subsequent meeting, I insert here.]

THE NATURE OF THE HUMAN SOUL.—ITS IMMORTALITY.

TO comply with your request, I have endeavored in this paper to explain briefly the nature and attributes of the human soul; and in order that you may the better seize on my meaning, I have supposed that, as I proceed, you will try to verify in your soul what my conscience prompts me to say of mine. I shall note its mental features, you will strive to look at your fac-similes of them, and again, when I sketch the extent and sweep of the mental faculties, do you endeavor to test my description by self examination. First, then, I would have you note that you live, think, reason, and will, in order that you may understand the character of your soul, not by directly looking into it, for this you cannot do, but by studying it in its intellectual acts. Reflect, too, how the soul elicits desires and forms purposes, how it feels, wills, freely determines itself, and reasons; and how, again, the senses having done their part, it originates all these intellectual acts by an immanent intrinsic power of its own. This incessant activity, the internal sense, if closely observed, will teach you, and furthermore will indicate that you can study the phenomena of mind in this interior world of the soul as effectually at least as you can the phenomena of nature in the exterior world around you. Conscience then testifying, you will realize the fact that your soul is the principle by which you live, and know, and purpose—the seat of the immanent vital acts of sensation, of mind, of will, of memory.

"In this introspection of your faculties, I would call your attention to two leading facts;—the first is, that the phenomena of thought, of wish, of sensation, which you note, lead up necessarily to the substance from which they proceed, much after the manner that the phenomena of inertness, extension, quantity point to the substance which supports them. Those mental phenomena, however, pass; thought succeeds thought; desire, desire; sensation, sensation; but their subject, that which produced them, conscience tells us, remains always the same—quickening thoughts, putting forth desires, receiving impressions, shaping purposes, and giving new sanctions to the projects of the soul. That subject is called by Aristotle spirit, soul. The second fact which I would have you observe is the soul's activity, or how it is self-energizing, self-moving, and controlling, according to its choice, the ebb and flow of mental and vital emotion. This manifold immanent activity, which the internal sense tells me that the soul possesses, it communicates at its will to the body, so that the body moves or rests just as the soul wills. Now, as experience must have taught you, activity or motion is the sign of life;

The Nature of the Human Soul. 313

when the body moves not, it is lifeless; when the heart beats not, it is dead. This you yourself must have witnessed in all animated nature, since among animals and plants it is movement or activity of some kind that separates the living from the dead. Here then we have two constituents, so to say, of the human soul, namely, that it is a substance and that it is the principle or source of human life; it is it which forms and perpetuates our personal identity; it recalls now what it had thought or willed before, and thus makes the individual to be the same yesterday, to-day, and forever. It is it which informs and unifies the body,—giving to it its nature and communicating to the senses their vital action. The human eye and ear, for instance, have a vitality of their own, but the first principle of that vitality is the soul itself.

"Those premises having been laid down, I will now ask you to observe some of the special attributes of the soul. Attend to how it declares the oneness and simplicity of its nature by its unifying power, by the dictate of conscience, by its individualizing influence, by its oneness of thought or judgment, so that each one can know that the principle from which proceeds all this vital activity within him is not compound, but most singularly a simple unit, an unextended reality. Observe also, that this living principle of activity within us takes in the concept of God, pre-eminently simple, of virtue, of being, of the universal; that it desires the good, the true, and the beautiful, and that, as being thus, the recipient of these simple ideas itself must be simple, or immaterial.

"Those delicate threads of thought, I am aware, are apt constantly to escape one's grasp, but, when held for a time by habit or reflection, lead to intellectual enjoyment. Here then are a few more of these threads which I will ask you to hold; they are wound around the making of knowledge, and if well unravelled will show that they are spun, so to say, by the immanent acts of the intellectual soul out of what is simple and spiritual. Look into the knowledge you have of any sensible object, reduce it to its first elements, and you will find that it was first photographed on your sense, then that, over the image thus formed in the imagination, was shed the pure light of the active intellect, and that image, the intellect, by the power of abstraction, dematerialized and elevated to the intellectual order. The intelligible thus becomes the stuff out of which knowledge is made, and the thing known, idealized by the mind, becomes somehow one with it in its act of cognition. But by what manifold process is this end arrived at! "Instinctively, even though unconsciously, we are ever instituting comparisons between the manifold phenomena of the external world, as we meet with them, criticising, referring them to a standard, collecting and analyzing them. Nay, as if by one and the same action, as soon as we perceive them, we also perceive that they are like each other, or unlike, or rather both like and unlike at once. We apprehend spontaneously, even before we set about apprehending, that man is like man, yet unlike; and unlike a horse, a tree, a mountain, or a monument, yet in some, though not the same respects, like each of them. And in consequence, as I have said, we are ever grouping and discriminating, measuring and surrounding, framing cross classes and cross divisions, and thereby rising from particulars to generals, that is, from images to notions."[1]

"To bring out more prominently the truth of the thesis I am putting before you, examine for a moment the other side of the question. Suppose the soul to be material, and then, as in all its parts a thought should exist, the thought would be manifold and not one product of the mind, as conscience tells us it is; or should it be said that the thought permeated the whole material subject, then thought would be divisible, an absurdity which needs no refutation. Indeed, physicists generally make no difficulty in admitting that thought is incompatible with unorganized matter, but by no means, they say, with matter organized under certain conditions; for in the human, material brain, they affirm, there is a capacity for 'ideation,' sustained or developed by fancy, sensation, nerve-force, or nerve changes. As you perceive, this theory runs on the assumptions that there is a causal relation between nerve-excitement and thought or wishes, and that consequently the nerve-force, as a cause, contains implicitly the thought as an effect; in other words, as nerve-power or brain-action can be measured or calculated, so can thought, and then the force of the nerve will be the force of the thought—every ploughman will be a Newton. Another assumption is, that a condition is a cause; that, since nerve-impression is necessary for forming the sensible image from which the intellect abstracts an idea of the ob-

---

[1] "Grammar of Assent," by Cardinal Newman, p. 28.

ject, therefore the nerve-impression is the cause of the idea, which is like saying that, since light is necessary for seeing, it is light, and not the eye, which sees. Furthermore, it is assumed that material power, at least in its highest form, sensation, can transcend its own nature, which is acknowledged to be the sensitive, and perform acts of an order wholly above it, namely, the purely moral and intellectual. That is, the sensitive organ, the supposition is, be it internal or external, through nerve-changes or the nerve-cells, can apprehend the abstract, the universally true, the good, the just, or high beyond the level of individual existence; can examine the universals, being, humanity, or, in general, man, horse, or tree, etc., a function which belongs exclusively to the intellect. But your own experience clearly teaches you that your thoughts and volitions are not limited by your organization; that far above the world of sense you can hold converse with your own soul about God and His attributes, about mathematical truths, and legal judgments, and constitutional maxims. And as you can take the abstract and universal from the sensible, you consequently possess faculties above it.

"The proofs hitherto given for the immateriality of the soul have been mainly derived from the operations of the intellect; like proofs of the same fact can be taken from the operations of the will. An insight into these will distinctly show you, what indeed you are conscious of, that within you there is a twofold inclination—that which tends to the sensible, and that which can reach forward to the ethical. By a law of our nature we cannot desire a thing without having known it; or knowledge must precede desire. Now, as we have seen, the immaterial cannot be apprehended by a material principle, and consequently cannot be desired by the same. We know the morally good and the morally true taken in their sense of universals, and therefore in their relation to the absolutely good and true; and thus God, and virtue, and wisdom become the objects of our will. This, as being a faculty of the soul, manifests, by desiring those objects, its spiritual nature, just as the mind does by apprehending them. Again, under another point of view, the range of our intellectual faculty was a premise from which we argued to the immateriality of the soul; we concluded that it was only a spiritual being that could encircle, as it were, the universe by its faculties, and ascend in thought along the scale of beings from earth to heaven. But whithersoever the intellect reaches, thither also the will aspires; unlike the sensitive will in animals, which tends only to particular sensible objects, the will, as a rational faculty, seeks directly good in general, which is its object, and desires and loves it under the eye of reason, because of the qualities of goodness which it possesses. What is intellectually true is that which for the will is desirably good. The good that is in things the rational will reaches immaterially; the purely virtuous it takes in, as it were, instinctively. In every created being, it finds something to content it, but still, by reason of its ever widening capacity, it can never be filled by any limited goodness. By extending the circle of its power in its aspirations towards the good and the beautiful, it rises higher and higher, until it reposes on the bosom of Him who is the infinitely Good and the infinitely Beautiful. Thus, again, within this sphere of thought, in a twofold way, by the exercise of its faculties the soul reaches God,—by seeking for the true through the intellect and by seeking for the good through the will; but in the doing of this, it is evident that, in the latter as well as in the former case, the soul must be immaterial, spiritual.

"I fear I have fatigued you by these two long explanations on this point, and still I will ask you to allow me to add another reflection. Your own experience teaches you that it is the freedom of your will that makes you most intimate with your soul; by it you can check the sensitive appetite, by it also you can determine on your choice, taking into account volition, and the moral law, and your relation to the end for which you act. You also feel that, even if your limbs were shackled, still in the sanctuary of your soul you would be free. Now that freedom of action, that superior force of soul, to be intelligible, must be rooted in a self-active principle, or in one entirely distinct from all that is corporal.

"The most of what has been hitherto said is grounded on two axioms of the schools, (1) namely, that "the action is according to the nature or essence of the agent"[1] (2) and that "what acts by itself also exists by itself,"[2] or is a substance. The inorganic operations of the intellect and will have shown you that the soul in which they are rooted is

[1] "Modus agendi sequitur modum essendi."
[2] "Quidquid per se operatur, et per se existit."

The Nature of the Human Soul. 319

a simple, immaterial substance, the source of human life and activity. In our studies, we have also seen that the soul subsists by itself, because it can act by itself, and though, in the preliminaries of thought depending objectively on the senses for the sensible images of things, subjectively, or in itself, it rises above the sensible,—taking in the nature of things in universal conceptions,—reasoning on the abstract qualities and relations of objects and searching for truth and looking for good even in the highest regions of the spiritual world. This fact, testified to by every conscience, proclaims that the soul is not merely an immaterial but also a spiritual substance; that in itself it is an independent entity, having the properties of a substance, and subsists by itself, though destined to union with the body; the sensitive brute-soul is, indeed, in itself immaterial, with a necessary dependence, however, on the material. The body and soul of the brute form but one principle, from which all its operations proceed. In these it depends altogether on the body; it cannot think beyond its senses, nor desire but what its appetite desires. It has no freedom of will, no power of abstraction, but is drawn to its object by unchangeable instinct, and has no progressive faculty because it has no choice of means. As the brute-soul, then, is necessarily dependent on the body, it dies with the body.

"It is otherwise with the human soul; we know the immaterial, as we have seen; even the material we know by an immaterial process. We are conscious, too, that we can prefer the spiritual to the material, and that sometimes at great sacrifice. All which vital acts prove that the intellect and will are inorganic faculties, intrinsically independent of matter. And since a faculty cannot be more perfect than the principle from which it proceeds, the soul, in which intellect and will are rooted, must, by its nature, be independent of matter, and consequently spiritual. In forming the human body as its substantial form, the human soul has thus independent operations of its own through its powers of reason and abstraction. In its own entity, independent of the body, it never dies. And as this is the point, I think, in which you are mainly interested, I shall, in discussing it, claim your closest attention.

"And in the premises, I beg you to recall the data already established; to wit, that the human soul is an immaterial, spiritual substance, subsisting by itself, possessing independent, inorganic activity, and, though informing the body, superior to it, and but using it for its service. In the light of these truths, consider the severing process of death; see how by it the body is rendered cold, motionless, lifeless; how its former graceful living features are replaced by the ghastly, blank expression of the corpse which people care not to look at, about which there is a loneliness which penetrates one with the thought that it is only the remains of a human person; then consider how after a short time decomposition sets in; the outward material form gives way, flesh and bones, muscles and tissues of every kind yield to decay and corruption and are finally reduced to their original elements. Still, though the body as such is wholly dissolved, these elements, like those of all other material substances, remain unannihilated. The human body is corruptible because it is material; and precisely for the contrary reason, the human soul is incorruptible, because it is a purely spiritual substance. Death cannot touch it by decomposition, because it is not composed. Men can kill the body, because it is organized matter; but they cannot kill the soul, because it is self-subsisting. It is beyond the reach of pistol or dagger, and lives on, a disembodied spirit, in spite of the purposes of the self-murderer. It was the soul which, by its union with the body, made it to be human, gave to it its being and nature;—but now, that the tie which bound them is broken, as a distinct, independent substance, the soul subsists in its own incommunicable essence. The intellect and will, for whose exercise the soul needed remotely the imagery of sense, now, after death, directly attain their objects; they live untrammeled by the sensible; in their own atmosphere, they are, so to say, in contact with the supersensible and intelligible, and immediately apprehend them. I say, then, that the soul naturally, or by reason of its own essential constitution, survives the dissolution of the body. If the soul depended necessarily on the body for its subsistence, if its acts commingled with those of the body, and reached not beyond them, as in the case of brutes, then, the body perishing, the soul also should perish. But having its own subsistence and operation as a spiritual substance, the soul is not touched by death, and retains consequently, in another life, the exercise of its peculiar faculties of intellect and will.

"Reflect impartially, and you will observe how the

soul, by its natural operations, is continually proclaiming its own immortality. It lives and is perfected in its rational nature by the imperishable. The incorruptible, the universal abstracted from things is its food; its standard of excellence is the ideal, and the higher it rises above the material world, the greater the perfection it acquires. That perfection for the human soul, inasmuch as it is rational, lies in knowledge and virtue. Now one and the other of these attain their highest excellence in proportion as they are farthest separated from the sensible nature or the bodily form. The past will teach you that the grandest speculations of genius, the loftiest exercises of pure reason were those which most transcended all material elements. By lofty thought minds seemed to have broken the ties that held them to their bodies, and to have lived in the intellectual world, invigorated by the contemplation of being and its relations,—of principles and their consequences. You have only to look into the writings of St. Augustine or of St. Thomas Aquinas, to see how immortal souls, assimilating to themselves immortal thought in the highest spheres of mental speculation, broke for the time with the external sense and with fancy, and lived, as it were, in another world.

" The longing for immortality indicated by reflex thought is shown perhaps more strikingly still by the exercise of virtue. Virtue, as you are aware, supposes the conquering of passion, the subjection of the body to the higher law of the spirit; and the more the body is subject to this law, the higher shall the soul rise above all natural sense, and the greater and the more refined shall be its acts of virtue. Looking for goodness or the object of its love in created things, the will finds that it is more capacious than they are, and mounts higher and higher in search of the Supreme Good. Now notice this feature of the will,—namely, the more it partakes of what suits its spiritual nature, the more it aspires to what is greater: it is not tired by the possession of what it loves, nor by the separation from what is sensible, but on the contrary, the greater the separation is, the more perfect the will becomes, and the nearer it approaches God, who is goodness itself unchangeable, the more strength and permanence it acquires. Such facts will furnish you with the data for interpreting the lives of many saintly men and women of the past. They lived, to be sure, in the body, but not for it; their thoughts and desires ran beyond changeable things to eternal truths, and were perfected by them, so that on earth, by the delights of soul which they experienced, they had a foretaste of their future immortality.

"But besides the perfection resulting to the human faculties from the contemplation of the universally true and good, there is in the soul a natural longing for everlasting existence. By nature, all desire to live. And as the inherent tendency of anything is a sure index of its nature, the soul's yearning for never-ending existence shows that the soul itself has been created for immortality. In this argument, the only point which seems to require proof is, that there exists such a yearning in the soul as that which I have just mentioned. Remember that there is question here of the rational soul, in which desire or longing follows the cognitive faculty. The soul yearns only for what it knows, and its knowledge consequently gives the mode and measure of its longing. Now, as I already remarked, the special object of human knowledge is, in the first instance, the universal, that is, what is not limited by time or space; and hence the rational soul apprehends existence undetermined by limits, whether temporary or local. The sensitive soul of the brute looks only to its present existence, or at least to its perpetuation by generation according to the species; all brute operations are directed to the preservation of the body or to the satisfaction of animal appetites; for this brutes live, and with this they die. It is otherwise with the human soul. Centre your mind for a moment on existence, and you will immediately find that it spontaneously rises from the present and the particular to the perpetual and general, that is, that it takes in existence apart from limit, as a thing interminable, and as such unreservedly desirable. Existence thus specified alone gives contentment to the will and satisfies the yearning of the heart for perfect happiness;—since happiness that is to come to an end will have always in it the pain of its ending one day. Suppose, for an instant, that this yearning for immortality is not to be realized, that it has no object proportioned to it, and you will have to admit that human nature as originally fashioned belies itself, that it naturally hopes for what it can never have, and that its innate tendencies have been given to it as for self-deception. All other creatures have their natural tendencies realized in this world, their instinctive capacities satisfied to their full; man alone, in this hypothesis, will remain stunted in his aspirations, and he who is the lord of creation must become the sport of nature, since he has a flaw in his very constitution. The absurdity of this supposition points directly to the immortality of the soul as being alone commensurate with the nature and dignity of man.

Viewed historically, belief in the immortality of the soul has been interwoven every-where and at every time with the history of the human race. It is a most prominent feature in the records of the most ancient religions of antiquity, but under three distinct forms. (1) One is the simple idea of the survival of the soul after the death of the body, without, however, any determined moral state being assigned to it; (2) another is similar to that taught by Christianity: after death judgment takes place, and the lot of the deceased, according to the life spent in this world, is settled for good or for evil eternally; (3) and a third form is that of metempsychosis, or the return of souls to actual life, either as men or animals, while their new condition is allotted to them in view of their former lives on earth. Relatively, however, this doctrine, it is admitted, is of recent origin.

In this century, the graves of ancient Chaldea have been made to bear witness to the belief in the immortality of the soul, as held by the ancient Assyrians. The explorations of Mr. W. K. Loftus and others in those ancient lands have shown with what superstitious care the dead were treated in view of their passage to another world. In their coffins or tombs they put provisions, lamps, arms, etc. " The same practice," writes Mr. Loftus, "is, I believe, continued among the Arabs, who conceive that these articles are necessary to give the spirit strength on its long journey."[1]

In ancient Egypt, belief in the soul's immortality was a fundamental doctrine of religion. A clear proof of this is found in "The Book of the Dead," as old, it is said, as the Egyptian nation itself. It consists of prayers which the dead were expected to recite, in order to secure for themselves a favorable judgment. For this end, to refresh their memories, a copy of the book, more or less perfect, was laid in the tomb with each mummy. The book also describes how man after death will be conducted by the god Horus before the tribunal of Osiris to receive judgment. There he will have to plead his cause before forty-two judges on forty-two different species of sin. This belief in immortality was brought before the eye on all sides in Egypt. It was written on papyrus, was carved, under some sensible form, on walls, on tombs, on public monuments. It was also the belief of ancient India, of China, of Greece, and pagan Rome.

From the very beginning, the Hebrew race steadily adhered to the doctrine of the immortality of the soul as to a first principle. For them as a people, it required no proof, as being a truth which could not be gainsaid; moreover, it underlay all Hebrew tradition, and was assumed by the doctors of the Law as an undeniable postulate. The Hebrews knew that death was a punishment for sin, and not the complete annihilation of man. This, their firm belief, they manifested in various ways.

[1] Travels, p. 213.

In his obituaries of the patriarchs, Moses ends his narrative with these significant words, "and he was gathered to his people," words which rationalists interpret as meaning that the patriarchs were buried in the tombs or among the graves of their fathers. This interpretation, at first sight plausible enough, is, however, contrary to the facts of the Mosaic narrative. Abraham was buried in Hebron, while his father Thare died at Haran in Syria, and Abraham's ancestors died and were buried in Chaldea. Jacob died in Egypt, and months elapsed before his body was buried in Mambre, in the land of Chanaan, and yet Moses writes of his death, "and he was gathered to his people." Aaron died on Mount Horeb and was buried there, away from every Israelite; Moses himself died on Mount Nebo, but the place of his burial was not known, and still both Aaron and Moses are said to have been gathered to their people. These and many other such texts clearly prove that for the Hebrew mind the aforesaid phrase meant that the soul of the lately deceased friends lived on beyond the grave, in the company of the souls of other deceased acquaintances.

This meaning is determined still more minutely by the fact that in the ancient Hebrew Scriptures a place was designated in which the souls of the departed dwelt. In Hebrew it was called *scheol*, the Latin *infernus*, and the English *hell*. In the books of the Old Testament, written before the captivity of Babylon, the word, it has been calculated, occurs sixty-five times; in the Pentateuch alone it occurs seven times. The Septuagint version of the Scriptures translates the word scheol by the Greek *hades*, the place which the Greeks assigned for the dwelling of the souls of the dead; only twice does the Septuagint translate the word θάνατος, death. Scheol is indeed a general term,—not designating specially the abode of the just or that of the unjust. Hence, even in the Apostles' Creed, we say of Christ that "He descended into hell," that is, into Limbo, where the souls of the just under the Old Dispensation were detained. When Jacob, according to the false report given to him, imagined that his son Joseph has been devoured by a wild beast, he exclaimed: "I will go down to my son into hell, (scheol) mourning." Not certainly into the hell of the wicked, since he and his son were just men. And on the other hand, it is written of Core and Abiron, who with their followers rebelled against Moses, "that the earth broke asunder under their feet, and opening her mouth, devoured them with their tents and all their substance. And they went down alive into hell"[1]—clearly the hell of the damned. But the Hebrew faith in the different states of the just and unjust in another world and the rewards that are there assigned to them is given at length in the fifth chapter of the Book of Wisdom.

In other books of the Old Testament, such as the Books of Kings, Job, the Psalter of King David, Ecclesiasticus, the Prophecy of Isaias, allusions are often made to the doctrine of the immortality of the soul, not of purpose, as if it were a matter of controversy, but incidentally, and, as it were, to unquestioned convictions that spring up naturally from a

[1] Numbers xvi. 31—33.

common, settled, national belief. Indeed, so popular and so absorbing, even for the Hebrew mind, was the doctrine of immortality, that some persons, in spite of all prohibitions, grossly exaggerated it and fell into superstition. The Israelites believed not only in the survival of the souls of the dead, but some among them by superstitious rites evoked and consulted them, and even made offerings to them as if they were adorable. This practice is expressly mentioned and condemned in the Book of Deuteronomy; it is also spoken of in Leviticus, in the Books of Kings, in the Prophecy of Isaias. Sinful, undoubtedly, as it was in itself, as being a superstition, the practice points directly to the faith in the soul's immortality; it was, indeed, a corruption of that faith, but even by its extravagance it speaks to us of the vividness with which men then believed in the future existence of souls.

The books from which I have just quoted antedate the Babylonian captivity, but, again, those that follow that date bear also the most ample testimony to the Hebrew belief in the immortality of the soul. In them all, through the ages, the same voice, in grave strong undertones, seems continually to repeat: "It is therefore a holy and wholesome thought to pray for the dead, that they may be loosed from sins."[1]

Now bear in mind that in the present argument I take those books merely for authentic history,—wishing only to ascertain in them what was the extent of the *consensus* of the human family in relation to future existence; and how it was that the Semitic

[1] II. Machabees xii. 46.

race in particular during its eventful history testified to the soul's immortality. Considered in time and place, the testimony given, as we have seen, was universal; belief in a future undying life seemed to be taken as a postulate of reason, and to live forever in the unseen world was held to be but the natural development of human life on earth. Say, if you like, that this belief sprang from a special tradition, which itself came from revelation, and then, I reply, this tradition, being in conformity with the nature of man, recommended itself to his reason and was accepted by it. Consequently, in either case, since the doctrine has been universally held by the human race, it must be inevitably true; the mind cannot be cheated of its object, and hence the universal subjective apprehension of immortality as a truth necessarily correlates its objective existence as a fact.

Intrinsically, or by its own nature, then, the soul is immortal; but a further inquiry is, whether it is also so extrinsically, or whether annihilation may not await it in another world, either by the power of the creature or by that of the creator.

Following the principle that the action of a being is a sure gauge of its nature, we have recognized that the human soul is an immaterial, a spiritual substance, that it has a spiritual agency independent of and superior to the body, and consequently has not, as the brute-sensitive soul, been educed by vital seminal action from the potency of matter. Being a distinctly spiritual substance, it could not have sprung from the changes or from the power which generation implies, since then it would have been corporeal; it could not have arisen from the purely spiritual, since then one spiritual substance would have generated another, a hypothesis which is directly in conflict with their nature. Neither of these hypotheses being admissible, it follows, first, that God Himself immediately creates the human soul and mediately, through natural generation, forms the human body; secondly, that from parents the human body comes immediately and is so conditioned that, by a requirement of its nature, it is to be informed by an animating soul. Thus parents become such, precisely, because of them is born a person, a child composed both of soul and body.[1] All this being premised, I say, that as the destructive power of the creature is proportioned to its productive capacity, the human soul cannot possibly be annihilated by any created being. No creature can create itself, consequently no creature can annihilate itself.

But if the creature cannot annihilate itself, it will be said that God can. To see the bearing of this objection, you will do well to remember that the power of God may be taken in a twofold sense, (1) either as implying its absolute nature,—or again, (2) its relation to creatures and to the wants which their condition supposes. In the former sense, of course, God could annihilate all creatures, since He would have only to withdraw from them His sustaining power, and instantly they would dwindle into nothingness. The proposition, thus considered,

---

[1] Homo sibi simile in specie generat, in quantum virtus seminis ejus dispositive operatur ad ultimam formam, ex qua homo speciem sortitur.—St. Thomas, "Summa contra Gentiles," lib. ii., cap. 89.

is most strictly true, but in our thesis it is beside the question. It is not what God could do in any possible hypothesis that we discuss, but what he will actually do as the Lord and Supreme Ruler of His creatures. Their corruptibility or incorruptibility depends *directly* on the properties of their nature, and not on the divine power. The soul, being in itself incorruptible will be sustained in existence according to divinely established law, and will have to live on forever, in spite of the dreams of pantheists or Buddhists. It will not be absorbed into the infinite, since this would be contrary to the very nature of the infinite; it will not vanish into Nirvana, since it is not self-destructive. The existence of his soul is not left to man's discretion. On the other hand, the absolute unity of the divine nature necessarily implies the most absolute harmony between the divine attributes. God cannot do what His wisdom and goodness forbid. He will not deny to the creature that which its nature requires, and undo that which He did by creation. In other words, He will not make mortal a soul which by nature he created immortal. Of this even all material nature seems to give us a warrant, as scientists teach that, whatever be the transformations of matter, not a particle of it is ever annihilated.

To be sure, to the pessimist non-existence seems better than existence; the extinction of the soul is for him the close of the evils as well as of the obligations of life. But divine justice cannot have it so. By its laws, crime, somewhere and somehow, must have its retribution and goodness its reward; if the wicked choose to live and die in their wickedness, justice requires that therefore they should pay the penalty; if, on the other hand, the good die virtuously, the same justice dictates that they should be rewarded. Whatever men do in this world to evade the payment of their dues to each other, they cannot cheat God, by any device whatever. "What things a man shall sow, those also shall he reap." Now you have only to look out into the world to see how unevenly justice seems to hold the scales. As a rule, virtue suffers and is ignored, the poor are despised and cast aside, while, on the contrary, vice often prospers and is not infrequently enthroned in power. Through society every-where there runs the same unevenness of rewards and penalties, the same imperfect system of unrequited goodness. Take away the full future supplement of justice beyond the grave, or suppose for a moment that there is no real personal immortality, and justice itself will have lost its character, injustice will have recoiled on God, and of all men the virtuous will be the most miserable. Reason revolts against such conclusions and points them out as some of those vain excuses with which vicious persons sometimes flatter themselves. Not to be would to them be better than to be, if they could have it so.

"And they cannot. "But the just shall live for ever, and their reward is with the Lord, and the care of them with the Most High." But "the wicked," writes the prophet Job, "whose houses are secure and peaceable," and who "spend their days in wealth, in a moment they go down to hell."

CHAPTER IX.

Conscience as a Witness to God.[1]

[According to agreement and by invitation, the gentlemen on the day appointed met, shortly after ten o'clock, at the mansion of Mr. Western, on the heights above New Brighton, Staten Island. During the morning a thick mist hung over the bay, shutting out from sight both earth and sky. But as the sun ascended the heavens, objects gradually came out to view, until the harbor with its crowded shipping lay before them, in all its picturesqueness. From the elevated site occupied by Mr. Western's residence the naked eye could easily take in some of the general features of New York City; on the left, it could discern the outlines of the North River almost as far as Weehawken, and on the right, those of the Sound, up to the Narrows. Along the eastern gable of the mansion ran a large veranda, shaded by a profusion of convolvulus and honeysuckle, and there it was that the party decided to hold their symposium and to hear Mr. Netterville.]

"THE study of man's body, of his senses in their adaptation to their objects, and of his organs in their use, is ground sufficient to the minds of many

---

[1] Some writers consider the proof from the moral law as only supplementary to the other arguments given for the existence of God.

persons for the proof of theism. It is absurd to suppose that blind forces, without any pre-ordaining intelligent power, could give to the human hand its latent capacities, to the human voice its flexibility and sweetness of tone, or to the ear its delicacy of structure and sensitiveness to sound. These speak to the reflective mind of God. Studying man in the constitution of his moral nature, or in the extent and force of duty under which he lives as a moral agent, one reaches God, however, more quickly perhaps and with more vividness than by examining the anatomy of the human frame. It has been proved that in the moral world in which we live God reveals His attributes in those fundamental distinctions that essentially separate the good from the bad, as well as from the necessity of an object that will completely answer to the tendency of the human faculties for the true and the good.

"To-day I purpose to survey,—conscience being my guide,—the moral kingdom of the soul, in search of Him who founded it and governs it. Throughout that kingdom, as signs from which the nature of its constitution can be inferred, are found general postulates of equity as resulting from right reason in its relation to the morally good or morally evil. Wherever one looks in that kingdom, he finds it proclaimed, that justice, modesty, temperance, etc., are in themselves laudable, and that to worship the Deity is of its very nature a commendable act. In these general moral judgments of reason the moral world without man and the moral world within him commingle, as it were, and he comes to know the great outlines of that world. He knows the good and the bad as they objectively exist, and that as such they are not of his making. Good or evil, to be man's own, must be his by his very acts; he is personally accountable only for what, directly or indirectly, he personally does.

"But that which holds together the moral kingdom of the soul and runs through all its grades, is law. This appears in the aptitude which men have for performing acts and for reaching ends peculiar to their nature, as well as in those rational principles by which they duly proportion means to ends and establish order in their being. Passively considered, law, indeed, is found to exist, though differently, in all creatures. In rational beings, it, as a product of reason, is said properly to exist as law, since it is in keeping with their nature; in all other creatures, animate and inanimate, it is only by a certain analogy that it is said to reign. All nature, therefore, being measured and bound by law, proclaims that there must be One who with supreme wisdom has measured and bound it, and has thus made His creatures to be sharers of His own eternal law. Of this law the traces are most noticeable in man; they are of course only limited, since he is finite, but are so vivid in their expressiveness that the mind, by its innate power, immediately feels their force. By them man directly perceives what becomes the dignity of his nature and the end of life, and on the other hand, what is contrary to both. By them he forthwith recognizes that within him, in the form of law, is a certain power that imposes on him an obligation urging him to do good and forbidding him to do evil. This law, wound up with man's nature, is unchangeable and universal, and will hold him inevitably in its embrace, through life, under all circumstances, and in every condition. Laws that spring from education, or custom, or human legislation change, but this inborn law of man's nature never changes. 'Est hæc non scripta sed nata lex.' On a scroll of Egyptian papyrus or on a baked brick of ancient Babylon, law will survive as a dead letter, a relic of antiquity, but the law written on the heart has given to it a living tongue that proclaims its binding force and will not be silenced by any power. Now this law, so definite in its commands and prohibitions, unmistakably points to Him who made it and wrote it in indelible characters on the human heart. When the dead inscriptions on brick, by the admission of all, speak of a lawgiver, a living rational dictate, incorporating in itself the great principles of natural equity, ought surely to be accepted as bearing evident testimony to the existence of its Author.

"'God,' writes Father Kleutgen, 'makes Himself felt within us by His moral law, as an august power to which we are subject.'

"The moral kingdom of the soul, then, is indestructible because its fundamental law is unchangeable. This, the natural law, though it can be violated by man, and its teaching falsely interpreted, can never be altogether eradicated. On it, human legislation, to be just, must be founded, and the duties of life, to be obligatory, must be in conformity with its principles.[1]

[1] "It (the natural law) is found in Pagan writers connected, no doubt, with Pagan systems of religion, but it is independent of them and above them, and has been accepted by the Christian world as the outcome of right reason, and as a proof that God never left the nations without evidence of Himself and of His eternal law.

"The history of the world shows us that usurpation and tyranny, whether political or sectarian, always fosters rigidity of doctrine, and as often as the modesty of nature has been so outraged, history bears witness to a reaction into the foulest libertinism."[1]

"Of that moral realm, resting immovably on law, and built upon it, the natural guardian is conscience. According to St. Thomas, conscience is a dictate of reason,—the proximate rule of human actions, the eternal law being their remote rule. In itself, the natural law is universal in its bearing, and does not contemplate this or that special case, but conscience applies the law to all particular actions. It is their immediate measure, not only in the present, but in the future and in the past. It does not make the law, but is its executive; it specifies, interprets, or applies it. In its practical working, therefore, conscience runs on two judgments; the one by which it decides that in a certain sphere of action a definite law exists; the second, by which it dictates that this law binds in this or that instance, and ought to be followed. The former judgment can be erroneous; reason, from want of due reflection, or under the influence of prejudice or passion, can take the false to be its rule of action or the rule of life, and then the latter judg-

---

The early Fathers of the Church wisely accepted this testimony of Pagan philosophy, but they never admitted that they needed it to complete their own conception of the natural law. This they found clearly expressed in the Old Testament before Greek philosophy existed; but as the law was given by nature, and not by revelation (strictly understood), they explained it by human reasoning and in the words of the Greek philosophers, and cleared it of such Pagan taints as it had got mixed up with. Nothing was better understood or more clearly delineated in the earliest Christian philosophy than the law of nature, and so it has continued without the slightest alteration to the present day, not in stagnation, but in ever vigorous application to the constantly altering circumstances of human actions."—"Dishonest Criticism," by James Jones, S. J., p. 19.

[1] Ibidem, p. 20.

ment will be radically tainted by the error of the former. This error may be indeed removable, and then man's actions consequent on it will be imputable to him; or the error may be insuperable for the time being, bringing no guilt to him who follows it in good faith. But in either case, the actual dictate of man's conscience is to be his rule of action for the time. Sometimes, from want of due formation, or from the strain of false maxims, conscience will be led astray; sometimes, also, overweighted by mere worldly teaching, it will almost have lost its living fibre; or again, through the sway of passion, it will be overruled by the will, and in these conditions, having lost its hold of the rudder of life, will be the sport of impulse or fancy. Yet, though almost dethroned as a teacher, it does not fail to make itself felt, and declares vice to be vice and virtue to be virtue.

"In the adoption, therefore, of erroneous views and in living up to them in practice, it is not conscience strictly defined, that is at fault, but principle; conscience only sorts for use, or applies to action, what has been presented to it by the mind. Let expediency, or inclination, or false doctrine be adopted as a rule of life, and the function of conscience becomes distorted. The law which it measures to action is false, and the principle which it interprets is baseless. Thus the irreligious, the criminal, the trivial, even the unnatural, can, by man's perversity, be made by him the materials for action, on which conscience has to work. He does not care to inquire on what that conscience rests, or how it has been formed, whether it be grounded on passion or prejudice, but holding rather to self-will and to the side which he has taken, he will suffer, perhaps die, for his passion. Men will call him a martyr, forgetting that it is the cause and not the mere dying that makes the martyr. Manicheans and Cathari of medieval times, adopting as their laws of living unnatural, anti-Christian doctrines, were burnt at the stake by the state-power. Were they, therefore, martyrs? They professed to follow the dictates of conscience, but that conscience was seared all over by false principles and corrupt practices. Before Brutus killed Cæsar, he tried, no doubt, to justify himself to himself, and before Nero caused his mother to be assassinated, he strove to make his inhuman, monstrous instincts minister to his act. I have dwelt at some length on this point, in order that it may appear that the abuse of conscience no more invalidates the proof drawn from it for our thesis, than the abuse of reason disproves the teaching of reason.

"From what has been said and, indeed, from the constant experience of every one, it is evident that in the moral kingdom of the soul conscience is witnessing to law since it is witnessing to obligations. In these silent judgments of the mind on the lawfulness or unlawfulness of actions there is continually implied a recognition of a superintending power which binds us and which, objectively considered, can be no other than God. Reason cannot impose an obligation on man, since it is of him and not his superior. To impose an obligation, reason and all human legislation teach, implies authority and jurisdiction in him who imposes it, or it implies a distinction between the subject and the ruler, between the lawgiver and the governed. Individuals can impose precepts on themselves for certain ends and in certain spheres of duty, but they can no more frame a universal law for reason, such as the natural law is, than they can make a law for the ruling of the planets. Obligation that follows man every-where, that holds him to what is naturally repugnant to him, that forbids him pleasure or the following of inclination, that has its monitor in conscience for reproving or directing, such obligation is surely, as every one knows, not of man's making. Uphold that it is, and then man can undo what he once did, he can pull down the moral kingdom within him, and reduce the whole moral world to a state of hopeless anarchy. 'Reason, therefore, is for us not a principle for creating obligation, but for recognizing it, and hence cannot be looked on in any other light than as a herald, which speaks to us in the name of the Author of nature, and by means of which the Author of nature promulgates to us His orders.... Since, as I have said, the judgment which orders or forbids anything implies thereby the idea of a certain superior, whom if we disobey we contemn his authority. Thence springs that moral necessity, arising from the obligation of law, and consisting properly in this, that man cannot resist the rule of law without contemning, not only the order of reason dictated by divine wisdom, but also without transgressing the will of a supreme legislator.'[1]

"Conscience, then, though as a dictate of reason it is actually to be followed, does not on that account

[1] Liberatore, "Institutiones Ethicæ," pp. 91-92.

make the false principle on which it is grounded true, nor take out of false doctrine its evil, or out of crime its wickedness. In this discussion there is question of conscience informed by natural law. But when conscience receives the light of faith and is strengthened by grace and charity, it comes to have a broader and a more intimate knowledge of God's law, realizes His Presence more keenly, and has a deeper feeling and conviction of the nature of right and wrong. The Christian conscience is a new witness and a new power for the natural conscience. It elevates, directs, and enlightens it, enables it to know better, both God and the soul, and points out distinctly the way of living that leads to eternal happiness.

"As the vindicator of law, natural conscience (since it is of it I speak) points more directly still to Him by whose authority it has a voice.[1] Under this aspect it is especially imperative, since it is thus that it sensibly approves or disapproves conduct. It actually summons the sinner before his Lord to answer for his guilt. In secret, when no mortal eye is on him, shame and confusion cover him, should he have lapsed into some immorality. He blushes. At what? Man does not blush at his shadow, or before a tree, or a horse, or a stone. The sense of shame implies the consciousness of the presence of a person; it is the sense which the presence of a parent begets in the child for its wrong doing. Thus, though the sinner's act be in itself pleasurable, he feels distress of heart, and self-reproach, and a certain fretting of soul, because he is conscious, he

[1] See Cardinal Newman's "Argument," ch. 10.

does not know how, that the eye of God is on him, that it has seen his sin and noted it for judgment. Shame is one of these furies that pursue the sinner, and fear is another; even when his sin is a secret one, unknown to the world, fear frequently pierces his conscience with a certain apprehension of impending evil. He seems to live sensibly under a threat of penalties, and though he has the secret for himself, he can scarcely keep it. 'Murder will out,' is a saying that bears witness, not only to a fact, but also to a truth. The truth is the recognition of the Supreme Judge who has seen the murder,—and who recalls the remembrance of the words, 'the voice of thy brother's blood cries to Me from the earth.' The fear of the murderer arises from the dictate of his conscience, which tells him that he has done evil, that he has violated the law of an all-seeing and all-just Judge, to whom he owes obedience and to whom he is responsible. Do what he may, he can scarcely shake off the feeling that suggests to him that the curse that fell on the first murderer has not seemingly died with him. Those who have followed his example and have shed human blood, have, as history teaches, something like the isolation of Cain around them; they seem to live—'hidden from the face of the Lord.' What has been just said of the murderer is in part true also of every grievous sinner. He is often haunted by a dread of some coming calamity; and of him it has been written, —'the wicked flee when no one pursues.' 'Then why does he flee?' asks Cardinal Newman; 'whence his terror? who is it that he sees in solitude, in darkness, in the hidden chambers of his heart? If the cause of these emotions does not belong to this visible world, the object to which his perception is directed must be supernatural and divine; and thus the phenomena of conscience as a dictate avail to impress the imagination with a picture of the Supreme Governor, a Judge holy, just, powerful, all-seeing, retributive, and is the creative principle of religion, as the moral sense is the principle of ethics.'

"A fiercer fury still for the guilty soul is remorse. It sets the sinner, as it were, against himself, tortures him and demeans him in his own eyes, and fills his soul with a bitterness worse than that of gall. Do what the unrepenting sinner may, he can never altogether lay that remorse in the dark; it haunts him, and amid the gaieties and revelries of life frequently does not leave him. It is the worm that never dies. How are we to account for this working of remorse, this shrinking of man from himself, this wringing of the conscience? Remorse springs from self-reproach, and this again from wrong doing. An offence offered to a friend will recoil on the heart of the offender. He will feel his soul immediately ruffled, will feel the sting of remorse, and will be urged to repair the injury done. After a like manner, the sinner is pressed to make reparation to God. For his sin, unknown perhaps to all save himself, he is free from the reproach of his fellow-men, and yet, no sooner has he committed it, than an eye seems to glare upon him, and conscience seems to grapple with him and force him to appear before a tribunal for judgment. What else is this but a sanction of law now violated as well as a summons to repentance for revolt against the will of an all-just God. In this case, therefore, remorse evidently correlates a Supreme Being, to whom the sinner feels himself responsible. 'Pride may cloud and darken our mind; sensuality may blunt our sensibilities; a long neglect of God may harden us against the powers of conscience; but its light cannot be extinguished. The diamond point is there; the shock of sudden visitation may bare the soul to its light and sting once more; or, if death comes quicker than repentance, then drops the veil, then vanishes the pride, then stands the soul face to face before the conscience, with its dark record as her witness before the justice of God.'"

As Mr. Netterville finished, he remarked, that he reserved for the discussion other notes that he had made on the subject.

"With the general tone of the dissertation just read," said Mr. Clayburne, "I have been pleased, but there were some points in it which seemed to me not to come out conclusively enough. I am at a loss to see how, with so many exceptions to it, the natural law of right and wrong can be said to be universal, which, however, it should be, were it written on the heart."

"I think, sir," answered Mr. Netterville, "it is with nations or tribes, in point of morals, pretty much what it is with individuals. A man, by self-will, can warp his moral sense, and by passion, or prejudice, or custom, create for himself a false standard of moral action in a certain line or degree. Still, with all that, he retains the power of perceiving what is essentially right or wrong. People may differ, as

Sir James Mackintosh suggests, as to what is right or wrong, but all the while, they believe that there is something right and something wrong. They have a rule of morality given to them, but they err in the application of it. This truth has been strikingly confirmed by travellers. Of one of the most degraded tribes of Africa, Livingstone writes —'after long observation, I came to the conclusion that they are just such a strange mixture of good and evil as men are every-where else.' What Livingstone has said about these African tribes has been said, in different ways, by other travellers, of savages, wherever met with. They have all been found, though indulging often in some immoral practices, to possess a clear perception of right and wrong. In regard to pagan civilized nations, the moral principles taught by their legislators and accepted by their respective peoples prove, I think, even in spite of their most fatal errors, that unity of the fundamental principles of morality exists among them. 'The sacred books of the East,' along with much that is false, trivial, and foolish, contain many maxims of pure moral teaching. Among European peoples and their descendants through the world, it is not denied that there exists a clear perception of what is morally right or wrong. Every-where, and by men of every condition of life, actions are held to be good which have for their ends justice, or gratitude, or temperance, or fidelity to promises; while, on the contrary, actions opposed to those ends are invariably held to be bad. That is, men cognize the matter of the natural law, though, from want of culture of their moral nature, they may not be able to define for themselves, in all cases, that law as a rule of right and wrong."

"From what has just been said," rejoined Mr. Clayburne, "I infer that after all it is not the law written on the heart which man perceives, but something of which he has a sense much in the way that he has a sense of the beautiful. His actions will be good or bad, not because they are forbidden by law, but because he happens to like or dislike them; now if that be so, what becomes of the argument for theism, which has been constructed from conscience."

"Excuse me, sir," said Mr. Netterville, "you seem to have misapprehended my meaning. We perceive directly, I maintain, that such or such an action is good or bad as the case may be, that, for instance, an act of treachery towards a benefactor is wrong, and that an act of charity towards the poor is virtuous. This intuition of the virtuous or the wrong in itself, or of the approved or disapproved, conveys to us the notion of the moral order, and, furthermore, that some actions are ordained and others forbidden. From these the mind necessarily gathers the idea of law, and from the law naturally ascends to a lawgiver. I say, however, this mental process is naturally wound into the frame of our minds, and is not derived from observation. 'The wrong' and 'the virtuous' are outside the range of phenomenal experience, but in actions are apprehended by the mind as self-evident moral truths as infallibly as are mathematical truths. I perceive as clearly that an act of hatred of God is wrong as I do that the whole is greater than its part. In the intuition, then, of primary, fundamental moral truths I have a knowledge, though vague and obscure, of God; but by inference I make that knowledge distinct and conclusive.

"It is not then, sir, the law as such that I immediately perceive in my cognition of moral truths, but the matter of the law, and consequently I hold that, as far as the natural law is concerned, acts are not objectively good or bad, precisely because they have been ordained or forbidden, but because they are good or bad in themselves. 'The perception of the morally good or morally bad is anterior to the perception of the law, though that perception is ultimately resolvable into that of the will of the Almighty,' while moral action, which implies obligation and sanction, is resolvable into the recognition of the authority of Him, as Supreme Ruler and Judge. Sin is sin because forbidden by law."

Mr. Clayburne having nodded assent to the answer just given, Mr. Ferguson interposed, saying, "Would it not seem, sir, that the changes recorded of morals from age to age prove that morality has not an absolute but a relative value, and that 'expediency' rather than any 'absolute morality' is the basis of human actions. The rights of conscience to-day are much in advance of what they had been in the past, and morality has come to be considered to be progressive, not stationary."

"I said, sir, in my introductory essay," answered Mr. Netterville, "that the first principles of morals remain always the same, that the intrinsically 'wrong' is always 'wrong' and the intrinsically 'right' always 'right,' or that the rational intuition of every one reveals to him irresistibly the objective law of 'absolute morality.' To this fact the conscience of each one bears testimony. But though the first great moral principles remain the same, the application of them varies with the condition of men and the circumstances of the age. Honesty in our dealings with the neighbor remains ever the same moral principle, but the forms of contract through which that honesty is pledged are in many instances not now what they had been. Moral science has also light cast on moral action by the development of other sciences, of physiology, for instance, and political economy, and has been enabled to solve questions which formerly it could scarcely have reached. In its manifold application, therefore, and in the consequences drawn from its teaching, morality, though in its first principle always the same, may be well said to be progressive and not stationary.

"But in regard to these rights, which, it has been said, conscience has acquired, I confess to a little confusion. In the proper sense of the word, I would remark that it is only persons that have or acquire rights; only by a figure of speech can mental faculties be said to possess them. The natural right, or rather function, of conscience is to interpret law for the occasion, to dictate, to approve, or disapprove. Now, I conceive that in this respect it will be granted, that conscience has gained no rights; it is exactly to-day what it was in the days of Cain. Its proper sphere of action as a dictate of reason lies within the bounds of the law and is limited, informed, and enlivened by it. Hence it may not dictate what it wists, since its field of duty is the lawful. No man, then, has a right to do wrong, since might is not right, neither has he a right to wish or to propose what is wrong. And if it be asserted that God speaks to man through his conscience, it should not be forgotten that many do not listen to Him ;—by the principles which they adopt or by the prejudices or passions which they follow, or by the beliefs which they have embraced, it is they themselves who, from the evil that is in them, speak to their own consciences. By them, 'conscience is taken to be a license to believe what they please and to do what they like.'

"In his letter to the Duke of Norfolk, Cardinal Newman writes,—' when men advocate the rights of conscience, they in no sense mean the rights of the Creator, nor the duty to Him, in thought and deed, of the creature; but the right of thinking, speaking, writing, and acting according to their judgment or their humor, without any thought of God at all. They do not even pretend to go by any moral rule, but they demand what they think is an Englishman's prerogative, to be his own master in all things, and to profess what he pleases, asking no one's leave, and accounting priest or preacher, speaker or writer, unutterably impertinent, who dares to say a word against his going to perdition, if he like it, in his own way. Conscience has rights because it has duties; but in this age, with a large portion of the public, it is the very right and freedom of conscience to dispense with conscience, to ignore a lawgiver and judge, to be independent of unseen obligations. It becomes a license to take up any or no religion, to take up this or that and let it go again, to go to church, to go to chapel, to boast of being above all religions and to be an impartial critic of each of them. Conscience is a stern monitor; but in this century, it has been superseded by a counterfeit, which the eighteen centuries prior to it never heard of, and could not have mistaken for it if they had. It is the right of self-will.'"

"I did not imagine," replied Mr. Ferguson, "that the natural conscience is different in our days from what it has ever been; my contention is that in relation to external authority it has now rights recognized as such which it formerly had not."

"I am glad to learn," continued Mr. Netterville, "that the gentleman disclaims the idea that modern times have created a new conscience, and I presume he would also disallow that they have created a new morality. Now I admit that wide-spread error has in those few past ages necessitated a new civil polity, by which freedom of worship is allowed by states. The Catholic colony of Maryland under Lord Baltimore was the first to inaugurate this polity. But I am at a loss to see how this liberty of profession founds any innate right for conscience; it enlarges, indeed, in civil life man's sphere of action, but as to conscience in the soul, it leaves it just as it was. This new polity does not make error truth, nor badness goodness; it does not justify a false conscience, nor does it create a right one; as always before, man's conscience remains in his own keeping. For its condition he is accountable to his Maker; his good faith in unconscious error will make acts resulting from it excusable, but all the while good faith is only a temporary expedient that exempts an action from guilt, and not a principle that ever remains a rule of right conduct. Error in itself is always error; men can extol their freedom under this new liberty, but we all know that men are truly free, only ' with the truth with which Christ has made us free.' "—" Still," rejoined Mr. Ferguson, " you will admit that there is an advance in this, namely, that men's consciences were in other times formed for them, whereas now they are formed by themselves; in other words, the individual conscience has taken the place of the ' corporate conscience.' "

" I am aware, sir," said Mr. Netterville, " that the words ' corporate conscience,' have been used, ignorantly and, I will add, in mockery of truth. But, perhaps, I shall best solve the difficulty proposed by some familiar illustrations. Let me then suppose that, in a complicated state of things, A. finds it more difficult to know his duty than to do it: he appeals to B., who is perfectly conversant with the state of things and knows, with the fulness of unerring knowledge, its religious and moral aspect. As he has divine authentic credentials for the commission which he exercises as a teacher, he secures the confidence of A. and marks out for him his line of duty with infallible authority; he does not, remember, speak as a mere human agent, but as one instructed and delegated by God. A., satisfied with the authenticity of the credentials presented and with the clear, definite tone of the teaching of B., becomes settled in his convictions, and in the light shed upon his mind sees clearly his duty, while his conscience bids him to fulfil it. His decision proceeding, as it does, from an unfaltering consciousness, his act is most intimately his own; and thus his conscience in the case, resting on infallible authority, elicits an act which embodies the deepest conviction and is most intensely personal. The conscience thus formed, built upon divine truth and on the divine appointment, will stand any trial to which it may be subjected; it will support a man, as we learn from history, when his flesh is being roasted by a slow fire, or when, as the case may be, he is led out to be hanged or crucified.

"On the other hand, let me suppose the case of C., who has the same difficulty in regard to his duty as A. He goes to his friend D. to be directed by him. D. has his own peculiar views on religious and moral problems. These views may or may not be true. He professes to have no authentic guaranty that they are true, except his own private judgment. But such as they are, he gives them to C., who hesitates and claims that, after all, his own judgment may be as reliable as his friend's. D., however, insists and urges the views of the denomination to which he belongs. Whereupon C. asks whether it has, for its teaching, credentials other than human, and upon being answered in the negative, overrules the argument of D. as being a false plea. He takes a decision, however, but with some hesitation; his soul, not having deep convictions on the subject, is not wholly in his action, and his conscience being somehow in suspense, is replaced, as it were, by some act of self-will, formed out of the demands of duty, and of doubts about the same. His act is a personal one, to be sure, but is not based on a secure, unfaltering conscience."

"This illustration shows, if I mistake not, that the securer the convictions are, the better fitted is conscience to judge of the lawfulness or unlawfulness of an act—a function which is the main point in this controversy."

"But let me suppose," added Mr. Ferguson, "that C., by due examination, masters knowledge enough to see wherein his duty lies; then his act will be more personal than that of A."

"Then you change the case," said Mr. Netterville;—"and still, even in the new hypothesis, C's act is not more personal than that of A. In the premises there is this difference between them, that the latter is directed by truth, the former by opinion; but the ultimate practical judgment as to what is to be actually done or omitted is in the power of each."

"It looks to me," suggested Mr. Neufchatel, "as if the conclusion arrived at upturns the whole argument. The drift of the reasoning, as I took it, was based on the fact of man's sufficiency for himself; out of his 'inner consciousness,' it was supposed that he could develop morality; in his heart he could read the law and his duties to the Creator. But now we are told he cannot do so, that he wants a tutor from without to direct him, and that apart from such aid he cannot fulfil his destiny and reach happiness."

"Among the fallacies enumerated by Jeremy Bentham," answered Mr. Netterville, "is this one,—'The Fallacy of Distrust,' or 'What is at the Bottom.' This fallacy supposes that one introduces an argument in order to refute it and adopt another project. This is what the gentleman seems to suppose that I have done. I have asserted simply man's power to read and observe the moral law, and I am told that I do away with it by calling in another to aid him in difficult circumstances to read and observe it. Absolutely speaking, man has the bare power of fulfilling the natural law; but taking him as he is,--morally, he will not do so; he will often read it wrongly and through passion, prejudice, or ignorance,--will distort, or curtail, or misinterpret it. In proof of this, it is not necessary to go back to prehistoric times; the record of every day shows how many there are who read the moral law inversely, or doubt of its meaning, and make out that to be the law which through inclination or bias they fancy it to be. Is not this too largely the record of the past? Seeing the hesitancy of the human mind as well as the faltering of the human will, and in view of man's destiny for supernatural blessedness, God from the very beginning elevated and confirmed the moral order of things. By revelation He enlarged on what He had written on the human heart, and thus the traditions of the new words of the law were taken by men into every country, were embodied in the forms of thought and language of every people. In the course of ages, that those traditions might be preserved with greater definiteness, the inspired legislator Moses wrote them out, added to them new revelations, and thus formed a code of laws for the government of the Jewish people. To the divine revelation, prophets, also inspired of heaven, added much, until at length, in the fulness of time, the Son of God Himself became man and dwelt with men. He confirmed the moral code, developed it, and defined it, and made it by His own teaching to be a new Law, a new Dispensation. That this may be preserved pure in all its bearings, He entrusted it to the keeping of the Church established by Him."

As no exception was taken to this answer, the conversation turned on the motives of moral action. After some remarks from many gentlemen, a debate arose between Messrs. Randolph, and Mattison, on pleasure, as an end of human conduct. The latter insisted that pleasure is the great spring of human acts, and that on it men base their sense of duty. Mr. Randolph argued that this supposed that every duty is of a pleasurable nature, a supposition which, to say the least, is very questionable. He then instanced the case of two men who have exactly the same duty to perform; the one performs it with great ease, the other at the cost of much self-sacrifice. By all impartial men, the act of the latter will be judged more virtuous than that of the former, inasmuch as there is more self-denial in it; that is, the absence of pleasure makes his act more virtuous. " Would you not grant so much?" asked Mr. Randolph.—"I am not called upon, sir, to solve puzzles," was Mr. Mattison's reply—"Davus sum, non Œdipus;" and he then went on to explain at some length the philosophy of pleasure. When he had finished, Mr. Randolph, in a somewhat vehement tone, remarked, "If I understand the gentleman rightly, he tells us that we are all voluptuaries, though we do not mean it; that we are Epicureans, though we think we live as Stoics."

"There is a feature in the exposition given," said Mr. Walters, "which does not come out clearly enough to me. The morality of human acts, it has been said, is ultimately resolvable into the eternal

Law of God, while it has been affirmed that the same morality is also unchangeable. Now, since all law depends on the will of the lawgiver, I cannot see why God, if He so willed it, could not change the morality of an act and make that lawful which before was unlawful. Human law frequently changes, why could not the divine law do the same?"

"There is this essential difference," answered Mr. Netterville, "between the purely human and eternal law, that the human law regards only the external acts, while the eternal law in God, or its counterpart, the natural law in man, relates not only to what is external in human acts, but much more to what is internal in them. The reason of the distinction between the goodness and badness of things ordered or forbidden by the natural law comes not immediately from the ordering of the divine will, but from their agreement or disagreement with the order of things as apprehended by man in the light of God's reason, which is the eternal law. Logically, therefore, the intrinsic, objective morality of actions in their relation to divine wisdom precedes that which they have from their relation to the divine will commanding or prohibiting them, or, within the sphere of the natural law, the good is commanded because it is good, and the evil is forbidden because it is evil."

"But," resumed Mr. Walters, "we have been told that God can change or suspend the laws of nature,—why then cannot He change the laws of morals?"

"The plain reason is," answered Mr. Netterville, "that physical laws are not connected with the eternal essence of things, whereas the essential laws of morals are. The former relate only to a passing or contingent order, the latter to one that is unchangeable and necessarily connected with divine wisdom. This order cannot be changed, because God cannot be unjust; He cannot undo the ordinance of his own divine counsel; He cannot make the essentially bad, good; nor the essentially good, bad. 'God continueth faithful,' says St. Paul, 'He cannot deny Himself.' "[1]

"I candidly acknowledge," said Mr. Babbington, "that much that has been said in this present session is unintelligible to me. In the modern school of ethical science, I have learned that the notions of good and bad which men have are but 'the inherited effects of continued experiences;' that, 'conscience is a hoarded fund of traditionary pressures of utility.' What our ancestors liked or disliked was woven into their nature and has thus, through the medium of various generations, been transmitted to us as qualities affecting our emotional faculties; what is called conscience is only a sense of the agreeable or disagreeable, a sort of 'twist' in our nature, an inheritance of the sensations of the pains and pleasures

---

[1] II. Tim. ii. 13.

"Præcepta ipsa decalogi quantum ad rationem justitiæ quam continent immutabilia sunt; sed quantum ad aliquam determinationem per applicationem ad singulares actus (ut scilicet hoc vel illud sit homicidium, furtum, vel adulterium, aut non) hoc quidem est mutabile quandoque sola auctoritate divina, in his scilicet quæ a solo Deo sunt instituta, sicut in matrimonio et in aliis hujus modi; quandoque etiam auctoritate humana, sicut in his quæ sunt commissa hominum jurisdictioni; quantum enim ad hoc homines gerunt vicem Dei, non autem quantum ad omnia."—S. Thomas, "Sum. Theol.," Ia 2ae, q. 100, a. 8.

"Dicendum est, proprie loquendo non dispensare Deum in aliquo præcepto naturali, sed mature materiam ejus, vel circumstantias sine quibus præceptum ipsum naturale non obligat ex se et absque dispensatione."—Suarez, "De Legibus," l. ii., ch. 15.

of life. As we have a hereditary sense of seeing, so have we a hereditary conscience of judging."

He had hardly finished speaking, when Mr. Maxwell said, "To the blind, sir, everything is dark; a thing may be unintelligible not only because of the nature of the object, but also by a defect in the organ of understanding. Hereditary conscience, sir, hereditary nonsense, sir." These words were uttered with a harshness of tone which shocked all. Mr. Maxwell immediately felt it, and after a moment's pause, turning to Mr. Babbington, said:—"I beg you to pardon, sir, my rude manner and my harsh words; it was not so much your reflections as my own sense of self-reproach that prompted them. Ten of the most precious years of life I have spent in the branch-schools of that institution of which you have spoken. I accepted their theories as the latest expression of truth and as the guide of my opinions. Lately, since I have had the good fortune of falling in with my friends here, I have carefully reviewed the data of those opinions. Putting aside the authority of my masters and trusting to my own common sense and to the help derived from the writings of the greatest intellects, I have found that my knowledge, such as it was, was composed, for the most part, only of 'such stuff as dreams are made of.' This, sir, is the reason, when I look into the past, why I can scarcely have patience with myself. You will excuse me, I hope, gentlemen, for this personal explanation. In regard to the views which you have put forward on conscience, I have found that one's own sense of duty is the best refutation of them. That sense distinctly teaches that the acts of conscience are supremely personal, and that they make the doer of them to feel his responsibility for them. Conscience, without any reference to ancestral traditions, threatens, or blesses, or reproves; it is of the soul,—a judgment on what is actually lawful or unlawful, not an instinct, as everybody knows, nor a physical sense, nor a 'twist' in our nature. This judgment, then, is what all conscientious men call conscience. Instinct is a tendency of nature, but conscience is the conclusion of a syllogism, whose major is the statement of a general principle, and whose minor is the enunciation of a special fact. Make conscience to be only 'the tribal judgment,' as Professor Clifford does, and you do away with a personal conscience altogether, and you put the reason for the grounding of conscience for the very dictate of conscience itself. It has been said by Cardinal Newman that conscience is not only a king, but a prophet and a priest likewise. 'Now, according to Clifford's theory (and here Mr. Maxwell read from his note-book,) conscience must be powerless as a king, and an impostor as a priest and a prophet. All its influence is, in fact, founded on a false prestige; and what Clifford and his school have fondly and foolishly imagined is that they can destroy the prestige and yet retain the power. They imagine they can remove the fulcrum and yet employ the lever.'

"I have found that the 'unknowable' of Mr. Spencer is the most knowable of all beings; that He is the 'Ultimate Reality,' 'the Father Almighty,' that He is eternal, infinite, the Source 'from which all things proceed.' By the logic of nature all things, animate and inanimate, lead up to Him;—my own mind and will, the order and design around me, the different modes of physical life, tell me that mind, and purpose, and life must be predicted of the cause from which they come.

"I have also discovered that evolution, about which I had read so much, in any true rational sense, so far from dispensing with God, necessarily supposes His existence. Evolution, which is simply a process of development of things that are, I foolishly took to be the first cause of those things, to be the law of their introduction, and not the law of their conservation, as it professes to be. I had supposed also that evolution is demonstratively true, but in the chain of proof I found that many links were wanting; and from Mr. Darwin himself I learned 'that our ignorance of the laws of variations is profound.' To my dismay, I found that on this subject also my teachers contradict themselves and each other. Mr. Huxley, a great admirer of Mr. Darwin, maintains in his Lay Sermon 'On Persistent Types of Life,' that paleontology furnishes no evidence of 'stages of promotion from lower to higher forms of life, and that it is not absolutely proven that any species has been originated by selection, whether natural or artificial.' But what disgusted me in my researches was the inconsistency of my teachers. They seemed to me to be in constant distress for truth, casting out for it now here and now there, and fancying that they had found it, because they struck on something that answered to their wishes. On fundamental questions I found them in conflict with one another, differing as to what is the very basis of knowledge, or what is its nature or object. Out of this jungle of thoughts and words I have, thank God, been rescued; and I now feel, by your co-operation, gentlemen, that I stand on the firm basis of truth.

"I should not, however, be true to myself nor explicit enough to you, did I not communicate to you some misgivings that still press on me. I have come out of Egypt, it is true, but I feel that I am not yet beyond the borders of the Philistines. I believe in God and know Him; I am conscious that I owe Him the homage of my whole being. His attributes lead me to suppose that He made a revelation of His will to men, and that He has done so, I have learned from authentic historical sources. But herein lies my difficulty. Who shall tell me with no faltering voice what that revelation is, who shall interpret it for me infallibly and guard me from error, both in faith and morals? I cannot trust myself, since my reason cannot reach truths that are beyond its range; and though my vision is bounded by the horizon, there is, I am conscious, a land beyond it which it behooves me at all costs to gain. Who shall be an unerring guide for me? My fellow-men are as fallible as I myself; and if the blind lead the blind, you are aware of the consequences."

There was something so pathetic in the utterance of those words, something that spoke so forcibly of the distress of a soul in its search for truth, that, swayed by a certain feeling of respect, all for a few moments remained silent. At length Mr. Jennings said,—"Mr. Maxwell, you have reasoned rightly; God, the Creator and Lord of heaven and earth has not abandoned men to their own conceits, but has given to them an unerring witness and teacher of truth. The credentials of that teacher you may examine for yourself, any day. They will tell you unmistakably of the mission which He has entrusted to this infallible organ of His word in this world. In examining the claims of that divinely appointed teacher, you may take as your test the history of every century, in order that you may see how those claims have been made good in the course of ages, how truth has been infallibly guarded, and defined, and interpreted, and how, though all the powers of the world have been arrayed against God's oracle on earth, they have not prevailed.

'Si monumentum quæris, circumspice.'

"But why should I not speak it out plainly to you, my friend, you, who crave to know the truth and the whole truth? The Catholic Church, founded by God, upheld by Him and guided by Him, will be for you the pillar and the ground of truth, the unerring interpreter to men of law natural and supernatural, the beacon of salvation.

CHAPTER X.

The Proof from Conscience Confirmed.

EXTRACT FROM "AN ESSAY IN AID OF A GRAMMAR OF ASSENT," BY CARDINAL NEWMAN.

"I assume, then, that conscience has a legitimate place among our mental acts; as really so, as the action of memory, of reasoning, of imagination, or as the sense of the beautiful; that, as there are objects which, when presented to the mind, cause it to feel grief, regret, joy or desire, so there are things which excite in us approbation or blame, and which we in consequence call right or wrong; and which, experienced in ourselves, kindle in us that specific sense of pleasure or pain, which goes by the name of a good or bad conscience. This being taken for granted, I shall attempt to show that in this special feeling, which follows on the commission of what we call right and wrong, lie the materials for the real apprehension of a Divine Sovereign and Judge.

"The feeling of conscience being, I repeat, a certain keen sensibility, pleasant or painful, self-approval or hope, or compunction and fear, attendant on certain of our actions, which in consequence we call right or wrong, is twofold:—it is a moral sense and a sense of duty; a judgment of the reason and a magisterial dictate. Of course its act is indivisible;

The Proof from Conscience Confirmed. 365

still it has these two aspects, distinct from each other, and admitting of a separate consideration. Though I lost my sense of the obligation which I lie under to abstain from acts of dishonesty, I should not in consequence lose my sense that such actions were an outrage offered to my moral nature. Again, though I lost my sense of their moral deformity, I should not therefore lose my sense that they were forbidden to me. Thus conscience has both a critical and a judicial office, and though its promptings, in the breasts of the millions of human beings to whom it is given, are not in all cases correct, that does not necessarily interfere with the force of its testimony and of its sanction, its testimony that there is a right and a wrong, and its sanction to that testimony conveyed in the feelings which attend on right or wrong conduct. Here I have to speak of conscience in the latter point of view,—not as supplying us, by means of its various acts, with the elements of morals, which may be developed by the intellect into an ethical code, but simply as the dictate of an authoritative monitor bearing upon the details of conduct as they come before us, and complete in its several acts, one by one. . . . .

" And again, in consequence of this prerogative of dictating and commanding, which is of its essence, conscience has an intimate bearing on our affections and emotions, leading us to reverence and awe, hope and fear, especially fear, a feeling which is foreign for the most part, not only to taste, but even to the moral sense, except in consequence of accidental associations. No fear is felt by any one who recognizes that his conduct has not been beautiful, though he may be mortified at himself, if perhaps he has thereby forfeited some advantage; but if he has been betrayed into any kind of immorality, he has a lively sense of responsibility and guilt, though the act be no offence against society,—of distress and apprehension, even though it may be of present service to him,—of compunction and regret, though in itself it be most pleasurable,—of confusion of face, though it may have no witnesses. These various perturbations of mind, which are characteristic of a bad conscience, and may be very considerable,—self-reproach, poignant shame, haunting remorse, chill dismay at the prospect of the future,—and their contraries when the conscience is good, as real, though less forcible, self-approval, inward peace, lightness of heart, and the like,—these emotions constitute a generic difference between conscience and our other intellectual senses,—common sense, good sense, sense of expedience, taste, sense of honor, and the like,—as indeed they would also create between conscience and the moral sense, supposing these two were not aspects of one and the same feeling, exercised upon one and the same subject-matter.

"So much for the characteristic phenomena which conscience presents, nor is it difficult to determine what they imply. I refer once more to our sense of the beautiful. This sense is attended by an intellectual enjoyment, and is free from whatever is of the nature of emotion, except in one case, viz., when it is excited by personal objects; then it is that the tranquil feeling of admiration is exchanged for the excitement of affection and passion. Conscience, too, considered as a moral sense, an intellectual sentiment, is a sense of admiration and disgust, of approbation and blame; but it is something more than a moral sense; it is always, what the sense of the beautiful is only in certain cases, it is always emotional. No wonder, then, that it always implies what that sense only sometimes implies; that it always involves the recognition of a living object, towards which it is directed. Inanimate things cannot stir our affections; these are correlative with persons. If, as is the case, we feel responsibility, are ashamed, are frightened at transgressing the voice of conscience, this implies that there is One to whom we are responsible, before whom we are ashamed, whose claim upon us we fear. If, on doing wrong, we feel the same tearful, broken-hearted sorrow which overwhelms us on hurting a mother; if, on doing right, we enjoy the same sunny serenity of mind, the same soothing, satisfactory delight which follows on our receiving praise from a father, we certainly have within us the image of some person to whom our love and veneration look, in whose smile we find our happiness, for whom we yearn, towards whom we direct our pleading, in whose anger we are troubled and waste away. These feelings in us are such as require for their exciting cause an intelligent being; we are not affectionate towards a stone, nor do we feel shame before a horse or a dog; we have no remorse or compunction on breaking mere human law; yet, so it is; conscience excites all these painful emotions, confusion, foreboding, self-condemnation; and on the other hand, it sheds upon us a deep peace, a sense of security, a resignation, and a hope, which there is no sensible, no earthly object to elicit. 'The wicked flees, when no one pursueth;' then why does he flee? whence his terror? Who is it that he sees in solitude, in darkness, in the hidden chambers of his heart? If the cause of these emotions does not belong to this visible world, the object to which his perception is directed must be supernatural and divine; and thus the phenomena of conscience, as a dictate, avail to impress the imagination with the picture of a Supreme Governor, a Judge, holy, just, powerful, all-seeing, retributive, and is the creative principle of religion, as the moral sense is the principle of ethics."

CHAPTER XI.

THE KNOWLEDGE OF GOD ATTAINABLE BY ALL MEN.[1]

"IN many places, Scripture declares, in the most express manner, that even for those to whom God has not manifested himself by His Prophets or by His Son, there exists a revelation of God in His works, and even within the mind of men, whereby they can, without any difficulty, cognize God, their Creator and Maker, as well as His sovereign law. It is not necessary to point out that Scripture does not in this speak of any (supposable) first cause, but of the Living and True God, who has created heaven and earth, and inscribed His law in the heart of man; and that, consequently, it speaks also of the moral order. Now it says in the same passages that men who do not thus cognize their God are without excuse; that they are insensate; that they deserve God's wrath and all His chastisements. It necessarily follows, then, that this manifestation of God by His works is such, that man cannot fail by this means to cognize God with certitude, unless he commit a grave fault.

"Assuredly, this does not mean that it is philosophical researches continued laboriously through obstacles and doubts, which can alone lead to

[1] "Scholastic Philosophy," by Rev. Joseph Kleutgen, S. J. Vol. i., pp. 226-232.

a knowledge of God. Very few men, in fact, are capable of these laborious researches: whereas Scripture speaks of all the heathens in general; and in the Book of Wisdom it is said expressly (xiii. 1.) 'All men are vanity who do not possess the knowledge of God.' The sacred writer even adds that this knowledge, to which he gives the name of 'sight' to express its clearness and certitude, ('cognoscibiliter poterit Creator horum videri,' v. 5.), can be obtained with as much ease (and even more) as knowledge of this world, which, certainly, does not fail any one capable of the least reflection. ("Si tantum potuerunt scire ut possent æstimare sæculum, quomodo hujus Dominum non facilius invenerunt," v. 9.). ...It is easier, therefore, to know God, the Governor of the world, than to know enough of nature to admire its power and its beauty.

"It necessarily follows, therefore, that there is a knowledge of God different from philosophical knowledge; a knowledge so easy to acquire and so certain, that ignorance and doubt on that head cannot be explained, except either by culpable carelessness or proud obstinacy. Such is also the common doctrine of the Holy Fathers; they distinguish that knowledge of God which is obtained by philosophical research from that which springs up spontaneously in every man at the very sight of creation. This latter kind of knowledge is called by them 'a witness of Himself,' which God gave to the soul at its creation; 'an endowment of nature;' 'an infused knowledge,' inherent in every man without preliminary instruction; a knowledge which springs up in some sense of itself, in proportion as reason is developed; and which cannot fail, except in a man either deprived of the use of reason or else given up to vices which have corrupted his nature. And when the Fathers of the Church declare unanimously on this head that this knowledge is really found and established in all men, the importance of their testimony is better understood by remembering that they lived in the midst of heathen populations.

"God has implanted in our reasonable nature everything which is necessary, that we know Him, and know Him with facility. Now He does not, after creation, withdraw Himself from creatures, but always remains near them, co-operating with them, exciting them to act, supporting and directing each one to its end, comformably to its nature. If this is true of all creatures, how could this concurrence be refused to the most noble of all creatures, to those whom God has created for the very purpose of their knowing and loving Him? Man, indeed, does not arrive at his end, except by using the powers which God has given him; but the Author of those gifts lends to man His concurrence, in order that he may make due use of them. Since that moral and religious life for which man was created is founded on a knowledge of the truths whereof we speak, God watches over man, in order that reason, as it is developed, may come to know them with facility and certainty. Observe, the question here is not of supernatural grace, but is (of the natural order)...

What would not be the misery of man (if there were no reasonable certainty without philosophical argument)? It is easy to show those ordinary men who are capable of any reflection at all, that their knowledge of the truth is not scientific; that they do not deduce it (reflectively and explicitly) from the first principles of thought; and, consequently, they cannot defend it against the attacks of scepticism. If, then, as soon as we come to know that our knowledge is not scientific, the conviction of its truth were at once shaken—what, on that supposition, would be the lot of man?....

The fact is, indeed, not so. That consciousness which every one can interrogate within himself attests its denial; and at every period the voice of mankind has confirmed that denial. As soon as we arrive at the use of reason, the voice of conscience wakes within us; whether we choose or no, we must cognize the distinction between good and evil. (Again) just as it is absolutely impossible for us to doubt our own existence (in like manner), we are absolutely compelled to regard as real the external world; (to hold) that further, there exists a Supreme Author of our being and of all other things; and that through Him there is a certain moral order. These also are truths which we cannot refuse to admit. No doubt we can do violence to ourselves in order to produce in ourselves the contrary persuasion, just as we may use efforts to regard the moral conscience itself as an illusion. But these efforts never succeed, or, at least, never succeed perfectly; and we feel ourselves even under an obligation of condemning the very attempt as immoral. The mind of man, in fact, is under the influence of truth, which has dominion over it, and which gives (man) certainty, even against his own wish. Truth manifests itself to our intelligence, and engenders therein the knowledge of its reality, even before we (explicitly) know what that truth is. Still, truth (I say) reigns over man and reveals itself to him—however great may be his resistance, as a sacred and sovereign authority, which commands him and summons him before its tribunal, and (standing) before that tribunal he is obliged to admit the immorality of even attempting to doubt. Just as he is bound to condemn the madness, I will not say of doubting, but of trying to doubt, the reality of the external world, so he is obliged to regard as an impiety (all) doubt of God's Existence and Providence.

Nor can it be here objected that conscience, in the proper sense of the word, moral conscience, gives no certainty, so long as its existence within us and its pronouncements are purely spontaneous. Of the conscience, more than of anything else, it may be said that it reveals to us its own truth; that it compels us to acknowledge an absolute good and a sovereign rule over our wills and actions, even though we know not its innermost nature, not only as really existing, but as an august and sacred power which is (in authority) over us. Whatever efforts man may make to overthrow and destroy his own intimate persuasion on the truthfulness of conscience, he will never succeed in doing so. Even though he seeks by every possible means to persuade himself that nothing obliges him to regard it as truthful, nevertheless he will always feel himself compelled to acknowledge its authority, and even to condemn his own resistance to it.

It is true, indeed, that, though conscience very

often speaks against a man's inclinations (so loudly) as to confound, by its manifestation of its own truthfulness, all pride and all the sophistical dreams by which he might wish to stifle it,—still it does not *always* so speak and raise its voice, as to take from man the power of turning from it and refusing to listen. If he enters into himself and chooses to observe what passes within him, he will obtain that reflexive knowledge which, as we have said above, is required for actual certainty; he will know that he cannot prevent himself from acknowledging the truth of what the voice of conscience dictates. But it is in his power—if not always, at least often—to abstain from entering into himself and lending his ear to that voice. He has (often) the power of not hearing it, or of giving it so little attention that he withdraws himself from that influence which would make him certain. It is in this manner that, for a certain time at least, notwithstanding the habitual certainty [1] which nature gives him, he may remain undecided on the truthfulness of conscience, supposing that he has not yet acknowledged that truthfulness by philosophical reflection, or again, that he does not seek to know it. But, even though we were not able to demonstrate by the intimate experience of every man that the doubt whereof we speak is contrary to the principles of morality, we ought, nevertheless, to be persuaded of that truth by the judgment of all mankind. Among civilized nations, in every time, the necessity of philosophical studies has been admitted, and those have been

---

[1] By "habitual certainty" as he has explained just before, Fr. Kleutgen means to express the *proximate power* of actual certainty.

held in high esteem who devoted themselves thereto and who were regarded as sages. Nevertheless, though the nations, it is true, accepted at the hands of philosophers the solution of many questions, they have never ascribed to these men a decisive judgment on all truth without exception. As to those first truths, on which all our convictions rest, humanity bears within itself the consciousness, or intimate persuasion, of knowing them with certainty. Philosophers may make these truths the subject of their speculations, but they are not allowed the right of pronouncing a definite judgment on these truths; and if their researches lead them to deny or doubt them, those very persons who would otherwise be the disciples of these philosophers, rise up against them as judges and condemn them. Was there ever a nation which did not regard it as madness to doubt an external world? A nation which did not hold in horror a man so perverted as to acknowledge no truth superior to the senses, and reject all distinction between virtue and vice? Has not atheism among all nations been accounted a crime? And, by the fact of seeing culpability in the denial of these truths, does not the world declare that they cannot possibly be unknown to men of good will?"

(Translated from the French edition in "Essays on the Philosophy of Theism." By William George Ward, Ph. D.—Vol. ii., p. 216 and following.)

CHAPTER XII.

St. Augustine's Soliloquy with God.[1]

"Not with doubting but with assured consciousness, do I love Thee, Lord. Thou hast stricken my heart with Thy word and I loved Thee, yea also *heaven, and earth, and all that therein is,* behold, on every side they bid me love thee; nor cease to say unto all that *they may be without excuse.* But more deeply wilt Thou have mercy on whom Thou wilt have mercy and wilt have compassion on whom Thou hast had compassion; else in deaf ears do the heavens and the earth speak Thy praises. But what do I love, when I love Thee? not the beauty of bodies or the fair harmony of time, nor the brightness of the light, so gladsome to our eyes, nor sweet melodies of various songs, nor the fragrant smell of flowers, and ointments, and spices, not manna and honey, not limbs acceptable to embracement of flesh. None of these I love, when I love my God; and yet I love a kind of light, and melody, and fragrance, and meat, and embracement, when I love my God, the light, melody, fragrance, meat, embracement of my inner man; where there shineth unto my soul what space cannot contain, and there soundeth what time beareth not away, and there smelleth what breathing disperseth not, and there tasteth, what eating diminisheth not, and there

[1] "The Confession," Book x., sec. 6, Oxford Translation.

clingeth what satiety divorceth not. This it is which I love when I love my God.

"'And what is this?' I asked the earth, and it answered me, 'I am not He;' and whatsoever are in it confessed the same. I asked the sea, and the deeps, and the living, creeping things, and they answered, 'we are not thy God, seek above us.' I asked the moving air; and the whole air with its inhabitants answered, 'Anaximenes was deceived, I am not God.' I asked the heavens, sun, moon, stars: 'Nor (say they) are we the God whom thou seekest.' And I replied to all the things which encompass the door of my flesh: 'Ye have told me of my God, that ye are not He, tell me something of Him.' And they cried out with a loud voice, 'He made us.' My questioning them was my thoughts on them, and their form of beauty gave the answer. And I turned myself unto myself and said to myself, 'who art thou?' And I answered, 'a man.' And behold, in me there present themselves to me soul and body, one without, the other within. By which of these ought I seek my God? I had sought him in the body from earth to heaven, so far as I could send messengers, the beams of mine eyes. But the better is the inner, for to it, as presiding and judging, all the bodily messengers reported the answers of heaven, and earth, and all things therein, who said: 'We are not God, but He made us.' These things did my inner man know by the ministry of the outer; I, the inner knew them; I, the mind, through the senses of my body. I asked the whole frame of the world about my God; and it answered me, 'I am not He, but He made me.'

"Is not this corporal figure apparent to all whose senses are perfect? Why then speaks it not the same to all? Animals small and great see it, but they cannot ask it, because no reason is set over their senses to judge on what they report. But men can ask, so that the invisible things of God are clearly seen, being understood by the things that are made; but by love of them, they are made subject unto them: and subjects cannot judge. Nor yet do the creatures answer such as ask, unless they can judge; nor yet do they change their voice, (*i.e.*, their appearance) if one man only sees, another seeing asks, so as to appear one way to this man, another way to that; but appearing the same way to both, it is dumb to this, speaks to that, yea rather it speaks to all; but they only understand, who compare its voice received from without with the truth within. For truth saith unto me, 'Neither heaven, nor earth, nor any other body, is thy God.' This their very nature saith to him that seeth them, 'They are a mass, a mass is less in a part thereof, than in the whole.' Now to thee, I speak, O my soul, 'thou art my better part; for thou quickenest the mass of my body, giving it life, which no body can give to a body, but thy God is even unto thee the Life of thy life.'

.... "Thy servant, who here confesseth unto Thee, far be it, that, be the joy what it may, I should therefore think myself happy. For there is a joy which is not given *to the ungodly*, but to those who love Thee for Thine own sake, whose joy Thou Thyself art. And this is the happy life, to rejoice to Thee, of Thee, for Thee; this is it, and there is no other.... Where then did I find Thee that I might learn Thee? For in my memory Thou wert not, before I learned Thee. Where then did I find Thee, that I might learn Thee, but in Thee above me? Place there is none; *we go backward and forward*, and there is no place. Every-where, O Truth, dost Thou give audience to all who ask counsel of Thee, and at once answerest all, though on manifold matters they ask Thy counsel, Clearly dost Thou answer, though all do not clearly hear. All consult Thee on what they will, though they hear not always what they will. He is Thy best servant, who looks not so much to hear that from Thee which himself willeth, as rather to will that which from Thee he heareth. Too late I loved Thee, O Thou, Beauty of ancient days, yet ever new! too late I loved Thee."

APPENDIX.

"A Refutation of Darwinism."

"If one speaks only theoretically and reasons on possibilities and not on facts, it is certain (if we except the spontaneous generation of the first being, which is impossible) that God could have created the world according to the "transformist" system, that is to say, He could have created one only being capable of developing itself gradually and of producing the different organisms of all actually existing beings.

(1) But that is not the question. We are not concerned with what *could have been* but with what *is* in reality. Now, the fact contradicts the doctrine of Darwin. He is unable to give any direct proof of the transformation of species; he is obliged to acknowledge that there exist many breaks between the different species, and that the passage from one to the other is by insensible degrees, a passage which grounds the system, but which has not been proved; he affirms, then, as real that which is only possible, although *a posse ad actum non valet consecutio*.

(2) Not only does Darwinism affirm more than it can prove, but it is in plain contradiction with the best authenticated facts. It affirms the *variability* of specific types; now, history and geology, on the contrary, prove their stability.—In the ruins of Her-

culaneum and Pompeii, buried more than 1800 years ago under lava from Mount Vesuvius, there has been found, in the house of a painter, a collection of shells and, in the store of a fruit-dealer, vases full of chestnuts, of olives, and of nuts—all in a perfect state of preservation. These shells and fruits are nowise different from the shells and fruits of to-day. Aristotle described, more than two thousand years ago, a great number of plants and animals. His descriptions answer exactly to the actual species and show that, during that interval of time, these species have undergone neither variation nor change. —During this century, there have been discovered in the tombs of ancient Egypt the seeds of different plants, and many species of embalmed animals that had lived much farther back than the epoch of Aristotle, even as far back as the fourth dynasty. These seeds and animals are the same as those of our day. (3) Geology permits us to go much farther back in the past,—far beyond the limits which history can reach, and its testimony is the same. Darwin has been obliged to acknowledge that the skeletons of animals have not been changed since the glacial period. (4) According to Agassiz the southern extremity of Florida has been formed by the accumulation of the corals of the tropical seas, and, if his calculations are correct, the formation of those coral reefs required no less a period than two hundred thousand years. Now, if we compare the zoophites which have formed the uppermost ledges of these reefs with those which formed their lowest strata, we cannot verify any difference between them. (5) The comparison of the flora of the glacial period with that of our time leads to the same results. There has been discovered near Hohenhausen, in the canton of Zurich, in the midst of a peat-marsh, quite a collection of the flora of those ages. These *debris* are embedded in peat whose formation, according to certain geologists, must have taken place between the two glacial epochs. The yew-tree, the wild pine, the larch, the birch, the maple, the nut-tree, in its two kinds, have been recognized as having existed in an age certainly anterior to ours. They have been compared with the same species as they now grow, and no difference has been found to exist between them. In a word, history and natural sciences prove the stability and permanence of the species: Darwinites cannot cite one historical instance of the gradual transition of one species to another; their system is therefore in contradiction with facts. Nature is not "transformist," and Moses spoke the truth when he said that God had created plants and animals according to their kind."[1]

The great flaw in Darwin's system is that he takes what is accidental or relative in a species for what is substantial and absolute. Environment, heredity, natural selection, struggle for life, these serve to give variations to the species, but do not change substantially the original constituent type of the same.

"All known living beings, animal and vegetable, are divided into definite groups by the two following characteristics,—the *genetic* and '*morphologic*.' Within the groups themselves the fecundity is un-

[1] (Manuel Biblique. Par. F. Vigouroux, Prêtre de Saint-Sulpice, T. i., pp. 282, 428, 429),

limited, but, as passing from one group to another, it is not or is limited to certain generations.

"The members of each of these groups can undergo organic variations more or less considerable, but these modifications are as so many oscillations around a type in a state of stable equilibrium. These '*morphologic*' variations tend of themselves to disappear, when it is only circumstances that lead to their growth. Each of these groups, commonly called a *species*, and the '*morphologic*' oscillations, more or less established by inheritance and by the constancy of the circumstances which produced them, constitute the different races of the same *species*. It has been calculated that there are more than five hundred thousand groups distinguished by the characteristics of stability which I have just indicated. This stability is absolute even in domestic species, the most plastic of all others. . . . Now it has been always the same as far back in the past as our observations can reach in history, in prehistoric times, in the geological ages. *There are then 500,000 facts in direct opposition to the change of species, the fundamental basis of the hypothesis of the transformists, while they have not one to cite in their behalf.*" [1]

"ENCYCLOPÆDIA BRITANNICA." ART. THEISM.

In the last volume of the "Encyclopædia Britannica" there is an article on theism by the Rev. Robert Flint, D. D., LL. D., Professor of Divinity, University of Edinburgh. The general conclusion which

[1] Etudes Religieuses, etc., Mai 1888, p. 111.

the professor reaches in the said article is favorable to theism, but is somehow halting by reason of the sceptical views that run parallel to it. The historical proof of primitive monotheism he seems to surrender to his adversaries without even a protest. According to historical criteria of their own invention they claim that "the opening chapters of Genesis" rest on no sure historical basis. The professor apparently assents; and this though Christ distinctly refers to the 27th verse of the first chapter in the 19th chapter of the Gospel according to St. Matthew. In the text of Genesis we read: "And God created man to his own image, to the image of God who created him, male and female, he created them." Christ says: "Have you not read, that he who made man from the beginning, made them male and female?" But from the second chapter, which is only a development of the first chapter of the same Book, Christ quotes the express words of Moses: "For this cause shall a man leave father and mother and shall cleave to his wife, and they shall be two in one flesh." But apart from this reasoning, which tells against the too liberal admissions made in the article, there are historical grounds on which, according to the authentic rules of historical criticism, he might have met and vanquished his opponents. Some three hundred years before Christ, a Greek version of the Hebrew Scriptures was made at Alexandria. This version is commonly known as the Septuagint. It is from it that the Apostles and early Fathers generally quote. In their eyes, it was therefore an authentic copy of the original Hebrew text. Now in that version "the opening chapters of

Genesis" are found. Here then, we have clear historical proof that those chapters had been accepted by generation after generation of Hebrew teachers as authentic revealed Scripture and as part of the Book of Moses. Following up Jewish tradition, scholars have also been able to trace the history of that book in its completeness from the age of the Machabees to that of the Judges, and beyond it.

But granted, argues the professor, that "the opening chapters of Genesis" are authentic, they furnish no proof of primitive orthodox theism. "Then," he writes, "although these chapters plainly teach monotheism and represent the God whose words and acts are recorded in the Bible as no mere national God but the only true God, they do not teach what is alone in question, that there was a primitive monotheism,—a monotheism revealed and known from the beginning." This phrase we are enabled to interpret by one that comes after it. "The one true God," continues the writer, " is represented in Genesis as making himself known, by particular words and in particular ways, to Adam, but is nowhere said to have taught him that He only was God." It was not necessary that He should. He can speak to His creatures by the words of the mind without any oral articulate expression; but in the instance in question facts alone sufficed to show that He alone was God. From the formation of Eve, Adam knew God to be the Creator; he also knew Him to be the Lord of every living thing, to be the great arbiter of life and death, the author of the moral code and of these laws by which species are propagated. In other words, he knew Him to be the only one true God. The absolute, independent sovereignty of God was clear proof to Adam of the necessarily exclusive nature of that sovereignty. The plain, unsophistical reading, then, of "the opening chapters of Genesis" shows that they teach " primitive monotheism,—a monotheism revealed and known from the beginning."

To confirm his interpretation of the chapters of Genesis, the professor next appeals with confidence to the records of all ancient religions. " The assertion," he writes, " that history every-where or even anywhere shows religious belief to have commenced with monotheism is not only unsupported by evidence but contrary to evidence." This is a bold assertion, and in view of the facts given in the text is altogether unwarranted. In a few phrases he brushes aside whatever had been said by deeply read, professional scholars in favor of primitive monotheism. His thesis is that, " it is impossible to prove historically that monotheism was the primitive religion." But, singular to say, after having endeavored to prove this thesis from ancient history, he then undertakes to refute it. He had resolutely denied that ancient Egypt or Assyria could furnish any proof of monotheism as being its primitive religion, but now, turning over a leaf, he gives the refutation of what he had asserted. " In one of the most ancient of books, for example," he writes, " and probably the oldest manuscript in the world, the maxims of Patah-Holep, a wise Egyptian prince of the fifth dynasty, God simply (*mutar*) is often spoken of without a name or any mythological characteristic, and in a way which in itself is quite monotheistic.

Thus, 'if any one beareth himself proudly, he will be humbled by God, who maketh his strength.' 'If thou art a wise man, bring up thy son in the love of God;' 'God loveth the obedient and hateth the disobedient.' Sentences like these," he adds, "standing alone, would be pronounced by every one monotheistic; and even when standing alongside with reference to 'gods' and 'powers,' they show that said gods and powers were not deemed by the Egyptian sage inconsistent with oneness of power and godhead, or exhaustive of their fulness." From Babylonian-Assyrian religious history he quotes the following: "O my Lord, my sins are many, my trespasses are great, and the wrath of the gods has plagued me with disease, with sickness, and sorrow. I fainted, but no one stretched forth his hand! I groaned, but no one heard! O Lord, do not abandon Thy servant; in the waters of the great stream do Thou take his hand; the sins which he has committed do Thou turn to righteousness." In these passages, with the recognition of inferior deities, we find a clearly defined belief in the sovereignty of one supreme God. It was disfigured, undoubtedly, in various ways, but remained uppermost in the minds of the people. To-day it rises like a pyramidal shaft amid the ruins of past greatness, to point to monotheism as to the faith that first prevailed in Egypt and Babylonia.

"THE SACRED BOOKS OF THE EAST."

In an article entitled "The Sacred Books of the East" in the *Quarterly Review* for July, 1886, the writer says: "Let us confess it boldly. The sacred books of the East are not edifying reading. Instructive they most certainly are. But they are instructive least of all in the direction in which their authors thought they would be most so. They teach us not so much what to believe or what we ought to do, as what the purblind have believed and what the foolish have done.... There are isolated passages in these books of great beauty, of deep religious feeling, even of rare insight into the realities of life. But there is much more that is monotonous, mistaken, wooden, even absurd. We must not turn to them for the sake of any expected revelation of sacred mysteries. Their interest is a real human interest—an interest like that which we take in watching the mind of a child unfold itself, and gather strength and shape, and struggle, through ignorance and even much misconception, into comparative freedom and light. Light has arisen in the East. But those who, with poetic fervor, have hoped that from the wisdom of the East would come the glorious, many-tinted light of truth, will be disappointed to find that it is only the clear, cold, and, withal, somewhat dry light of stern, historical fact."

"THE END DOES NOT JUSTIFY THE MEANS." [1]

To justify his act, not only the end which a man proposes to himself must be lawful, but the means thereunto, or the act itself, must also be lawful, together with the circumstances that accompany or qualify the act. The badness of an evil end there-

---

[1] This article, though not connected with the main subject of the work, has been suggested by some views set forth in the proof from the Moral Order.

fore, affects means legitimate in themselves, and means that are vicious vitiate an end otherwise laudable, while the very circumstances that qualify an act may often render it unlawful. A man who steals in order to give alms sins by his act; a man who gives alms in order to gain applause sins also, and a man who, to the great detriment of his family, gives large alms, acts also unlawfully. His obligation to his family springs from justice, and justice here goes before charity. To make an act lawful, then, the end, the means, and the circumstances must combine;—either of these three conditions failing, the action becomes unlawful, according to the axiom accepted by all Catholic writers: "Bonum ex integra causa,—malum, ex quocunque defectu."

On this subject an old calumny is periodically revived. In spite of proof and protest to the contrary, the saying that "the end justifies the means" is flung out upon the world as if it were a maxim of Catholic teaching. It is one of those lies that never die. Some time ago it was brought out again by Bishop Cox in a letter to the *Churchman* and reprinted with a refutation in the *New York Herald*, January 9, 1888. In this letter the Bishop repeats the charge with an assurance which seems to challenge all denial. The authority to which he appeals and that which he considers final on the subject is an article on the Jesuits in the "Encyclopædia Britannica." The article in question (and a more dishonest one, be it said, could scarcely have been penned) was written by Dr. Littledale of England, well known in controversial literature. It is with the same reverend Doctor that Father James Jones deals in "Dishonest Criticism." The undisguised "end" which the Doctor proposed to himself in a letter to the *Pall Mall Gazette* as well as in the article in the "Encyclopædia," was to show from the works of St. Alphonsus Liguori and other approved Catholic moral theologians that the Catholic Church is immoral in her teaching. With this end in view he proceeds to his work, attributes to those Catholic theologians opinions which are in conflict with their teaching, says of them what they do not say, misrepresents, mistranslates, and falsifies their text in order to gain his end. "The means adopted for this end," writes Father Jones, "are not only equivocation but sheer and repeated falsifications.[1]" That is to say, Dr. Littledale, Bishop Cox's great and final authority, is found out practising adroitly what he charges Catholic writers with. With him the end, the dishonoring of the Catholic Church, justifies the means thereunto, or the falsification of Catholic teaching.

The originator of the false maxim, that the end justifies the means, was, according to Littledale, the Jesuit writer Busenbaum, who lived in the beginning of the 17th century. In proof of this, words taken out of their context in his work are quoted. For instance, he writes, "to whom the end is lawful, the means also are lawful." "Busenbaum is speaking of means of their own nature honest, and indicated by natural law as the fit means for a lawful end, but which are not allowed unless in certain circumstances. The question regards the conjugal state, in which the end and the means are legalized by the

[1] P. 29. See also pp. 65 et seq.

circumstances of wedlock. If the end is admitted to be lawful, the lawfulness of the fit means can be proved from it, and *vice versa*. In this, as in similar questions, theologians say that the circumstances, including the end, *cohonestant actum*, that is, add the required extrinsic legality to an act of its own nature honest and good. Surely, this is very different from justifying a wrong or evil act, the meaning which Dr. Littledale unwarrantably attaches to Busenbaum's words. This also is the sense given to them by St. Alphonsus"[1] (l. c., 934).

But on this subject a clearer proof still is found in various passages in Busenbaum's work, in which he lays down principles directly contradictory of the maxim attributed to him. I shall here cite a few of these passages. In his article on "Duelling" he asks, "what is duelling, and is it lawful?" To the latter clause he answers: "Duelling is not lawful to prove truth, or justice, or the innocence of the charge alleged, or to decide a dispute; because it is a fallacious, nay, a *superstitious means* for that *end*."—Again, in treating of the eighth commandment, he asks: "Is it lawful to disclose another's crime in order to escape grievous torments? Answer 1°: It is when the crime is true, because it does no injury to the other, since one has a right to reveal it (the crime) provided it be necessary to reveal it. Answer 2°: If the crime be false, it is not lawful (to reveal it) because it would be a pernicious lie." Alms is in itself a good end, and still Busenbaum decides that, "it is not lawful to give alms out of goods obtained by theft, or which ought to be restored."—In fact, the

[1] "Dishonest Criticism," p. 115, note.

whole teaching of Busenbaum is directly at variance with the maxim falsely attributed to him and of which most probably he had not even a conception.

Busenbaum, according to Littledale, was the first to originate the maxim in question, and Gury was among the last to confirm it. Now here are a few words of the latter, bearing on the point:—" It is never lawful to do evil, no matter how trivial, to obtain a good, whatever it may be ; for, according to the well known axiom derived from the Apostle, 'evil is not to be done that good may result.' Thus *it would not be lawful for you to tell a lie to save the life of a man.*" (Vol. i., p. 10.) In his standard catechism Cardinal Bellarmine, a Jesuit, also asks : " Is it lawful to tell a lie for a good end? Answer: No ; for a lie being intrinsically evil, no reason or motive can excuse it." Littledale would lead us to suppose that it is only within those last centuries that the charge we discuss has been laid against members of the Church, but he is wrong.; the reproach was made to St. Paul, as we learn from these his words: " And not rather (as we are slandered and as some affirm that we say) let us do evil, that there may come good ; whose damnation is just " (Rom. iii. 8). Upon which words another Jesuit, Cornelius à Lapide, comments,—" observe here with care that no sin, not even the smallest venial sin, is a means that may be chosen or put into execution for the purpose of avoiding the very gravest sin." And this teaching is exactly in conformity with what St. Ignatius lays down in the " Spiritual Exercises," when in the meditation on the three degrees of humility he defines that the second degree consists in this, that we be determined for no end whatever, be it the greatest human happiness or even the preservation of life, to commit a venial sin.

Different Names of God.

To God, though in Himself most simple, we give different names to express even imperfectly our knowledge of Him. As we cannot comprehend His essence in itself, we can know Him only through His perfections as they are manifested in creatures. "And since," writes St. Thomas, "we cannot name a thing, only inasmuch as we understand it, (since names are but the signs of intellects) we can name God only from the perfections found in creatures whose author He is. And because perfections are many, the names of God are many. Hence, though His different names in reality signify the same thing, they are not, however, synonymous. Names that are synonymous signify the same thing and represent the same intellectual conceptions. Therefore, as the different names of God embody the different conceptions our intellect forms of Him, they are not synonymous."[1] Thus we say of God that He is most good, most wise, and just, etc.; "these names signify the divine substance, but this they do imperfectly, as created things also represent it imperfectly."[2] But there are names for God which He Himself has revealed. These signify the same eternal Being, but under different aspects."

[1] "Compend. Theol.," pp. 16, 17.
[2] "Sum. Theol.," p. 1, q. 13, a 2.

The first revealed name of God which we meet with in Scripture is Elohim. "In the beginning," writes Moses, "God (Elohim) created heaven and earth." In nearly every verse of the first chapter of Genesis the same name occurs. It is in the plural number, and according to Gesenius is a developed form of El, which, radically, means power. Other scholars would derive it from the Hebrew word "Alah," to swear. What is peculiar about the name is that, though in the plural number, it is constantly, when used for the one true God, joined with verbs and adjectives in the singular. And on the other hand, when applied to denote false gods, it is invariably united to verbs and adjectives in the plural. This marked distinction in the use of the name has thoroughly convinced some rationalists of the original monotheism of the Hebrew race. On the subject Ewald writes the following:—

"In Hebrew, the difference between monotheism and polytheism is perfectly expressed even by the very use of the word Elohim, which is not considered as plural but when there is question of false gods or their adorers. This difference upheld in the use of this word is most significative and changes altogether the spirit and the sense of the discourse.... Now, as that use, so peculiar and important, is found every-where in Hebrew, before as well as after the time of Moses, even as far back as the patriarchal epoch, without any change, since the patriarchs are presented to us as using the same language, we are necessarily led to admit that faith in the oneness of the true God dates not merely from Moses, but that the patriarchs already considered their God as the one only God, and became distinct by that belief from all pagan peoples."[1]

Another peculiar feature of the name Elohim is, that it has a singular Eloah, which, though not used by Moses, is found in Job and Habacuc, as Pererius points out.[2] Again when Elohim is united to a verb in the plural, (which occurs, in any form, critics say, at most only twelve times against some two thousand instances for the contrary usage) its sense is determined by the word Jehovah which accompanies it. This constant use of the name Elohim, some theologians following the opinion of the Master of Sentences uphold, was not without design. By it Moses wished, they say, to indicate the Trinity of Persons in the Godhead, and by the singular verb to teach the unity of the divine nature. It is the thesis which the learned convert from Judaism, Chevalier P. L. B. Drach, maintains with great erudition in his work, "De L'Harmonie entre L'Église et la Synagogue." "Whoever is familiar," he writes, " with the teaching of the ancient Doctors of the Synagogue, especially of those who lived before the coming of the Saviour, knows that the Trinity in one only God was a truth admitted by them from the remotest antiquity."[3]

The name Elohim, however, as being generic, was sometimes given to created beings. "In Scripture," writes Pererius, "it is given not only to God, but also to angels, to judges, and princes. Since properly it signified those who, on account of their

---

[1] H. Ewald, "Jahrbücher der Biblischen Wissenshaft," quoted by F. Vigouroux in "La Bible et Les Découvertes Modernes," vol. iii., p. 55.
[2] "Comment. in Genesim," t. i., p. 11.
[3] Vol. i., p. 280.

great authority and power, especially in the vindication of justice, are objects of fear to others."[1] When men fell away from the true faith they called their gods and their idols Elohim.

The exclusive use of the name in the first chapter of Genesis seems to suggest that by divine inspiration it was chosen by Moses to denote the exercise of the power and beneficence of the one true God.

But the name which the Israelites looked upon as the proper name of God was Jehovah. It is derived, according to Hebraists, from the Hebrew (haia), "is," and means "He who is." The Jews style it "the name of substance," "the name of being," "the venerated and terrible name," "the name reserved or incommunicable," "the mysterious name," "the ineffable name," the name tetragrammatical (literally, the name, product of four letters,—a Hebraism).[2] Jehovah, therefore, as Masius, quoted by à Lapide says, is the same as, He "who exists from eternity, who is His own essence, and from whom depends the essence of all things."[3] So sacred was this name to the Jews that it was only the high priest who pronounced it, and that amid the most solemn rites. In common discourse or in reading the people substituted the name Adonai for Jehovah. Literally, Adonai means Lord, and this meaning the Septuagint version adopts, translating Jehovah by the word κύριος, while the vulgate renders it by the word "Dominus." Being first revealed to Moses, the name Jehova was not known to the patriarchs. To them God revealed Himself as the Almighty (El Shaddai), for

[1] Ad locum.
[2] Drach, op. cit., v. 1., p. 334.
[3] "Commentaria in Exodum," cap. vi., verses 2, 3.

thus He spoke to Moses: "I am the Lord, that appeared to Abraham, to Isaac, and to Jacob by the name God of Almighty (El Shaddai), and my name Adonai (Jehovah) I did not show them."[1]

Modern infidels have undertaken to prove that Jehovah stands for the sun, which in Grecian and Phenician mythologies is called, according to the different seasons, by different names.[1] They report that the Grecian oracle of Apollo at Claros said, "Jao is the greatest of the gods; he is styled Hades in winter, Zeus in spring, the sun in summer, and the tender Jao in autumn." This story, however, about the Grecian oracle has been rejected by all learned critics, among them, Gesenius and Jablonsky. The fabrication they attribute to one of the early judaizing gnostics. But in itself the story is puerile and sophistical. We prove from the authentic teaching and religion of the Hebrews, as far back as the time of Moses and Abraham, that they worshipped Jehovah as the one and only true God; —but, notwithstanding this evidence, opponents insist that for our proof we must go to Phenician and Grecian mythologies, even though these have no connection whatever in time or in place with the subject of our thesis; or, what the Greeks and Phenicians thought of their gods in the beginning of the Christian era, is to be the basis of proof for what the Hebrews thought about Jehovah in the time of Abraham. There is no need of enlarging further on the absurd in such reasoning.[2]

But so far were the Hebrews from worshipping

---

[1] Exodus vi. 2, 3.
[2] "La Bible et Les Découvertes Modernes," vol. 3, p. 63.

the sun that they were forbidden to do so under the penalty of being stoned, as we read in Deuteronomy. And on the other hand they were taught to sing, "Praise ye the Lord (Jehovah) from the heavens. . . . . praise ye him, O sun and moon; praise ye Him, all ye stars and light.[1]"

Another name generically used in Scripture for God is the word *El*. Primarily it means power; thus, in Genesis, Laban says to Jacob: "it is in my power (El) to return thee evil," and Moses, speaking to the people, says: "May thy sons and thy daughters be given to another people. . . . . and may there be no strength (El) in thy hand."[2] But generally *El*, when applied to God, takes an adjective denoting one or other of the divine attributes. Hence, as we have seen, he revealed Himself to Abraham as *El Shaddai*, that is God all-powerful and munificent (shaddai), while He revealed Himself to Melchisedech as "the most High" (Elyon). Of Abraham it is written, "I lift up my hand to the Lord God, the most High, (El Elyon) the possessor of heaven and earth."[3]

Besides the names just ennumerated and given by St. Jerome, he also adds El Sabaoth, that is, according to Aquila, "the God of armies." Strictly speaking, *Sabaoth* is not a name but a surname; hence, says à Lapide, "it is always united to some other name of God." Then, there is the name *Ja*, which is an abbreviated form of *Jehova* and is one of the component words of Halleluia, made up of *hallelu*, praise ye, and *Ja*, the Lord.

Such were the names which, while venerated and beloved in the spirit of a lively faith, held the He-

---

[1] Ps. cxlviii. 1, 3. [2] Deuter. xxviii. 32. [3] Gen. xiv. 22.

brew mind irrevocably to God. They spoke to the Israelite of the being, the power, the goodness, the holiness, of the Deity, and recalled to his memory the glories of his race. His God was the God of Abraham, of Isaac and Jacob, and not only of these, but of Noe, of Henoch, of Abel, of Adam. And these are the names which, with the glories of the faith in them and around them, still command the reverence and homage of every faithful Christian heart.

But in our days against those adorable names and against God Himself most blasphemous things have been spoken and written. To refute them in detail would require volumes, here all that I can do is, by way of refutation, to propose some general principles, suggested in the foregoing pages. First, then, I say, that for one who accepts the truth of God's existence as demonstratively true (and all men, if they follow the lead of reason, must so accept it), or who accepts it as a most distinctly revealed doctrine, whatever difficulties may be proposed, are so many questions that require a solution but that do not make a doubt. There is hardly a truth in the order of nature or of grace that is not beset with difficulties. Through them one may not be able to see his way, but being in the possession of the truth around which they lie, he is not unsettled by them. His inability to solve them is for him a proof, not of the uncertainty of the truth, but of the limitation of his reason. Boundless, as it were, in its speculative power, reason practically in the development of thought learns often how restricted it is. To reach a conclusion justly, it must follow law; to maintain the connection in a train of thought, it must also depend on law; and to be fully certain of the inferences it makes, it must be free from bias. Absolutely certain of the truth of its own existence, reason has at its roots problems which it cannot solve. It does not know *how* it thinks, it does not know *how* it abstracts thoughts from objects, and it does not know *how* with the will it sets the body in motion. Whatever objections, therefore, may be proposed against the demonstrated truth which one possesses, they ought not to disconcert him, even when he cannot answer them. He is, as it were, in an impregnable fortress and is conscious that, as long as he remains within its precincts, he is perfectly secure.

2. God, a necessarily self-existing Being, the Creator of all things, is limited by nothing and is therefore infinite in nature and perfection. The laws, consequently, of the physical and moral world, must be conformable to the laws of His wisdom and justice. There may be some provisions in those laws which seem to clash with the divine attributes, but since God is infinitely wise and just, one logically infers, *a priori*, that whatever He has ordained must be in accordance with wisdom and justice. Reason also teaches man that he neither knows nor can know the whole bearing of the ordinances of God as revealed in nature. Wheresoever he looks, his view is limited by the horizon; he sees at most only a few miles' distance; how then can he presume to lay the line along the boundless creation and judge from his imperfect measure what is the height, and depth, and length, and breadth of God's infinite wisdom? Hence he concludes that to argue with an atheist on matters touching the justice of the divine govern-

ment is to argue without a common premise for the basis of reasoning. Or, it is to descend from the high stand-point of the justice of God in order to judge of the loftiest causes according to the rules of mere legal procedure. The first thing to be done in the case is to try to convince the atheist of the truth of God's existence; if he refuses to admit that, there remains no other resource for reasoning with him than to point out to him how baseless, or how inconclusive, or false, is his logic.

3. God's dealing with men is grounded not merely on their external conduct, but principally on their internal acts. It is to what is in these, and not merely to what they seem to be, that God specially looks. In the eyes, consequently, of his fellow men one may be irreproachable in conduct; he has given no public scandal, and to all appearance has conformed to the observance of law and even to the proprieties of life, and still, in secret, before God, that same man can be guilty in his heart of all kinds of sin, of the violation of every law. "From within, out of the heart of men, says Our Lord, proceed evil thoughts, adulteries, fornications, murders, thefts, covetousness, wickedness, deceit, lasciviousness, an evil eye, blasphemy, pride, foolishness. All these evil things come from within and defile a man."[1] Within the heart, therefore, unseen by mortal eye, can be committed crimes innumerable that are amenable to divine justice alone. The murderous design, the treacherous project, the lascivious intent, should they be carried out in acts, are punishable by human law. The state vindicates right and upholds the majesty of justice by incarceration, by the confiscation of property,

[1] Mark vii. 21—23.

or by capital punishment. All this it does in virtue of the powers delegated to it by God. But the state is surely not the only means which God can use to punish crime; the creatures of His creation are at His command, and these He may use for the chastisement or punishment of those who in their hearts rebel against Him, and who will not be converted. And these acts will perhaps seem harsh, unjustifiable, nay, cruel, to an infidel or an atheist, who believes not in divine Providence or in man's accountability to his Maker, and who holds that the vindication of all justice whatever can come only from the verdict of a jury or from the sentence of a judge in a court of law.

4. To examine duly the facts that occur in the history of the divine government, it is necessary to keep always in view these truths: (a) that God is Supreme Law-giver, from whom, consequently, as from its primal source, all law, human, natural, and supernatural, derives its obligation; (b) that He is Supreme Lord, whose "is the earth and the fulness thereof, the world and all they that dwell therein;" (c) that He is Supreme Judge, to whom all things are manifest, and to whom appertains in the first instance the power of life and death. Considered, therefore, under this threefold character, God may exercise supreme dominion over things, persons, and nations. The first universal principles of moral law being excepted (since these are wound up with the essential order of things, and hence with divine wisdom), God can dispense in some particular cases with inferences drawn from these principles, or rather, as some writers prefer to say, He can

withdraw " the matter or the circumstances of a precept without which it has no binding force."

Even in civil life, circumstances sometimes take their criminality out of some criminal acts. By the divine law it is forbidden to steal or to take unjustly what lawfully belongs to another. And still the state decrees that indebtedness or some heinous crimes warrant the forfeiture of one's goods; nay, for national defence or utility, it may, in virtue of its sovereignty, oblige individuals to surrender their property on certain conditions. It is also forbidden by divine precept to take the life of another, and still the state, for certain specified crimes, justly inflicts capital punishment. A person also, in self-defence, in order to save his own life, is justified in taking the life of his assailant. Now the state and individuals act in such cases with power delegated to them by God. In His sovereign absolute right, therefore, as Supreme Lord of persons and things, He may, for His own high ends or for hidden reasons, transfer the property of one person to another and, according to His own wise counsel, decree or command the death of men. "And hence," writes St. Thomas, " when the children of Israel by the command of God took away booty from the Egyptians, they did not commit theft, because, by the sentence of God, what they took was their due. And likewise, when Abraham consented to kill his son, he did not consent to commit murder, because it was made lawful for him to kill his son by the command of God, who is the Lord of life and death: for it is He who has decreed the penalty of death against all men, just and unjust, for the sin of their first parents.

.... Thus, then, the very precepts of the Decalogue, as to the principle of justice which they involve, are immutable, but as to a certain determination of them in their application to some single actions, (that, for instance, this or that should be murder, theft, etc., or not) in this they are sometimes changeable by the divine authority alone,—'there being question of these things instituted by God only.'"[1]

The doctrine just stated, and the fact of sin being a punishable offence against the divine majesty being kept in view, it is easy to interpret the startling examples of the vindication of justice as we find them recorded in the Old Testament.

In the narration of them it is the punishment that most comes out to view, while the merciful patience of God is rarely noticeable. But in the 18th chapter of Genesis is found a striking record of the way in which God combines both His patience and His justice. " And the Lord said, the cry of Sodom and Gomorrha is multiplied, and their sin is become exceedingly grievous. I will go down and see whether they have done according to the cry that is come to me; or whether it be not so, that I may know.[2] And they turned themselves from thence and went their way to Sodom, but Abraham as yet stood before the Lord. And drawing nigh he said : Wilt Thou destroy the just with the wicked ? If there be fifty just men in the city, shall they perish withal? and wilt Thou not spare that place for the sake of the fifty

[1] " Summa," 1a 2æ, q. 100, a. 8 ad 3um.

[2] " I will go down, etc. The Lord here accomodates his discourse to the way of speaking and acting among men, for He knoweth all things and needeth not to go anywhere for information. Note here that two of the three angels went away immediately for Sodom, whilst the third, who represented the Lord, remained with Abraham."—Note of the Douay Version.

just, if they be therein? Far be it from Thee, to do this thing and to slay the just with the wicked, and for the just to be in like case as the wicked, this is not beseeming Thee; Thou, who judgest all the earth, wilt not make this judgment. And the Lord said to him: If I find in Sodom fifty just within the city, I will spare the whole place for their sake. And Abraham answered and said: Seeing that I have once begun, I will speak to my Lord, whereas I am dust and ashes. What if there be five less than fifty just persons? wilt Thou for five and forty destroy the whole city? And He said: I will not destroy it if I find five and forty. And again he said to Him: But if forty be found there, what wilt Thou do? He said, I will not destroy it for the sake of forty. Lord, saith he, be not angry, I beseech Thee, if I speak. What if thirty shall be found there? He answered, I will not do it, if I find thirty there. Seeing, said he, I have once begun, I will speak to my Lord: What if twenty be found there? He said, I will not destroy it for the sake of twenty. I beseech Thee, saith he, be not angry Lord, if I speak yet once more: What if ten shall be found there? And He said, I will not destroy it for the sake of ten. And the Lord departed after He had left speaking to Abraham, and Abraham returned to his place...... And the Lord rained upon Sodom and Gomorrha brimstone and fire from the Lord out of heaven. And He destroyed these cities and all the country about, all the inhabitants of the cities and all things that sprung from the earth...... And Abraham got up early in the morning, and in the place where he had stood before with the Lord. He looked towards Sodom and Gomorrha and the whole land of that country, and he saw the ashes rise from the earth as the smoke of a furnace."

5. To estimate rightly the exercise of divine justice in this world, it is altogether necessary to keep in view the fulfilment or completion of that justice in the next. The time of man's life here is a time of probation. During it, he has to make good, divine grace aiding, his hopes of happiness hereafter, or, if he will have it so, by sinful living to lay up for himself wrath in the day of judgment. Now it is of the character of this probation that he who undergoes it should be tried in various ways, that he should give proof of sincerity in the service of his Maker, and of attachment to the divine law in spite of all opposition. The world and fortune will not unfrequently be against him, and justice, in the course and changes of human affairs, will often seem to have lost its aim. The good and just suffer, as history teaches, nay, frequently they appear to be born only for trial, while the wicked often prosper and seemingly have all things to their liking. Within the moral world, to the rationalist, things must seem to be wofully out of joint, so great is the disproportion, in this life, between virtue and its rewards. In the present order of things, therefore, to understand how justice will be righted, we must look to the rewards as well as to the punishment of a future existence. Then virtue shall be fully requited and sinfulness adequately punished; then every one shall receive according to his works, and the wicked "shall go into everlasting punishment, but the just into life everlasting."

6. To him who in ignorance and arrogance poses

as a censor of divine justice, St. Paul answers: "O man, who art thou that repliest against God? Shall the thing formed say to him that formed it: Why hast thou made me thus? . . . . ." For who hath known the mind of the Lord? Or who hath been His counsellor? Or who hath first given to Him and recompense shall be made him? For of Him, and by Him, and in Him are all things; to Him be glory forever. Amen."

www.ingramcontent.com/pod-product-compliance
Lightning Source LLC
Chambersburg PA
CBHW051242300426
44114CB00011B/855